SAGE was founded in 1965 by Sara Miller McCune to support the dissemination of usable knowledge by publishing innovative and high-quality research and teaching content. Today, we publish over 900 journals, including those of more than 400 learned societies, more than 800 new books per year, and a growing range of library products including archives, data, case studies, reports, and video. SAGE remains majority-owned by our founder, and after Sara's lifetime will become owned by a charitable trust that secures our continued independence.

Los Angeles | London | New Delhi | Singapore | Washington DC | Melbourne

RECONCEPTUALIZING
INDIAN
DEMOCRACY

RECONCEPTUALIZING
INDIAN
DEMOCRACY

The Changing Electorate

Bidyut Chakrabarty
Rajendra Kumar Pandey

Los Angeles | London | New Delhi
Singapore | Washington DC | Melbourne

First published in 2020 by

SAGE Publications India Pvt Ltd
B1/I-1 Mohan Cooperative Industrial Area
Mathura Road, New Delhi 110 044, India
www.sagepub.in

SAGE Publications Inc
2455 Teller Road
Thousand Oaks, California 91320, USA

SAGE Publications Ltd
1 Oliver's Yard, 55 City Road
London EC1Y 1SP, United Kingdom

SAGE Publications Asia-Pacific Pte Ltd
18 Cross Street #10-10/11/12
China Square Central
Singapore 048423

Published by Vivek Mehra for SAGE Publications India Pvt Ltd, typeset in 10.5/13 pt Adobe Caslon Pro by AG Infographics, Delhi.

Library of Congress Cataloging-in-Publication Data

Names: Chakrabarty, Bidyut-author. | Pandey, Rajendra Kumar-author.
Title: Reconceptualizing Indian democracy: the changing electorate/Bidyut Chakrabarty and Rajendra Kumar Pandey.
Description: First. | New Delhi, India; Thousand Oaks, California: SAGE Publishing, 2020. | Includes bibliographical references and index.
Identifiers: LCCN 2020005386 | ISBN 9789353882730 (hardback) | ISBN 9789353882747 (epub) | ISBN 9789353882754 (ebook)
Subjects: LCSH: Political participation–India. | Representative government and representation–India. | Democracy–India. | India. Parliament. Lok Sabha–Elections. | India politics and government–1977-
Classification: LCC JQ281.C426 2020 | DDC 320.954—dc23
LC record available at https://lccn.loc.gov/2020005386

ISBN: 978-93-5388-273-0 (HB)

SAGE Team: Amrita Dutta, Sandhya Gola and Sonam Rana

Dedicated to the sacred memory of
Professor Mohit Bhattacharya—the doyen of political science
and public administration in India—who inspired and groomed
generations of scholars through his lifelong endeavours in
teaching and research.

Thank you for choosing a SAGE product!
If you have any comment, observation or feedback,
I would like to personally hear from you.

Please write to me at **contactceo@sagepub.in**

Vivek Mehra, Managing Director and CEO, SAGE India.

Bulk Sales

SAGE India offers special discounts
for purchase of books in bulk.
We also make available special imprints
and excerpts from our books on demand.

For orders and enquiries, write to us at

Marketing Department
SAGE Publications India Pvt Ltd
B1/I-1, Mohan Cooperative Industrial Area
Mathura Road, Post Bag 7
New Delhi 110044, India

E-mail us at **marketing@sagepub.in**

Subscribe to our mailing list
Write to **marketing@sagepub.in**

This book is also available as an e-book.

Contents

List of Tables

List of Abbreviations

AAP	Aam Aadmi Party
AIADMK	All India Anna Dravida Munnetra Kazhagam
BJD	Biju Janata Dal
BJP	Bharatiya Janata Party
BJS	Bharatiya Jana Sangh
BSP	Bahujan Samaj Party
CPI	Communist Party of India
CPI (M)	Communist Party of India (Marxist)
DMK	Dravida Munnetra Kazhagam
JMM	Jharkhand Mukti Morcha
JP	Jayaprakash Narayan
NCP	Nationalist Congress Party
NDA	National Democratic Alliance
OBCs	Other Backward Classes
RJD	Rashtriya Janata Dal
RSP	Revolutionary Socialist Party
RSS	Rashtriya Swayamsevak Sangh
SAD	Shiromani Akali Dal
SP	Samajwadi Party
TDP	Telugu Desam Party
TMC	Trinamool Congress
UPA	United Progressive Alliance
YSRC	YSR Congress

Preface

Being immensely socio-culturally diverse and politically puzzling and multidimensional, India has always been an attractive and also intellectually enriching area of academic enquiry. Given what India is, it is difficult, if not impossible, to provide a universally valid conceptual/theoretical framework. The task does not seem to be easy. Nonetheless, attempts have constantly been made to build intellectually persuasive models, based on individual author's choices and preferences. As a result, what we have at our disposal are a large number of well-researched monographs dwelling on various aspects of Indian polity, providing useful inputs for further probing. This is undoubtedly a healthy trend because not only does it enrich the plethora of literature on Indian polity, but it also provokes scholars to embark on projects for exploring the phenomenon with new zeal and excitement. It will not be an exaggeration to suggest that 'the wonder that is India' is perhaps one of those areas of enquiries which attracted scholars with different ideational inclinations. In other words, the theme of Indian polity is clearly a sought-after *problématique* in the academia presumably because it always provides new ideas and new challenges to those seeking to grasp the phenomenon afresh. Ours is an endeavour in this direction. Given our interdisciplinary academic training, we were drawn to the processes leading to gradual, but steady, democratization of India since it became politically free in 1947 following the withdrawal of British from India. As independent India's polity is inherited in view of the continuity of the Westminster model of governance, one has to be sensitive to its distinct historical past. What it suggests is the claim that for an academically persuasive understanding of the phenomenon, the scholar is required to take into account India's historical past; otherwise, the assessment is bound to be faulty and argument shall have no validity. Hence, our aim, while embarking on this project, was to account for India's changing politico-ideological texture by reference to a thorough analysis of the elections since 1952. Our purpose is to provide an explanation of the entire process of transformation by exclusively focusing on these elections with a historical perspective. Couched in a narrative mode, *Reconceptualizing Indian Democracy* is a unique endeavour, for it is not only a study of elections but also an account for the twists in the voting behaviour of the Indian electorate. Broadly speaking, the book is an initiative at conceptualizing Indian democracy on the basis of a socio-psychological scanning of human preferences in the regularly held elections.

Acknowledgements

For us, this book is the outcome of our efforts, but there are many who have contributed significantly to our endeavour. First of all, this book is clearly a continuity of our earlier exercises as we believe that an author builds his/her argument on those foundational points which he/she makes earlier. We are thankful to our publishers for being so cooperative because without their support it would not have been possible for us to put our thoughts in the public domain. By extending unconditional support to our academic endeavour, our parents helped us remain focused on our goals. We would not have been what we are, had they not been around. Our teachers shall always remain an important source of inspiration; without their guidance, we would not have had the confidence that we evince now. One cannot forget the friends who, by being appreciative of what we have been doing, sustained our zeal and the determination to work even in adverse circumstances. Being teachers, we cannot forget our students here and abroad; without them, we would have lost many battles which we had to fight, as the circumstances in which we worked were not always in our favour. Finally, our family deserves to be profusely thanked for being generous in extending the support that we badly needed to sustain our academic creativity.

In the course of completion of this book, we are shocked to learn about the untimely passing away of our teacher Professor Mohit Bhattacharya, who trained generations of researchers in the disciplines of political science and public administration. In the fond memory of our revered teacher and mentor, we dedicate this tract to the departed soul.

The preface remains incomplete unless we formally acknowledge the contribution of Vivek (Mehra) of SAGE because without the support that he had extended, it would not have been possible for us to undertake such a mammoth task. Cheers to you, Vivek. We are thankful to the SAGE team, especially Amit, Indrani, Rajesh and Amrita. Their role is immensely significant in bringing this book out for public consumption. We are blessed to have received support from many of our friends, which is a rare thing in this context of uncertainty and distrust. The book is an outcome of support of our friends and well-wishers who, by being persuaded by our tenacity for academic works, always remain just 'a phone call away'. We know that this is not at all enough to acknowledge our debt to them, though we thought it to be appropriate for the time being to put on record our appreciation for their sustained support for our academic zeal.

Introduction

Etymologically, democracy means the rule of people since it is derived from the Greek word *demokratia* which is a combination of *demos* (people) and *kratos* (rule). As per the history of democracy, the rule by people had begun in Athens in the middle of the 5th century BC. The system that the rule by people established was not absolute, but controlled by the rule of law or the constitution, as it is commonly known. In its ideal manifestation, democracy as a form of governance is structurally perfect and ideologically persuasive since it leaves no room for decisions, whimsically made; this is a system in which governance is meant to be non-discriminatory and people driven in the strict sense of the term. Hence, democracy is defined as a government by the people, of the people and for the people. It is a much clichéd definition. Nonetheless, it draws our attention to the core of governance which is democratic in spirit and substance.

An analytical scan of the functioning of democracy in the real world however reveals that democracy manifests in three different forms: (a) there are political systems which are democratic in character in the sense that elections are held and the *vox populi* is respected; but governance defies the very principles in which democracy is articulated. A majority of the countries, ruled by the 'man on the horseback' follow this pattern. (b) Some of the so-called democratic countries, despite being appreciative of the structural distinctiveness, tend to deviate from the core values, norms and principles while governing the demos on their behalf. Driven by the leaders, the political system becomes their hostage. It was B. R. Ambedkar who conceptually articulated this when he forewarned his Constituent Assembly colleagues of the devastating politico-ideological consequences of what he defined as 'the Bhakti' syndrome in the Indian politics. Fascist states, both their classical and contemporary forms, belong to this category. (c) There is a third pattern which is visible in those political systems which are democratic in both spirit and substance and yet are subject to tendencies to the contrary; as a result, there are occasions when democracy loses its grip in the political system and seemingly endorses the duly-elected political authority's politico-ideological preferences. Prominent examples are Brazil and India. In case of the former, the 1945 Constitution, which was promulgated after the ouster of the dictatorial regime, led by Getúlio Vargas, upheld democracy as fundamental to the political system that had emerged. The journey was halted in 1967 when the military dictatorship adopted Institutional Acts, a set of supra-constitutional laws to supersede the 1945 Constitution. The year 1988 however marked a new dawn in Brazil's political history; a new constitution was adopted which was not only democratic but was also receptive to those ideas that have gained salience in the context of the global drive towards creating inclusive societies. This is an endeavour for democratizing governance to the extent which was inconceivable in the recent past.

India's democratic trajectory does not seem to be radically different from that of Brazil and other sister countries where democracy, despite being casualties on occasions, thrived presumably because it was not, at all, a window dressing, as was apprehended at the dawn of constitutional democracy in India, but has become integral to her existence as an independent and also vibrant polity. Like their Brazilian counterpart, the *demos* in India confronted an authoritarian regime during the 1975–1977 Emergency which, instead of diluting their faith in democracy, reconfirmed that it was perhaps the best mode of governance in a diverse country like India; it further confirms that the 'Bhakti' syndrome was at the root of devastation of the system and degeneration of the beliefs that formed the core of democratic agility for which the Indians stood out. Barring these two years in the 1970s, India's constitutional democracy did not seem to have faced threats to her existence to the extent that Brazil had faced intermittently in the last two decades.

In view of the fact that the constitutional democracy has evolved deeper roots in India than those decolonized countries that also had adopted democratic form of government, it can safely be argued that it is primarily due to the consolidation of a supportive mindset which is strong enough to scuttle the tendencies to the contrary. This has two serious implications which need to be taken into account for conceptualizing constitutional democracy and also theorizing its grip in India: first, the strengthening of constitutional democracy in India redefines its conceptual parameters and theoretical contours in contrast with what the classical liberal theorists, such as James Mill, J. S. Mill, S. M. Lipset, among others, argued in defence of their contention that a socio-economically diverse society like India was neither fit to be democratic nor a liberal polity. Second, India's democratic experiences confirm that the role of the democratic structure of governance cannot be undermined in initiating and also consolidating the supportive inputs at the grassroots. This means that the privileging of the context does not seem to be theoretically as persuasive as is made to be. The democratic political system also contributes by creating a template supportive of the processes of democratization which complements the drive in its favour.

There is no doubt that India has matured as a democracy with the slow but steady consolidation of representative institutions, the separation of powers and increased participation of the people in elections. Even the prevalence of staggering inequality, which B. R. Ambedkar had highlighted during the drafting of the 1950 Constitution, did not seem to have deterred the processes of democratization. This is certainly a great achievement, especially in the context of India's South Asian neighbours that, despite having the same colonial legacy, are still struggling to establish democracy on a solid politico-ideological foundation. What it entails is the argument that the mere prevalence of an institutional structure purportedly supportive of democracy does not always create circumstances in which democracy thrives not just as a structure of governance but also as a process contributing to the consolidation of a mindset in its defence. By being democratic since the inauguration of the 1950 Constitution, the text that has emerged out of India's experience helps us discern a new mode of conceptualization which is theoretically innovative and politically persuasive.

Besides seeking to understand how constitutional democracy evolved in India in the wake of colonial rule and its aftermath, the aim of this exercise is also to comprehend and conceptualize its changing texture. The outcome of the 2014 national elections and the recent Uttar Pradesh assembly elections confirms that the voters remain supreme and the political leaders hardly possess an authority in case they are alienated. In others words, voters are neither predictable nor indecisive, as is generally believed, but are clear-headed while making their preferences in the polling booth.

Despite the continuity of constitutional democracy in India for more than seven decades, questions are being raised about the depth of our democratic consciousness. For instance, have we been reduced merely to being 'voters' who remain contended with the casting of votes in elections, or do we need to become 'democratic citizens' acting as a shield against the tendencies, both the state-driven and otherwise, towards undermining the very ethos, values and principles of democracy? Is it merely adequate for us, as citizens of democratic India to elect and leave the representatives to always decide for us? Is there a need to devise mechanisms other than the available ones to make the Indian democracy more accountable, participatory and deliberative?

India's democratic trajectory is full of turns and twists which make the effort towards understanding its nature theoretically innovative and conceptually enlightening. By directing attention to the changing texture of democracy since the inauguration of the 1950 Constitution of India, the book seeks to grasp the processes contributing to the way in which it is being reconceptualized.

II

The democratic fabric of India's governance is based on the constitutionally guaranteed values and norms which evolved gradually both during colonialism and its aftermath. There is no denying that India is an inherited democracy, the Westminster type, presumably because of the continuity of the British administration which transmitted liberal democratic ideas in the wake of its rule. There is also an equally important aspect of this argument that these ideas were held by the nationalists while being opposed to the alien rule. As a result, there had emerged a system of thoughts leading to a creative blending of both derivative and indigenous values and norms. In other words, what appeared to be 'purely derivative' was not exactly so, since these ideas had also been indigenized once they were adopted by the nationalists in the context of the freedom struggle. The process that had begun during the campaign against the British rule in India continued even after freedom was won following the dismemberment of India into two sovereign states, India and Pakistan. So it was not a matter of accident that the founding fathers who made the 1950 Constitution seem to have been overwhelmed by the Enlightenment values, though they were equally inspired by Mahatma Gandhi's notion of 'village swaraj'; they were persuaded to such an extent that the arguments for village swaraj never received the attention that they deserved. The story that captured the evolution of the 1950 Constitution is a testimony to this argument.

The making of the Indian Constitution is an interesting chapter in independent India's political history for a variety of reasons. Not only was the Constitution an outcome of deliberations on the floor of the Constituent Assembly, it also acquired a clear centralized bias reflective of the trauma of the 1947 partition. Furthermore, while the Constitution is a continuity, at least in structural and procedural terms, there is also a clear break with the past since the Constitution seeks to articulate the political in decolonized India. There can be no greater evidence of the spirit of accommodation and reconciliation and commitment to constitutionalism and rule of law on the part of the founding fathers than the Constitution that they framed despite serious difficulties in the wake of transfer of population, following the vivisection of the subcontinent. The commitment to liberal democratic values, as the Constituent Assembly proceedings suggest, remained paramount in the making of the Constitution.

The Constituent Assembly was set up as a result of negotiations between the nationalist leaders and the members of the Cabinet Mission over the possible constitutional arrangement in the post-war India. The Assembly was elected by the members of the provincial leg-islative assemblies. The Congress secured an overwhelming majority in the general seats, whereas Muslim League had a clear sweep in almost all the reserved seats. There were members also from the Scheduled

Castes Federation, Communist Party of India and the Unionist Party, located in Punjab. The Muslim League boycotted the Assembly when it began and following the partition, a large chunk of the League members, elected from the Muslim-majority provinces, left for Pakistan. Only 28 members of the Muslim League joined the Assembly. As a result, the Assembly ceased to become 'Indian' presumably because of the over-representation of the Congress, which constituted almost 82 per cent of its total members. The Assembly thus became 'a one-party body in an essentially one-party country'.[1] Was it possible to make the Assembly more democratic in those circumstances? The answer is invariably no for two reasons: first, the Congress was the only political party that had a widespread network across the country due to its historical role in the nationalist struggle; and second, the electoral process could not have produced a representative body because the franchise that followed the Sixth Schedule of the 1935 Government of India Act, was highly restricted. Furthermore, the Congress was not party in the narrow sense of the term, it became an umbrella organization representing the country as a whole as 'the Congress has', argued Nehru, 'within its fold many groups, widely differing in their viewpoints and ideologies [which made the Congress] the mirror of the nation'.[2] The 1950 Constitution was thus a serious endeavour of accommodating diverse socio-economic interests.

In view of the fact that India's political freedom was marred by the trauma of partition, India's Constitution was born, thus notes Paul Brass, 'more in fear and trepidation than in hope and inspiration'.[3] There is hardly a strong argument to dispute this proposition presumably because of the context in which the Assembly began and concluded its proceedings. It began its deliberations on 9 December 1946, and concluded with the passage of the Constitution on 24 January 1950. This period, slightly over three years, was one in which the joy

---

[1] Granville Austin, *The Indian Constitution: Cornerstone of a Nation* (New Delhi: Oxford University Press, 1999), 8.

[2] Jawaharlal Nehru, *Unity of India* (London: Lindsay Drummond, 1948), 139.

[3] Paul Brass, 'The Strong State and the Fear of Disorder', in *Transforming India: Social and Political Dynamics of Democracy*, eds. Francine Frankel et al. (Delhi: Oxford University Press, 2000), 60.

of freedom was severely marred by national trauma, associated with the partition and violence, that resulted in the killing of Mahatma Gandhi, besides the butchering of innocent people in the wake of the transfer of population in the immediate aftermath of the declaration of freedom. The Constitution was thus a pragmatic response to the reality that the Assembly confronted while drawing the roadmap for free India. The founding fathers practised 'the art of the possible' and never allowed [their ideological cause] to blind them to reality'.[4] This further confirms that the Indian Constitution was not exactly ideology driven, but was an outcome of the considerations that the founding fathers deemed appropriate to create a politically united India.

Despite being appreciative of India's pluralistic social texture, there was a near unanimity among the Assembly members for a strong state. Even those who were critical of the Emergency provisions also defended a centralized state to contain tendencies threatening the integrity of the country. Emergency provisions in the Constitution were justified because 'disorder' or 'mis-governance' endangers India's existence as 'a territorial state'. Such concerns could only have reflected, argues Paul Brass, 'another kind of continuity' between the new governing elite and the former British rulers, namely 'an attitude of distrust' of the ordinary politicians of the country and 'a lack of faith' in the ability of the newly-franchised population to check 'the misdeeds' of their elected rulers.[5] Nonetheless, the fear of 'disorder' was probably the most critical factor in favour of the arguments for a centralized state despite its clear incompatibility with cherished ideal of the national-ist leaders for a federal state. B. R. Ambedkar's contradictory stances on federalism, for instance, thus may appear whimsical, independent of the circumstances. In 1939, Ambedkar was clearly in favour of a federal form of government for its political viability in socio-culturally diverse India.[6] By 1946, he provided a radically different view by saying that 'I like a strong united Centre, much stronger than the

---

[4] Austin, *The Indian Constitution*, 21.

[5] Paul Brass, 'India, Myron Weiner and the Political Science of Development', *Economic & Political Weekly* 37, no. 29 (July 20, 2002): 87.

[6] B. R. Ambedkar, *Federation versus Freedom* (Poona: Gokhale Institute of Politics and Economics, 1939).

Centre we had created under the Government of India Act of 1935'.[7] While presenting the final report of the Union Powers Committee, he unequivocally declared,

> We are unanimously of the view that it would be injurious to the interest of the country to provide for a weak central authority which would be incapable of ensuring peace, of coordinating vital matters of common concern and of speaking effectively for the whole country in the international sphere.[8]

As evident, federalism did not appear to be an appropriate structural form of governance in the light of the perceived threats to the existence of the young Indian nation. Hence, the Constitution makers recommended for a strong centre because the constitutional design of a country is meant to serve 'the normative-functional requirements of governance'. The Constitution was to reflect 'an ideology of governance' regardless of whether they articulate the highly cherished ideals of the freedom struggle that a majority of the Assembly members nurtured while participating in the freedom struggle. As G. L. Mehta believed, 'we have to build up the system on the conditions of our country [and] not on any abstract theories'.[9] In the same tune, A. K. Ayyar argued, 'our constitutional design is relative to the peculiar conditions obtaining here, according to the peculiar exigencies of our country [and] not according to a prior or theoretical considerations'.[10] In the making of the constitution for governance, they were guided more by their views on statecraft, which would surely have been different without the traumatic experience preceding the inauguration of the Constitution in 1950. Hence, one can safely suggest that 'hard-headed pragmatism and not abstract governmental theories' was what guided 'the architects of our Constitution'.[11]

---

[7] CAD, vol. 1 (1946), 99.

[8] CAD, Report of the Union Powers Committee (20 August 1947).

[9] CAD, vol. 5 (1947), 79–84.

[10] CAD, vol. 9 (1949), 838–839.

[11] Mohit Bhattacharya, 'The Mind of the Founding Fathers', in *Federalism in India: Origins and Development*, eds. Nirmal Mukarji and Balveer Arora (New Delhi: Vikas Publishing House, 1992), 89.

The Constituent Assembly debates are a useful guide to understand the processes that finally culminated in the making of the 1950 Constitution. Yet it was not the entire Assembly that wrote the document. It was clearly the hard work 'of the government wing of the Congress, and not the mass party' and the brunt of the task fell upon 'the Canning Lane Group [because] they lived while attending Assembly sessions on Canning Lane'.[12] There is another dimension of the functioning of the Assembly, which is also instructive. According to Granville Austin, India's constitutional structure is perhaps 'a good example' of decision-making by consensus and accommodation, which he defends by examining the debates on various provisions of the Constitution.[13] Scholars however differ because given the Congress hegemony in the Assembly, views held by the non-Congress members were usually bulldozed. As S. K. Chaube argued that at least on two major issues—political minorities and language—both these principles were conveniently sacrificed. As regards political minority, there was no consensus and the solution to the language was, as Austin himself admits, 'a half-hearted compromise'.[14] By dubbing the Assembly as 'a packed house', the shrunk Muslim League expressed the feeling of being alienated from the house. Even Ambedkar underlined the reduced importance of the Assembly since on a number of occasions, as he admitted, 'they had to go to another place to obtain a decision and come to the Assembly'.[15]

Decision by consensus may not be an apt description of the processes of deliberation. But, as the proceedings show, there was near unanimity on most occasions and divisions of opinion among the Congress party members, who constituted a majority, were sorted out politically. As Shiva Rao informs, on a number of controversial issues, efforts were made to eliminate or at least to minimize differences through informal meetings of the Congress party's representatives in

[12] Austin, *The Indian Constitution*, 17, 317.

[13] Ibid., 311–321.

[14] Granville Austin, 'Language and the Constitution: The Half-hearted Compromise', Chapter 12, in *The Indian Constitution* (New Delhi: Oxford University Press, 1999), 264–307.

[15] CAD, vol. 11, 1094.

the Constituent Assembly.[16] If the informal discussion failed to resolve the differences, 'the Assembly leadership ... exercised its authority formally by the Party Whip'.[17]

Two important points emerge out of the preceding discussions: first, the making of the Indian Constitution was a difficult exercise not only because of the historical context but also due to the peculiar social texture of the Indian reality that had to be translated into the Constitution. The collective mind in the Assembly was defensive as a consequence of rising tide of violence taking innocent lives immediately after partition. Second, the founding fathers seem to have been obsessed with their 'own notion of integrated national life'. The aim of the constitution was to provide 'an appropriate ordering framework' for India. As Rajendra Prasad equivocally declared on the floor of the Assembly, '[p]ersoanlly I do not attach any importance to the label which may be attached to it—whether you call it a Federal Constitution or a Unitary Constitution or by any other name. It makes no difference so long as the Constitution serves our purpose'.[18] This is illustrative of the concern of the founding fathers for a template to create and consolidate a diverse society around certain widely accepted constitutional values and principles which the 1950 Constitution epitomized.

III

The Indian democracy is reckoned as one of the most vibrant democracies in the world. If one leaves the established democracies of the West, India has the impeccable record of conceptualizing, implementing and deep rooting its system of democracy in such a way that now it seems improbable that the democratic system of the country could face any credible challenge in the times to come. The basic factor that goes in making the Indian democracy a vibrant system has been the active and enthusiastic participation of the common people in the democratic

---

[16] Shiva Rao, *The Framing of India's Constitution*, vol. 5 (New Delhi: Universal Law Publishing, 2004), 835.

[17] Austin, 'Language and the Constitution', 315.

[18] Rajendra Prasad's statement, made after the Constitution was inaugurated on 26 January 1950, *The Times of India*, 29 January 1950.

processes. From time to time, whenever the general masses of the country are asked to identify the elements or systems that make them feel proud of being an Indian, the vibrancy of the democratic system of the county comes out on the top. It is therefore not surprising to find that Indians have now learned the art of defending their democratic institutions in case they are threatened to be destabilized. In this regard, the response of the people to the imposition of Emergency in 1977 for a short span of time could be seen as the exemplary resoluteness of the Indians to guard against any threat to democracy.

While democracy as a value system remains ingrained in the psyche and routine behaviour of the people, its institutional articulation is ensured through the holding of periodic elections to enable the common masses elect their representatives. In turn, such representatives go on to facilitate the formation of the government that eventually gives the sense of satisfaction to the people that they are ruled by no other than their own representatives. Thus, elections have great instrumental value in making, sustaining and improving the structures and processes of democracy. In fact, free and fair elections are considered as the litmus test of a vibrant and functional democracy in place of a morbid and structural one. As a matter of fact, there are a number of countries in the world, including many of India's neighbours, who did decide to go for a democratic system of government at the time of their independence. But in the course of time, the basic functional imperatives to ensure the vibrancy of their democracies were disrupted, thereby leading to the eclipse of democracy in such countries. Another pattern with regard to the perverted form of democracy can also be seen in many countries of Asia, Africa and Latin America. In such countries, there are provisions for establishment of democracy with elaborate structures and processes. But in reality, the absence of free and fair elections reduces democracy to a farce in these countries. As a result, though constitutionally these countries call their political systems democratic, in practice they are nothing but authoritarian political systems. In a nutshell, therefore, substantive shape to the democratic system of a country is provided by the system of free and fair elections held at regular intervals. In fact, the Western countries have been able to preserve their democratic systems only through the periodic elections. Here one needs to be sensitive to the role of the representatives who are expected to represent the voters of their constituencies in parliament or similar platforms; they are the voice of the people, though while articulating the voice they are also expected to be conscientious to the Constitution and the values on which it rests. Whether representatives, chosen by electorates, are free to act on their own is a matter of debate, especially in today's context when politico-ideological priorities are too diverse to be expressed in categorical terms. There is however a widely accepted view that voters continue to remain critical since the representatives are bound to come back to them in case they decide to carry on what they are.[19]

That way, India has been fortunate enough to not only have the constitutional provisions for establishment of a democratic system of government but also have a comprehensive and dedicated system for holding regular elections. An indicator of the significance of elections in the political and administrative system of the country has been the fact that when elections are declared in the country, all the systems get geared up towards the smooth, free and fair conduct of the elections. And, until the elections are complete, the administrative machinery remains on their toe lest any irregularity is detected in the process. The Constitution has elaborate provisions for the independent authority in the form of the Election Commission of India with enormous powers under Article 324 to conduct and superintend the electoral process. The impeccable record of the working of the Indian Election Commission has been well recognized in the world so much so that it is quite often invited by various countries to facilitate them in the holding of free and fair elections for their political institutions. In fact, the independent status of the Election Commission of India has been at the core of its autonomous functioning in organizing the whole set of activities in the process of holding the general elections. Barring a very few occasions, the political class in the country has also desisted from exerting any kind of undue pressure on this august body in performance of its duty. As a result, now, holding timely, free and fair elections has become part of Indian political and administrative

---

[19] Though little dated, A. H. Birch's *Representation* (London and New York, NY: Praeger Publishers, 1971) is a very useful text to unravel some of the complex conceptualizations of elections and electoral behaviour.

culture and all the stakeholders are well aware of their respective roles and responsibilities towards the festival of votes that has gone into vibrancy of democracy in the country.

IV

The inexplicable relationship between democracy and elections can be understood from the analogy that the two are also cause and effect of each other. As has been argued, the idea of democracy can never be conceptualized in the absence of having an efficient and effective system of elections. In fact, the concept of democracy inherently involves the right of the people to choose their rulers as against the authoritarian systems where the ruler is invariably an unelected entity and rules without the consent of the people. Hence, when the idea of democracy is conceived, it is unavoidably accompanied by a system through which people could express their choices for the people who could be their rulers. For instance, in the ancient times, the bodies such as sabha and samiti were the organizations where the representatives of the people used to find a place to decide upon the issues of governance and public welfare. Similar institutions used to exist in the ancient Greek city-states where the people used to decide their chores of life either themselves or through the representatives chosen by them for the specific tasks. Thus, what is being argued here is that the elections have been an inevitable part and parcel of any democratic system that has to be vibrant and functional. That way, democracy becomes the cause of elections and as long as democracy remains in existence in a robust and effective manner, the place for free and fair elections and the machinery to organize them will remain intact.

Democracy as the vital aspect of elections has been a well-established fact that has universally been recognized by both the theorists and practitioners of democracy alike. In other words, democracy takes root in a country only when its piousness and sanctity are ensured through the holding of free and fair elections to elect the people who would be steward of taking the democracy forward. Interestingly, even the freeness and fairness of election is not a formalistic but a functionalist paradigm. Given that the basic purpose of election is to ensure that the people elect their true representative who can be bestowed with the responsibility of taking vital decisions related to governance as well as public welfare, it becomes the wanton duty of the electoral system to make sure that the electoral process produces that result only for which people have expressed their opinion. Any deviation from this rule may ruin the sanctity of the elections. Thus, it is at this point that the hosts of malpractices such as money and muscle power become the debilitating factor in the efficiency and effectiveness of the electoral system. In countries where such malpractices are commonplace, the electoral process can never be an enabling factor for democracy as the true representatives of the people are likely to be replaced by the pseudo representatives through the process of electoral malpractices. On this count, India presents a mixed bag of results as the electoral processes in the country in the past have been vitiated by a number of electoral malpractices.

If the elections are the lifeline of democracy without the vibrancy of which the robustness of democracy cannot be ensured, the inverse of the same can also be true to a large extent. In other words, it is beyond doubt that the sanctity and vibrancy of democracy in a country cannot be ensured without an efficient and effective system for holding elections. But what happens to the electoral system in case the democratic system in a country is neither pious nor robust? Admittedly, in such a situation the electoral system can never be permitted to work as per the rulebook or the constitutional stipulations. In fact, that is exactly what happens in the countries that begin their journey towards a democratic system of government through comprehensive provisions in their constitutions for holding free and fair elections so that the democracy remains vibrant and functional. While such countries are able to make a perfect start, the problem arises midway when the turn of events leads to usurpation of the constitutional powers by an unwarranted person, most probably an army general. After such usurpation of power, though the constitutional system remains in existence, the implementation of its provisions becomes a ritualistic affair without any substance. In such a scenario, the lack of democracy in that country greatly compromises with the efficient and effective working of the electoral machinery in a free and fair manner. Almost all the authoritarian countries in different parts of the world disrupt this symbiotic relationship between democracy and elections that allows them to carry on with their authoritarian rule. It is therefore mandatory for all the democratic countries that the organic relationship between democracy and the electoral process is kept intact so as to make the two supplement each other as long as none of them goes out of existence.

Despite severe challenges from within and the consolidation and triumph of forces opposed to democracy in the neighbouring states, India's experience with democratic form of politics and government is rather successful. Although the British democratic tradition contributed immensely to India's democracy, equally significant is the role of the Congress party which sustained the democratic spirit at least institutionally since its inception. Not only did the Congress stalwarts absorb the democratic values, they played a role in legitimizing democratic rule as a whole. The general concern is not so much for the substance of political authority as the mechanisms entailing elections, representation and mandate obtained through adult suffrage derive their sustenance from the 1950 Constitution which provides for a specific structure of political life 'by allowing and encouraging (within limits) popular participation in the political system within a framework of rules, rights, structures and processes which must be broadly respected by both rules and ruled'.[20] Here probably lies the strength of India's democracy which has developed a different mode of legitimacy to consolidate itself in the context of challenges from within and outside its boundary.

V

Like all the other established democracies in the world, the sustenance of the democratic system in India has also been guaranteed to a large extent by the system of holding free and fair elections at regular intervals. Right from the time of the inauguration of the parliamentary democracy in the country, barring a very few, the country has not witnessed any occasion when the elections to the higher legislative bodies could not be held in defiance of the provisions of the Constitution.

[20] Achin Vanaik, *The Painful Transition: Bourgeois Democracy in India* (London: Verso, 1990), 103.

It is true that there can arise certain exigencies in a country when the holding of elections might not appear to be a plausible idea. For such situations, all the constitutions have specific provisions to permit the exceptions in holding the regular elections. Such exceptions are accepted as part of the constitutional system under which the democratic system of a country has been visualized. For instance, the declaration of Emergency in the country in 1977 has technically not been a violation of the Constitution and the government of the time was well within its rights to perceive and analyse the prevailing situation and take corrective measures to tide over certain unsavoury situations if that threaten to disturb the vital aspects of the public life or the unity and integrity of the nation. The problems arose in the country in the wake of high-handedness of the government under the garb of democracy, thereby robbing the people of their fundamental rights to become part of the democratic process of governance.

Conceptually, elections cannot be understood as a standalone and sterile exercise that does not have much to do with the different aspects of public life, on the one hand, and the vital institutions of democracy, on the other. To put it differently, elections need to be conceptualized as one of the most significant political and administrative exercises within a country that leave deep impact on the shape and nature of the public institutions. This can be truer in the case of the countries where most, if not all, of the public institutions are in phases of transition and are constantly reinventing themselves in order to keep abreast with the fast- changing situations within the country. That way, India can also be considered as a transitory society in which different vitals of the society and public life, including political and constitutional institutions, are always ready for reinvention in order to meet the challenges of the future. In this regard, the functional elasticity of the Indian democracy allows it to be reshaped and reinvented by a number of factors. Among such factors, the elections occupy a place of prominence given their symbiotic relations with democracy and their function as the bedrock over which the edifice of democracy subsists in the country.

The basic argument of this book is that the Indian democracy has been given its functional shape through a number of constitutional and political processes among which the elections stand out prominently.

In other words, the book seeks to reconceptualize the nature and dynamics of the Indian democracy through the prism of elections. As a matter of fact, each and every election held in the country to elect the members of the lower house of the parliament does leave valuable lessons and inputs for the democratic system of the country. Now any kind of laxity on the part of the Indian democracy to imbibe the lessons or values thrown up by the general elections may prove counterproductive for it. For, in that case, the democracy would not be able to reflect the contemporary realities of the time including the wishes and aspirations of the people. And, if a democracy is not able to reflect the current realities of the society for which it subsists within the broader constitutional framework, it places itself at the risk of becoming redundant. In that case, the people would not be left with any other option than to look for the alternative systems through which they can be able to express their opinions and choose their representatives to take charge of the political and administrative system of the country in place of the redundant democracy. On this count, fortunately, the Indian democracy has been very receptive and responsive to the issues, challenges and opportunities thrown up in the course of the periodic general elections. This permits the institutions of governance to take corrective measures well in time so as to respond to the changing needs and aspirations of the general electorate of the country. What is, however, of equal, if not more, importance is the fact that the democracy can also offer certain corrective measures to the common electorate in case it finds that all is not well on the part of the general electorate of the country.

VI

India's successful tryst with democracy and elections has placed it in the enviable position of providing useful inputs to each other. But there cannot be denying the fact that of the two, democracy is a much weightier and valuable aspect of the country than the elections. Hence, over the years, the successful conduct of a number of elections has indeed been able to provide numerous valuable inputs for the democracy to reinvent itself. As a matter of fact, notwithstanding the reality that democracy is more fundamental element of the political system of the country, the live and regular updates on the wishes and aspirations of the people from the democratic institutions are offered by the periodic elections only. That way, each of the general elections in the country has come out with significant pointers for the Indian democracy in such a way that the dynamism of the Indian democracy has been maintained right since the inception of the democratic system in the country. Interestingly, despite the bold decisions of the Indian Constitution makers to adopt democracy as the guiding principal of public life in the country, there has always remained certain apprehensions in the minds of all the stakeholders as to what extent the democratic experience in the country could be successful. But the general masses of the country have proved the apprehensions of all the people wrong and played an exemplary role in the deep rooting of democracy. However, the success of democracy in the country has very much hinged on the successful working of the electoral system in the country.

India has so far conducted 17 general elections in a grand manner with the latest election taking place in 2019. In a way, all of these elections may be considered as important landmarks in the democratic process of the country. Rather, the significance of the first few elections could be taken as more important than the later ones given the vital stakes that have been at risk during those days. The basic reason for this is that the people of India were given the right to vote at a time when they did not have any previous experience of voting or taking appropriate decisions as to the exercise of their right to vote. Yet the practical wisdom of the people weighed heavily on the textbook rules of voting and they became the harbinger of a wonderful democratic experience in the country. However, the lessons that these elections could have offered for the successful working of democracy would have been quite valuable for that time. Those lessons would surely not be as significant in the present times as they used to be during those days. Keeping this into consideration, the book skips the study of the elections held until the time of Nehru. In other words, the book begins its journey of analysing the critical inputs provided by the various general elections in the reconceptualization of the Indian democracy with the sixth general elections held in 1971.

Given that democracy is a dynamic idea that keeps on reinventing itself as per the changing dynamics of the time, the inputs for such reinvention could be provided by a number of institutions and processes. But of all these sources of inputs, the inputs provided by the elections may arguably be more, if not the most, significant in view of the symbiotic relations between the two. That way, what has been attempted in the book is a critical examination of the vital aspects of the general elections to discern the intricate process and products that have redefined the contours of democratic system of the country. For instance, one of the very important aspects of the democratic process in India has been the nature and extent of people's participation in the general elections. Theoretically, general elections are open to all, thanks to the adoption of the universal adult franchise, and everybody has same stakes in the electoral process given that the votes cast by them would determine the nature and texture of government that would govern them for the next five years. But the participation of people in the general elections in the country has never been uniform and stable. Earlier the elections used to be the bastions of the rich and mighty. But since the closing years of the 1980s, with the deepening of the democracy in the country, the participation of people in these elections has become quite broad based and diversified. This has imparted distinct viability and robustness to the democratic process in such a way that the government has become more responsive and public welfare oriented than before. Thus, the electoral inputs have helped in reinvention of the democratic system in the country to a great extent.

VII

Altogether, 12 general elections have been studied in the volume, which have chronologically been divided into 10 distinct chapters. This apparent incongruity between the number of general elections and chapters is due to the clubbing together of two elections in a single chapter at times. To be specific, there have been certain general elections that could not prove momentous for the reasons of fractured mandate as a result of which the mandate became meaningless because no stable government could be formed out of that mandate. In such cases, two elections have been studied in a single chapter. There has also been an occasion when the same kind of mandate has been repeated in the next general elections, as a result of which the same government got repeated. In such cases, there does not seem to be much variety or newness in the two similar mandates, thereby making the claim of their separate analysis redundant. Accordingly, the opening chapter presents a critical review of the sixth general election held in 1971 in which Indira Gandhi received a decisive mandate to overcome the hiccups that she faced in implementing her policies of social and economic development of the poor and marginalized sections of society. This is followed by a critical examination of the seventh general elections held in 1977, after the lifting of Emergency. The seventh general elections have in fact been the stupendous efforts of the common people of the country to redeem the democratic institution that had suffered a serious dent in the wake of the high-handedness of the government during the period of Emergency.

The focus of the third chapter has been on the study of the eighth general elections that took place in 1984 in the wake of the assassination of Indira Gandhi by her bodyguards. The basic argument of the chapter is that the eighth general elections went on to consolidate the dynastic politics in the country. In the following chapter, the ninth general elections have been analysed to find out how the anti-Congressism has emerged as the new foundation of the opposition unity. However, given the fractured mandate out of this election, the government formed in accordance with it could not last its full term and its unceremonious departure led to calling of the next general elections within a short span of just two years. In the fifth chapter, the verdict coming out of the 10th general elections have been analysed in terms of the social and political forces unleashed during the tenure of the previous government. The 10th general elections in fact produced the phenomenon of the primordialization of the democratic process of the country in such a way that the sectarian and caste loyalties of the people played profound role in determining the outcome of this election.

The sixth chapter consists of the study of two distinct general elections: 11th and 12th. These two elections took place in quick succession with each other within a short span of two years, 1996 and 1998, respectively. During the 11th general elections, the mandate was so fractured that no stable government could be formed out of it.

Rather, history of sorts was created in the aftermath of this mandate when the country saw three prime ministers assuming charge on the basis of the same mandate. Even this also could not ensure the durability of the government as a result of which fresh elections had to be called in 1999. The 13th general elections held in 1999 form the core content of the seventh chapter. It was during this election that some kind of decisive mandate was offered by the electorate as a result of which the first National Democratic Alliance (NDA) government was formed that lasted its full term of office. In the eighth chapter, again two general elections have been clubbed together, not because of their relative insignificance but because of the similar verdict delivered by the two general elections. Thus, during both the 14th and 15th general elections, the Congress-led United Progressive Alliance (UPA) was handed down a working majority in the lower house of parliament along with its alliance partners to form a stable government that lasted for 10 years in a row. The ninth chapter deals with the momentous 16th general elections in which the BJP, for the first time, was placed in a comfortable position to form the government at the centre. The last chapter critically examines the vital aspects of the latest general elections held in 2019 in which the Modi wave had swept the major players of the yesteryear into political oblivion. The stunning success of the incumbent ruling coalition, led by the BJP clearly indicates, if not confirms, that the grand coalition of the opposition parties (*Mahagathbandhan*) did not appear to have acted as decisively as it was expected in mobilizing voters in its favour. Instead of following the conventional path, the conclusion is not just a summary of the text, but raises those pertinent questions which will create a new template of understanding by being sensitive to the rapidly changing socio-economic and political realities. Articulating voters' preferences, elections provide critical inputs which this volume takes into account to seek to reconceptualize the Indian democracy in the new perspective in which the role of the globalizing forces is also significant.

VIII

On the basis of an analytical study of the elections in India since the first one, held in 1952, the book makes two major and one minor arguments. The first obvious argument draws on the narratives of the elections. As elections are held at regular intervals following constitutional norms, it can thus safely be argued that the electoral democracy has evolved organic roots in India, which further confirms that, despite occasional hiccups, the democratic fabric that gains strength from regularly held elections does not seem to be fragile at all. The second argument highlights the socio-psychological support that Indian voters extend to the liberal democratic framework of governance; otherwise, it would not have survived, let alone flourished. Here is a fundamental point: a mere constitutional guarantee hardly makes a polity democratic, which is possible provided the stakeholders uphold the system as their own. In other words, a system of ownership has emerged which contributes to the growth and consolidation of India's electoral democracy. Along with these two major arguments, the book also makes a minor argument by emphasizing the critical importance of the context in shaping the electoral behaviour. It is true that election pledges by the contestants do help in mobilizing support, but that may not always be adequate to ensure victory; what is needed is an extra push to champion one cause over another. As the 2019 national poll confirms, the surgical strike by the Indian Air Force in the terrorist camps in Balakot in Pakistan created an emotional and also nationalist euphoria that appears to have instantaneously made the BJP candidates invincible.

On the whole, the book provides an analytical statement on the basis of a historical narrative of the elections that hardly had a uniform character. This is however not a study of elections per se, but one that draws out those fundamental conceptual points which help us explain the distinctive character of the polity which, despite being guided by the 1950 Constitution, does not seem to be entirely oblivious of the popular psyche, as the repeal of Articles 370 and 35A in 2019 demonstrates. By referring to this specific example, showing how an electoral pledge charts a new course of action which was inconceivable in the immediate past, the book thus represents an endeavour suggesting that elections are not only mechanisms of change of political guards but also devices for reconceptualizing the politico-constitutional fabric on which the Indian polity rests.

CHAPTER 1

Political Ends, Economic Means

Elections have been one of the important variables that have imparted distinct shape and dynamism to the theory and practice of democracy in India. Interestingly, while some elections have served the instrumental purpose of getting an elected government in place, a few of them have indeed turned out to be momentous in witnessing such unconventional processes and products that might help in undertaking fresh theoretical explorations in conceptualizing the Indian democracy. In other words, elections have been visualized by the constitution makers in India as a workable method of affording common people an opportunity to express their opinion on putting in place a democratically elected government. Thus, elections have been conceptualized as a tool to be put in the service of democracy in the country. But at times, the democratic processes are put in service of elections in such a way that election becomes an end in itself through which the government seeks to serve its interest at the cost of democracy. The fifth general elections for Lok Sabha held in March 1971 are one of such elections in India through which the government of the day sought to sacrifice a number of vibrant though fledgling democratic conventions in the country on the altar of elections just in order to earn a fresh lease of life for it.

Undoubtedly, the fifth general elections marked the advent of a number of such political traditions which have not been experienced in the country in the past. For instance, government of the day headed by Prime Minister Indira Gandhi, for the first time, recommended the dissolution of Lok Sabha even before it was able to complete its term. Before that, each of the Lok Sabha was allowed to complete its full term of five years and elections for constituting a new Lok Sabha were held only during the stipulated period of time. Such dissolution of Lok Sabha also led to the delinking of elections for state legislative assemblies with the Lok Sabha for the first time in India. In other words, right from the time when the Constitution was implemented, elections for Lok Sabha as well as majority, if not all, of the state legislative assemblies were calibrated in such a way that the people got opportunity to vote for both the houses—central and state legislatures—at the same time. Thus, the simultaneous polls for both central and state legislatures not only saved a lot of money and materials but also acted to produce such electoral results which led to formation of governments by the same party at both central and state levels. Theoretically, such a proposition has a number of advantages that have not only been recognized by the political class of the country immediately after Independence but have also ensured smooth functioning of the democratic polity without much schism between the centre and states. These are only certain illustrative instances to show how democratic processes and constitutional provisions had been misused to gain benefit out of troublesome circumstances prevailing in the country at that point of time. In the present chapter, certain other theoretical ramifications of the fifth general elections are analysed in depth.

Prelude to the Elections

The fifth general elections were announced in such circumstances where the political situation in the country was underpinned by a number of uncertainties. Indira Gandhi's style of running the government had already strained her relations with the party stalwarts. The chasm between the government and the party was increasing with each passing day and culminated in the expulsion of Indira Gandhi from the Congress party on 12 November 1969.[1] After weighing the relative merits of her prospective trajectories, Indira Gandhi went on to split the party in order to charter an independent course for her including selective electoral adjustments with other parties.[2] Thus, Indira Gandhi was placed in a very precarious situation to tide over which was not an easy task for her in the given circumstances.

After split in the Congress party in 1969, though Indira Gandhi had emerged as a formidable political figure amidst the old guards of the party, her leadership of both government and parliament remained vulnerable for a number of reasons. Given that her party was reduced to a minority after split, she had to depend on a number of unpredictable parties for their support in Lok Sabha to maintain the majority for her government in the house. Although she carried the vision of her father to usher in the socialistic pattern of society in India, she was unable to translate her visions for such a society into action for reasons both political and judicial. At the same time, she was also subjected to many kinds of undue demands from the regional parties such as the Dravida Munnetra Kazhagam (DMK), supporting her government from outside, in so far as formulation of national policies on vital issues such as language was concerned. Thus, it was probably getting tough for her to run the government as per the priorities and programmes with which she parted ways with her parent organization.[3]

As a matter of fact, since the taking over of the reins of government, Indira Gandhi had to deal with such circumstantial difficulties in making of whom she played only marginal role. Not only was Indian economy in bad shape during that period, the formidability of political leadership that seemed must for dealing with such situations decisively was missing due to the precarious majority of her government in Lok Sabha. On the economic front, industrial and manufacturing activities were said to be static, investment was at its nadir and agricultural sector

[1] Robert L. Hardgrave, Jr., 'The Congress in India: Crisis and Split', *Asian Survey* 10, no. 3 (March, 1970): 258.
[2] Mahendra Prasad Singh, *Split in a Predominant Party: The Indian National Congress in 1969* (New Delhi: Abhinav Publications, 1981), 105.
[3] Iqbal Narain, 'Ideology and Political Development: Battle for Issues in Indian Politics', *Asian Survey* 11, no. 2 (February, 1971): 187.

was in doldrums.[4] Political analysts observe that during that period, 'India's economy, political leadership and military powers faltered badly'.[5] Whatsoever efforts were made by the government to tide over the economic difficulties met with resolute opposition not only from her political rivals but also conservative judiciary that did not seem to be in a mood to bear with the progressive economic reform measures of the government. As a result, both long-term structural and short-term strategic reforms could not be carried out by the government leading to a large degree of disaffection and resistance to the political class by the landless and other dispossessed sections of Indian society.[6]

During this time, Indira Gandhi faced formidable challenges mainly on two fronts. The first challenge that appeared before the government was to overcome the conservatism showed by the Supreme Court in its attitude towards examining the constitutional validity of the progressive measures initiated by the government for social and economic transformations in the country. In this context, taking the fundamental right to property as the primary reference point, the Supreme Court appeared set on the spree of declaring null and void the slew of progressive measures rooted in socialism such as the bank nationalization and abolition of privy purses and other privileges of the princes. The other difficulty before her arose on the political front from more than one quarter. In an effort to exploit the precarious position of the government in parliament, opposition leaders had become very active to introduce no-confidence motions in Lok Sabha. Although all such motions had been comprehensively defeated, thanks to support to government by the communist parties along with others, the fear psychosis created by such moves in the government appeared to be quite serious. At the same time, the

---

[4] M. S. Swaminathan, 'Fifty Years of Progress in Indian Agriculture', in *Independent India: The First Fifty Years*, ed. Hiranmoy Karlekar (New Delhi: Oxford University Press, 1998), 147.

[5] L. I. Rudolph and S. H. Rudolph, *In Pursuit of Lakshmi: The Political Economy of the India State* (New Delhi: Orient Longman, 1987), 390.

[6] L. I. Rudolph and S. H. Rudolph, 'Regime Types and Economic Performance' in *Politics in India*, ed. Sudipta Kaviraj (New Delhi: Oxford University Press, 1997), 182.

breakdown of the 'federal consensus'[7] created a lot of political com-
plications for the government as the provincial politics appeared set
to cast their shadows on national politics as well.

In such a scenario, Indira Gandhi was looking for certain safety
valves that could have helped her achieve multiple objectives in one go.
First, she did not have any other option than to go for such policies and
programmes which could have been backed by her political allies without any reservation, given the precarious position in which her government was placed at that time. Second, she also wanted to carry forward
the unmistakable mark of Nehruvian socialism on each and every aspect
of developmental programmes and policies through vigorous attempts
at structural reforms towards creation of an egalitarian society. Third,
given the political uncertainty staring at her, she also wanted to take
the political battle to the court of people where the matters could be
settled decisively. Showing the acumen of a seasoned politician, she had
almost made up her mind that the day-to-day political wrangling both
with the political parties supporting her government and the opposition
parties could not be resolved either by any sort of court politics or more
and more accommodation of the wishes and aspirations of different
political parties. She appeared convinced of the fact that the opposition
parties are relentlessly trying to portray her as a political novice who
had been trying to cling to power by hook or by crook under shadow
of the political legacy of her father. So what she wanted was to break
the political impasse as well as the public impression about her political
wisdom by going to people and securing a fresh mandate.

Amidst the multiple challenges facing the government, what
seemed to have tilted the scale in favour of the general elections was
the successive defeat of the state governments led by Indira Gandhi's
party. For instance, in September 1970, the alliance between the
Congress (R) and Chaudhary Charan Singh's Bharatiya Kisan Dal
(BKD) broke down leading to fall of the government in Uttar Pradesh.
This development was taken by Indira Gandhi as a kind of alarming
bell because it indicated that now the regional satraps are also taking
her party as relatively weak and vulnerable to political manoeuvring on

[7] Rajni Kothari, *Politics in India* (New Delhi: Orient Longman, 1970), 195.

their part. Her apprehensions proved true sooner than expected when there appeared a kind of action replay of the incidents of Uttar Pradesh in Bihar in December 1970. These events led to serious apprehensions in the minds of the Congress (R) leadership that political power at the provincial levels had fast been slipping out of hand of the party. For party leaders, there appeared a clear likelihood that the chain of events taking place in Uttar Pradesh and Bihar might expand to other states as well leading to the erosion of power of the party in large parts of the country. State of things, thus, appeared to be getting out of control of Indira Gandhi, and to arrest the situation she did not have many options. One way out available to her was to go for political manoeuvring and realignment of political forces at both national and provincial levels. But such activities were not likely to bring about any long-term benefit for the party. So she was left with no other option than to sacrifice her minority government and go for general elections.

The Elections

With the objective realities standing against her and strengthening of the opinion in support of going for fresh elections within her party, Indira Gandhi unhesitatingly recommended for the dissolution of Lok Sabha to the president on 27 December 1970. Further, in order to ward off any misinformation campaign being mounted by her opponents behind the motives for premature dissolution of Lok Sabha, she took to a special radio broadcast to address the common people and explain them the rationale behind such an unprecedented move in the annals of the Indian parliamentary system. In the memorable address to the nation, she averred:

> There comes a time in the life of a nation when the government of the day has to take an unusual step to cut through difficulties in order to solve the pressing problems with which the country is beset. The present is such a time. Therefore, on the advice of the Council of Ministers, the President has dissolved the Lok Sabha before its full term. In a parliamentary democracy this is not unusual but in India it has happened for the first time. Why did we do this when it is conceded from all sides that our government could have

continued in power for another fourteen months? It is because we are concerned not merely with remaining in power but with using that power to ensure a better life to the vast majority of our people and to satisfy their aspirations for a just social order.[8]

Indira Gandhi took this opportunity to showcase her tremendous efforts towards bringing about an egalitarian social and economic order in the country through the radical measures such as bank nationalization and abolition of privy purses along with the initiatives for land reforms. For her bold and unconventional decisions, her personality was likened to that of a 'parameter-altering leader'.[9] At the same time, she also came down heavily on her opponents whom she described as reactionary forces to put the blame on them for sabotaging her efforts for social and economic reforms. She emphasized,

> In the present situation, we feel we cannot go ahead with our proclaimed programme and keep out pledges to our people. These attempts to accelerate the pace of social and economic reforms have naturally roused the opposition of vested interests. Reactionary forces have not hesitated to obstruct in every possible way the proper implementation of these urgent and vitally necessary measures. Power in a democracy resides with the people. That is why we have decided to go to our people and to seek a fresh mandate from them.[10]

Thus, she sought to put the things in perspective before the people so that the imperatives of election are clear to them and they are able to exercise their franchise in a prudent and considered manner. Her speech in the backdrop of dissolution of Lok Sabha reminiscences the approach of her father to establish a direct dialogue with the common people of India in extraordinary and difficult times. This address helped portray a picture of Indira Gandhi as that of the harbinger of

---

[8] Publications Division, *Selected Speeches and Writings of Indira Gandhi: August 1969–August 1972: The Years of Endeavour* (New Delhi: Publications Division, Government of India, 1975), 75–76.

[9] Susanne H. Rudolph, 'The Writ from Delhi: The Indian Government's Capabilities after the 1971 Election', *Asian Survey* 11, no. 12 (October, 1971): 963.

[10] Ibid.

social and economic revolution in the country, which the reactionary elements of society were not allowing. Logically, what, therefore, was needed was a resounding mandate to the prime minister so that nothing is allowed to come in her way of bringing about remarkable social and economic transformations in the country.

In going for the Lok Sabha polls even before the expiry of term of the house, Indira Gandhi had also considered delinking the general parliamentary elections with the state assembly polls, a tradition which her father had sought to build so assiduously.[11] Taking her as the national leader who needed not be assessed on the issues of regional or local interests, she appeared convinced that her radical social and economic measures needed to be voted upon straightaway without any relation with the issues of state politics.[12] Thus, Indira Gandhi's deft handling of the prevailing political situation took her adversaries by surprise. Although initially they raised objections to her announcements and called upon the president to explore the situation for formation of an alternative government before dissolving the Lok Sabha, they later accepted the decision of the government and readied themselves for the polls. What however was remarkable in this context was the political wisdom of Indira Gandhi which made her assess the prevailing situation in perfect measure and take somewhat infallible corrective steps by going for delinked Lok Sabha polls with immediate effect.[13] Her decision was taken as a necessary step given the indeterminate political situation in the country. At the same time, it was also expected that the personal gamble of Indira Gandhi would result in a clear mandate as the issues critical in the elections were very much individualistic in nature and the voters' verdict on them would surely be a clear mandate for a definite course of action.[14]

[11] Ashok Mehta, *A Decade of Indian Politics: 1966–1977* (New Delhi: S. Chand and Company, 1979), 49.

[12] Stanley J. Heginbotham, 'The 1971 Revolution in Indian Voting Behaviour', *Asian Survey* 11, no. 12 (December, 1971): 1152.

[13] Romesh Thapar, 'Capital View: The Election', *Economic & Political Weekly* 6, no. 1 (January 2, 1971): 54.

[14] Rajni Kothari, 'The Parliamentary Elections: Case for a Clear Mandate', *The Times of India*, New Delhi, 4 June 1971.

Elections for the fifth Lok Sabha were argued to be different from the previous general elections on various grounds.[15] For instance, it was argued that instead of banking on the party organization as the foundation of electoral strategy, Indira Gandhi was seeking to contest the election on her personal promises and charismatic appeal. At the same time, in the face of her formidable challenge, the opposition parties hurried to form a combined platform against her, thereby brightening the possibility of putting up a straight fight against Indira Gandhi. Interestingly, for a Congressman, this election presented a great dilemma of choosing between Indira Gandhi and the syndicate.[16] Given that Indira Gandhi sought to fight the polls as a one-woman army, she did not wish to leave any stone unturned to not only project her positive promises before the people but also expose the weaknesses of the opposition. The gist of her campaigning strategy lay in branding the polls as monumental fight between her promise of *garibi hatao* (eliminate poverty) and the ominous portents of the grand alliance of opposition parties.[17] However, such arguments and appeals of Indira Gandhi to voters were not found to be quite impressive to the political analysts primarily for reasons of localized nature of election campaigning in the absence of a system of mass media in the country.[18] Nevertheless, the electoral campaigns of Indira Gandhi were filled with emotional appeals to the electors along with her promises of bringing about a radical turnaround in the social and political fortunes of the poor and downtrodden sections of society. Amidst such high pitched and intensely personal campaigns of Indira Gandhi, the stage was set for polling to constitute the fifth Lok Sabha.

[15] E. P. W. Da Costa, 'Fifth Lok Sabha Polls: Three New Factors', *The Times of India*, New Delhi, 9 January 1971.

[16] Rakhahari Chatterji, 'Political Development in India: The State, Civil Society and its Institutions—the First Half Century', in *Politics in India: The State—Society Interface*, ed. Rakhahari Chatterji (New Delhi: South Asian Publishers, 2001), 4.

[17] Rakhahari Chatterji, 'Democracy and the Opposition in India', *Economic & Political Weekly* 23, no. 17 (April 23, 1988): 845.

[18] Myron Weiner, 'The 1971 Elections and the Indian Party System', *Asian Survey* 11, no. 12 (December, 1971): 1155.

Electoral Outcomes

The conduct of the fifth general elections was the largest electoral exercise in the country post-Independence. With a mammoth 150 million people voting in 520 electoral constituencies, the conclusion of the elections in a largely, if not absolutely, free and fair manner, proved the capabilities of the Indian electoral machinery to carry out such exercises successfully. Since the elections were a costly risk Indira Gandhi had taken, the results of these elections paid rich dividends to her. As Francine Frankel wrote succinctly,

> If the 1971 general election was a gamble by Mrs. Gandhi that she could defeat both her opponents in the Grand Alliance and her competitors on the left through a direct class appeal that promised radical economic reforms through parliamentary methods, then the Prime Minister handsomely won that gamble.[19]

She came out with a stunning victory in these polls with her party winning as much as two-thirds majority in the lower house of parliament. Of the 441 seats she contested, the Congress (R) emerged victorious in 352 seats in a house of 518 members. Indira Gandhi was indeed able to turn the tables on her opponents and rivals in a decisive manner. The grapevine among the circles of the Congress (R) was that even the party itself was not sure of winning such a landslide despite the best efforts of its leaders. The poll outcome comprehensively decimated the rival Congress (O) into a non-entity in the Indian political system with the glorious legacy of the Indian National Congress wrested by the Congress (R), which was also viewed as the personal victory of Indira Gandhi.[20]

Interestingly, despite the high-pitched electoral battle, the voter turnout in these elections had not been as per expectations. It was

[19] Francine Frankel, *India's Political Economy, 1947–2004: The Gradual Revolution* (New Delhi: Oxford University Press, 2005), 436.
[20] R. N. Mathur, '1971 Lok Sabha Elections: A Brief Survey', in *Development of Politics and Government in India*, vol. 7, eds. V. Grover and R. Arora, (New Delhi: Deep and Deep Publications, 1994), 617.

anticipated by the political pundits that since the election was being fought on the basis of issues and promises that touch upon the daily chores of life of poor and common people, they would come out in huge numbers to extend their support to the respective ideological standpoints taken by different political parties. Such a lower turnout was tried to be reasoned out by the strategists of the Congress (R) on the plea of delinking of Lok Sabha polls with the elections for state legislative assemblies. Such an argument was also supported by Morris Jones who contended that the delinking of national and state polls had acted as dissuading factor for the voters given their somewhat decreased interests in the national issues and national political processes.[21] Notwithstanding the percentage of voting in different parts of India, there appeared to be a wave existing in favour of Indira Gandhi's party as her candidates were able to trounce a number of stalwarts in the electoral hustle. Given that her fight was primarily with the old guards of the Congress (R), it had been quite disastrous for the syndicates as they suffered all round defeat in almost all the states and union territories at the hands of the nominees of the Congress (R).

Indicative result of the elections presented in Table 1.1 show the relative position of different political parties along with their seats and percentage of votes. The number of seats won by the Congress (R) outpaced other parties with such a margin that did not appear to

Table 1.1 Results of 1971 General Elections

All India (518)	INC (R)	INC (O)	SWA	JS	SSP	PSP	CPI	CPI (M)	Others	Independents
No. of seats	352	16	8	22	3	2	23	25	53	14
Percentage of votes	43.7	10.4	3.1	7.4	2.4	1.0	4.7	5.1	13.8	8.4

Source: V. B. Singh and Shankar Bose, *Elections in India: Data Handbook on Lok Sabha Elections, 1952-1985* (New Delhi: SAGE Publications, 1986), 27.

[21] W. H. Morris-Jones, 'India Elects for Change and Stability', *Asian Survey* 11, no. 8 (August, 1971): 729.

be even a remote competition between the former and the latter. To put it differently, while the Congress (R) was able to secure a score of whopping 352 seats, the other political parties barring the Communist Party of India (Marxist) (CPI [M]) could not win even two dozen of seats. Similarly, while the vote percentage of the Congress (R) stood at convincing 43.7 per cent, the matching figure for other contenders could equal with that of the former only when the vote shares of all were combined together. Insofar as opponents and competitors of Indira Gandhi were concerned, their performance can be analysed by putting them in three distinct categories. First, given that Indira Gandhi's direct confrontation was with her erstwhile colleagues, who now constituted the Congress (O), they probably thought of posing the greatest challenge to her by carrying with them not only the party organization but also the old guards of the party. But in the electoral hustle, the Congress (O) was so comprehensively decimated that majority of its candidates lost their deposits, and its share of seats in Lok Sabha and percentage of popular votes dwindled beyond their imagination. As a result, the party was driven into oblivion in the Indian politics and the long-cherished legacy of the grand old party of India finally rested with the Congress (R).

Second, the major opponents of the policies and programmes of Indira Gandhi were the regional parties influential in different states and following varying ideologies and political affiliations. The debacle of these parties in the elections had been so deep that many of them could barely win a few seats just to mark their presence in Lok Sabha. The vote share of many of these parties dipped as low as that of just 1 per cent that reflected the voters' complete disapproval of these parties as prominent player of the Indian politics. As against these parties, the third group of political forces that stood as political competitor to Indira Gandhi was the leftist parties represented by the Communist Party of India (CPI) and the CPI (M). Although a section of the left parties had been supporting the government of Indira Gandhi in Lok Sabha in view of the progressive agenda of social and economic change pursued by her, they quite often tried to show the parliamentary minority status to the government on different issues. Despite that, there existed a great deal of overlapping between the policy orientations of the left parties that made them carry on with the government. So, in the electoral fray, the left parties entered the scene with quite similar, if not identical, agenda of social and economic transformations that had been pursued by the government of Indira Gandhi. Resultantly, left parties were able to save their face by winning respectable number of seats in Lok Sabha as compared to the performance of other opposition parties.

Clearly, it was the broadening of the social support base of the Congress (R) that helped it scale unprecedented heights in the electoral fray in 1971. Religion wise, the party was able to garner substantive support from all the major religious groups of India. As a matter of fact, since Independence, Muslims had been a solid vote bank of the Congress party on account of the secular, if not pro-Muslim, stance taken by the party. Right from the framing of the Constitution to the evolution of policies and programmes aimed at ameliorating the social and economic conditions of the minority community, the Congress had been well received by the community. A somewhat dilemmatic situation would probably have been arisen before the Muslim voters with the split in the party. But in these elections, they extended their overwhelming support to the Congress led by Indira Gandhi, taking it as the true custodian of the secular legacies carried forward by the party since Independence. The voting percentage of other religious communities such as Hindus and Sikhs has hovered around 60 showing the divisions in their political allegiances. Despite that, the Congress (R) remained the preferred choice of majority of these religious groups vis-à-vis other political parties. Thus, the liberal image and secular credentials of Indira Gandhi made her an acceptable leader across different religious groups that got amply reflected in the voting behaviour of the followers of different religions.

Caste dynamics of the Indian politics was also in full play during the fifth Lok Sabha elections with varying political preferences of different castes and social groups. Three major conventional patterns of voting behaviour on the basis of caste before the emergence of caste-based parties in the country during the 1990s were: first, high status, middle status, Harijans and Scheduled Tribes remained the steadfast voters of the Congress party ever since Independence. Even among them, the most solid support came from the Scheduled Tribes who voted overwhelmingly for the Congress (R).[22] That pattern continued in the fifth general elections as well with those caste or social groups shifting their loyalties to the personality of Indira Gandhi instead of the Congress as an organization represented by syndicates.

Although people of other caste or social groups also extended their strong support for her, a section of these groups also voted for the non-Congress parties as well. Second, the upper caste, merchants and upward mobile groups of people could not vote overwhelmingly for Indira Gandhi given their traditional loyalty for the parties such as the Bharatiya Jana Sangh (BJS). It was probably because of the support of these social groups that the BJS was able to show an impressive per-formance in the general elections despite an apparent wave in favour of Indira Gandhi. Finally, the lower-caste groups remained divided in voting for the Congress (R) and the lower-caste parties such as the Praja Socialist Party (PSP). In spite of the clear caste divisions, Indira Gandhi stood as the towering personality with attractive agenda for social and economic transformations that secured strong support for her from among all the social groups.

Voting behaviour based on economic status of different groups of people in both rural and urban areas for the Congress (R) reflected the deep impact that the electoral promises of Indira Gandhi left on psyche of the people. Undoubtedly, the low-income groups of people remained the most visible support base of the party. While not being sure of how the radical policies of government such as bank nationalization and abo-lition of privy purses would have impacted the life of the poor people, a feeling presumably was created in their psyche that the governmental move of arresting the private ownership of means of prosperity and erst-while royal privileges would eventually lead to economic empowerment of the poor people. That was the probable reason for massive voting by low-income group people for the Congress (R) despite not gaining much from the ruling by the party since Independence. As against that, the political stance of the high-income group people in rural and urban

[22] Llyod I. Rudolph, 'Continuities and Change in Electoral Behaviour: The 1971 Parliamentary Elections in India', *Asian Survey* 11, no. 12 (December, 1971): 1128.

areas showed a large variation. While the rich people in the rural areas did not have to fear much as land ceiling laws had already settled the land issues for them, the same group of people in urban areas appeared quite frightful in view of the moves such as bank nationalization which apparently seemed to be an assault on their hard-earned savings by the government. For the middle-class people, the state of things did not seem to be poised for any radical change and their voting behaviour was in consonance with the general trends in the country. Despite the great ambivalence in the attitude of different sections on the likely impact of radical economic measures of Indira Gandhi, they did not get scare away by such moves and preferred to vote for Indira Gandhi in the hope of a stable government.[23]

Congress (R)'s performance in the fifth general elections had been reflective of its regaining the widespread support of different social and economic groups of people as had been during the period of Nehru. In other words, the relative decline of the party during the 1967 elections by losing support among certain social groups such as upper and lower castes had been effectively arrested, and the umbrella nature of the party was re-established under the leadership of Indira Gandhi. At the same time, in the decisive battle over control of the legacy of the party, the syndicates were comprehensively voted out of existence. As a result, a new generation of the Congress leaders came into existence under the commanding leadership of Indira Gandhi who did not have much support of their own among the electorate. They depended on the charismatic leadership of Indira Gandhi not only for electoral victories but also for any kind of intervention in public life in the name of the Congress party. While on the one hand, all sorts of parochial considerations were wiped out of existence within the party, on the electoral pedestal, all the religious and caste groups voted for Indira Gandhi in support of her unflinching faith in the socialist ideals and blueprint for social and economic transformations in the country. Almost all the social groups appeared reassured of the protection of their interests under the leadership of Indira Gandhi.

[23] Jayant Lele, 'Understanding Indian politics: Are We Asking the Right Questions?' in *Indian Democracy: Meanings and Practices*, eds. Rajendra Vora and Suhas Palshikar (New Delhi: SAGE Publications, 2004), 186.

Regionally, quite expectedly, the magic of Indira Gandhi was in full play in the northern India that contributed as much as 86.6 per cent of total seats of the region. Such stellar performance of the party was indeed able to put effective check on the parochial caste-based politics attempted by the regional parties that had started eroding the widespread support base of the party in the northern states. Sweeping performance in the north was supplemented by grand performance of the party in east as well where the party was able to secure a respectable 62.1 per cent of seats of total seats in the region. Whatever competition was faced by the party in the east was offered by the left parties in West Bengal with the rest of the region going wholeheartedly with the Congress. In comparison to the east, party's performance in the west was compromised by the inroads made in this region by the rightist parties such as the Congress (O), the Swatantra Party and the BJS. These parties were able to capitalize on the fear psychosis of the erstwhile princes and royals induced through the governmental move towards abolition of privy purses and other royal privileges enjoyed by them. The prevalence of a number of princely states in the provinces of Madhya Pradesh and Rajasthan helped the opposition register better performance in comparison to the other regions such as north and east.

Comparatively, the most dismal performance of the Congress (R) was experienced in southern states where the gain of regional parties ate into the overall seat share of the party from south. For instance, the DMK was indeed able to maintain its hold on the Dravidian politics in Tamil Nadu that stymied the sweep of Congress (R)'s wave in the state. Similarly, good performance of a regional party, the Telangana Praja Samithi (TPS) in the Telangana region of Andhra Pradesh did not allow the Congress (R) to have a walkover in the electoral battle in Andhra Pradesh. As a result, south contributed the least number of seats out of its total seats spreading over the four states. The seat-wise break-up of the gains of the Congress (R) in different regions is also, more or less, reflected in the vote share of the party as percentage of total votes in a region. The most interesting part in this regard is the highest percentage of votes secured by the party in the western region, though the seat share was highest in the northern region. Such an apparent paradox between vote share and number of seats may be explained by the multi-cornered contest in the northern states as compared to the relative unity of the opposition parties in the west. For east and south, the vote share of the Congress hovered around respectable 36–37 per cent which translated in good number of seats for the party.

Although the regional figures on the performance of the Congress (R) show the pan-India appeal of Indira Gandhi in garnering support for her radical policies, the variation in its performance in different regions is indicative of two major tendencies of political economy of India. First, relatively backward or poor regions such as north and east had been excessively receptive of the radical policy measures promised by Indira Gandhi to bring about a rapid social and economic transformation in the country. Thus, sensing the bright prospect for certain degree of turnaround in their fortunes, the people in the two regions voted overwhelmingly for the party that helped it secure a high percentage of vote shares that transformed into good number of seats for the party in the Lok Sabha. Second, perceived animosity to the radical measures on the part of the erstwhile royals and other ruling classes in the western part of the country, on the one hand, and the deep entrenchment of the regional parties in their respective states in the deep south, on the other, did not allow the Congress (R) to walk over its rivals in these regions. As a result, both the vote share and the number of seats secured by the Congress (R) in these two regions did not supplement each other in the same measure as had been the case in the rest of the two regions.

Impact on Indian Democracy

The outcome of the fifth general elections had left indelible mark on the structures and processes of democratic polity of India including its party system. It marked the zenith of the process of democratic crystallization in the country.[24] The process of fragmentation in the Indian politics that began during the mid-1960s had heralded greater churning among different social groups on the basis of ideological

[24] Rajni Kothari, '1971 Election: An Interpretation', in *General Elections, 1971: A Study*, eds. Sham Lal, Girish Mathur, Rajni Kothari and Iqbal Narain (New Delhi: AIR Lectures, 1971, March), 12.

orientations provided by their proponents. The split verdict of the previous general elections was an outcome of such fragmentation as a result of which no party could secure a majority in the Lok Sabha. But during the 1971 general elections, Indira Gandhi's economic means for political ends had worked as magic wand that helped her not only trounce her political adversaries but also emerge as the undisputed leader of the grand old party. The prospects of a bright social and economic future embedded in the attractive promise of *garibi hatao* made people look beyond their primordial affinities and vote for a party and its leader who appeared to have genuine concern for their pathetic economic conditions. However, in practical realm, it was argued that though populism gave Indira Gandhi a landslide victory, it did not succeed in securing for her any kind of organized strength that could have been used to pursue the radical economic measures to their logical conclusion.[25]

These elections also brought back the phenomenon of one-party dominant system as Indira Gandhi's Congress (R) was indeed able to crystallize the disparate voters into one larger group that would vote for their economic emancipation in place of caste solidarities and alliances. However, the new party structure that emerged under the weight of 'Indira wave' was more pyramidal in nature as it was based on the voter's preference for an individual's promises of economic turnaround compared to the Nehruvian party structure.[26] During Nehru's time, the Congress party was a kind of umbrella organization with broader spectrum based on the collective legacies of its leaders' sufferings during the national movement. Thus, the outcome of these elections also heralded the onset of personality-based parties in the country. In the course of time, with Indira Gandhi's party getting more and more centralized around her personality, its name was also changed from Congress (R) to Congress (I) to indicate more explicitly the personality-dominated nature of the party.

[25] Sudipta Kaviraj, 'Indira Gandhi and Indian Politics', *Economic & Political Weekly* 21, no. 38–39 (September 20–27, 1986): 1701.

[26] Stanley A. Kochanek, 'Mrs. Gandhi's Pyramid: The New Congress', in *Indira Gandhi's India: A Political System Reappraised*, ed. Henry C. Hart (Boulder: West View Press, 1976), 93.

Further, comparing the nature of one-party dominant system during the period of Nehru with the re-emergence of one-party dominant system in the aftermath of the 1971 elections, analysts pointed out the democratic deficit in the new party system in comparison to the previous one. It was pointed out that during the Nehruvian phase, the one party system did not disregard the political dissent and ample scope was left in both the party and government to accommodate any political dissent that might emerge at any time.[27] On the contrary, the one-party dominant system during the times of Indira Gandhi was more and more oriented towards disregarding any kind of political dissent given her solitary contribution in making the Congress (R) as the new hegemon of the Indian political system. Thus, the 1971 elections acted to create democratic deficit in the structure of the Congress (R) that later became an alluring element for other political parties as well.

An important feature of the 1971 general elections had been Indira Gandhi's obvious gamble of delinking the Lok Sabha elections with the elections of state legislative assemblies in order to discourage the regional issues from influencing the national elections. But despite earning a landslide for Indira Gandhi, such a gamble could not fulfil her aspiration of separating national and regional issues from working at cross purposes with each other. In the finer analysis of results of 1971 elections, it was well established that in many of the states, the runner-up in terms of popular vote was not a national but a regional party proving that a large number of people were still swayed by regional considerations despite the national character of the election.[28] Thus, the regional factors remained formidable determinants of voting behaviour of the people despite the delinking of Lok Sabha and Vidhan Sabha elections. It were, in fact, these regional feelings that later emerged as the strong base for anti-Congress political formations in different parts of the country.

[27] Pradeep Kumar, 'The National Parties and the Regional Allies: A Study in the Socio-political Dynamics', in *Political Parties and Party System*, eds. Ajay K. Mehra, D. D, Khanna and Gert W. Kueck (New Delhi: SAGE Publications, 2003), 294.

[28] Myron Weiner, 'The 1971 Elections: India's Changing Party System', in *The Indian Paradox: Essays in Indian Politics by Myron Weiner*, ed. Ashutosh Varshney (New Delhi: SAGE Publications, 1989), 228.

Concluding Observations

The economic content in the 1971 general elections had acted as the game changer for Indira Gandhi in ways more than one. She emerged as the champion of poor and downtrodden of the Indian society whose miserable economic conditions she would alleviate through her concerted policy measures. Her valiant moves towards radical measures for social and economic transformations aroused so much curiosity and hope among the people that they could not resist the temptation of coming out for massive participation in the electoral politics. Such a mass though unpublicized participation of plebeians surely tended to snatch the realm of the Indian politics from elites to make it the theatre of mass popular participation.[29] Furthermore, the electoral outcome was conclusive in its indication that the people of India, cutting across caste, class or any other primordial consideration, valued the promises of amelioration of their economic conditions more than any other considerations. Such a crystallization of mass voting behaviour around economic issues helped in checking the political fragmentation in the country.[30] Moreover, caste-based divisions and other ideological alliances among different sections of society had tended to disappear for the cause of nation-building that hinged on the loftier objective of ameliorating the miserable social and economic conditions of the masses.[31] Thus, the strategic vision of utilizing economic means for achieving political objectives helped reap rich dividends for Indira Gandhi by outperforming her political rivals.

[29] Sudipta Kaviraj, 'On State, Society and Discourse in India', in *Rethinking Third World Politics*, ed. James Manor (London: Longman, 1991), 93.

[30] Rajni Kothari, 'Opposition in a Consensual Polity', in *Regimes and Oppositions*, ed. Robert Dahl (New Haven, CT: Yale University Press, 1973), 315.

[31] Iqbal Narain, 'Democratic Interlude for Nation Building: Fifth Lok Sabha Elections', *Economic & Political Weekly* 6, no. 38 (September 18, 1971): 2026.

CHAPTER 2

Jayaprakash Narayan and Re-democratizing 'Democratic' Institutions

The 1977 Shah Commission is illustrative of how government machineries were captured by the existing political leadership to fulfil an ideological mission in opposition to those who apparently posed threat to the democratically elected government. The Constitution of India became subservient to the Congress leadership and the deviant behaviour in public life was considered as inevitable in the light of the possible devastations in the country following the massive opposition mobilization against those in power. Conceptually, the 1975–1977 Emergency is an era of political corruption in India when public authorities were abused, beyond recognition, to accommodate the leadership-driven ideas of public well-being which however did not go well with the stakeholders once implemented. The outcome was the mass campaign, led by the firebrand Gandhian leader, Jayaprakash Narayan, which finally replaced the constitutional authoritarianism which the Congress supremo, Indira Gandhi, had imposed following the proclamation for internal Emergency in India. By challenging the corrupt administration which thrived during the Emergency, the mass campaign also confirms the argument that in a democratic polity, corruption cannot go unchecked because it creates its own enemy.

Translation of Jayaprakash Narayan's dream of creating a truly democratic India into reality through the sixth Lok Sabha elections in 1977 constitutes the focal theme of Chapter 2. Indira Gandhi's magical moves getting converted into bumper support for her in the previous general elections had somehow drove an impression in her to become a democratic despot whom people would adore and accept forever. Apparent result of this was the declaration of emergency and the dark phase of democratic experience in India. This, however, offered an opportunity to the people of India to relook at the empty rhetoric and false promises made during elections and turn towards the creative alternatives to such hoaxes. As a result, 1977 general elections proved to be historical in three senses. One, the common people of India showed their prowess in voting out a government whom they voted just a few years back to power with thumping majority precisely on account of the fact that the same government tried to curtail their constitutionally ordained basic rights and sabotage the democratic processes in the country. Two, for the first time, the country was to witness the inauguration of a non-Congress government consisting of a diverse range of ideological and identity standpoints in sharp contrast to what had been professed and practised by the Congress till date. Thus, the demarcation of Indian party system as 'Congress system' was decisively shattered through this election. Three, a refreshing theoretical perspective was provided to the idea of democracy through the ideas of JP who also acted as the conscience keeper of participatory democracy in the country. For JP, democracy has to be participatory enough to include all the sections, particularly the marginalized ones so as not to remain the bastions of the elite sections or a few individuals.

Battle for Corruption-free Governance

Baptized as a Marxist, Jayaprakash Narayan (1902–1979), popularly known as JP, engaged in sustained political activities to weed out corruption from public life. During the nationalist phase, he was also known as a crusader for justice for the downtrodden which was usually undermined because of the appropriation of the instruments of governance by the vested interests. He was the inner voice of the nationalist movement when it deviated from the well-established moral path and his Congress colleagues were reportedly appreciative of his role. Never being a part of governance, JP always remained an outsider and yet played a very critical role when he was needed to lead movements against corrupt or deviant government. The opportunity came in 1974 when the sarvodaya leader, JP, gave a clarion call to fight the misrule and corruption that seemed to have crippled governance in Bihar. The movement was organized under the non-political platform, Bihar Chhatra Sangharsh Samiti, which spearheaded the campaign under JP's leadership. What had begun in 1974 spread quickly beyond Bihar which, as shown in Chapter 5, led to the imposition of internal Emergency in 1975.

As argued above, JP's involvement in mobilization against misrule in 1975 was not an isolated case; in fact, one discerns a trend in his political life illustrating that he was always vocal against lack of ethics in governance which was often reflected in the desire of the political leadership to deliberately bypass the basic code of conduct. His role in the campaign against Emergency stood out. Given the fact that he was always associated in crusades for fair play and justice in governance, it will be conceptually enlightening to locate the campaign against Emergency within his wider concern for creating a social climate which is critical to, as JP strongly felt, corruption-free governance. The aim here is to understand the overall theoretical predisposition that JP held while conceptualizing his ideological priorities. In view of his sustained commitment to fight for just and fair governance, the battle in which he was involved during the Emergency was just a continuity of his desire that he so sincerely nurtured since he arrived on India's political scene. What JP thus provided is an ideological package which draws on the Marxist conceptualization of praxis, a creative combination of theory and practice in which neither is dwarfed for the other. The idea that runs through is also about a dialectical interconnection between what is known as derivative wisdom and practice. Despite being drawn on what he learnt out of its ideological convictions for the downtrodden, JP's model, being also context driven, is thus uniquely textured.

Plan for Reconstruction of Indian Polity

JP's growing frustration with the Marxian praxis and practical manifestation of its socio-economic and political order led him to evolve some sort of alternative order suitable to the specific requirements of the country. The adoption of the Constitution in the post-Independence times was taken positively by the majority of people with the hope that it would result in translating the high aspirations of the national movement. However, people like JP soon got disillusioned with the working of the democratic polity in the country. Later, JP embarked on a tour of various European countries ostensibly in order to get a feel of the structure and functioning of the governments in these countries. A basic flaw discovered by JP in the structure of most of the system of governments, including the one prevailing in India after the implementation of the Constitution of 1950, was increasing concentration of powers at the higher levels of government. This appeared quite distressing to JP as, being a true democrat, he wanted the powers to be vested in the hands of the people and only that much power need to be transferred to the higher levels of authority structure which would have been unavoidably required. Thus, in order to give a concrete shape to his ideas on comprehensive re-conceptualizing the nature and structure of Indian political system, he published the book *A Plea for the Reconstruction of Indian Polity* in 1959.

In advancing his plea for the reconstruction of Indian polity, JP appeared extremely influenced by the ideas of Sri Aurobindo as he found that the 'extraordinary, intuitive sweep of his vision [that] has laid bare the true nature of the foundations of Indian polity'.[1] Following Aurobindo's line of argument JP was convinced of the veracity of the ancient Indian political order based on the centrality

---

[1] Jayaprakash Narayan, *A Plea for the Reconstruction of Indian Polity* (Varanasi: Akhil Bharat Sarva Seva Sangh, 1959), 22.

of the self-governing village communities in that order. Indeed, JP's seemingly uncritical appreciation of the ancient Indian political order was so formidable that he argued that the conceptualization of the political system in post-Independence India was nothing but 'a question of an ancient country finding its lost soul again'.[2] Thus, JP's basic argument in calling for the reconstruction of the Indian polity was to reinvent and implant the village-based political order with the idea of decentralization underpinning the basic functional ethos and spirit of the system.

Significantly, JP called for the replacement of the prevailing politico-economic order in India based on parliamentary system of democracy and centralized planning with what is called the communitarian democracy and decentralized political economy.[3] In fact, JP was a staunch critic of the parliamentary system of democracy, denouncing it from all probable quarters. But the most intolerable defect of such a system of democracy, to JP, was its inherent tendency towards centralism which appears to be a contrast in terms in itself. In other words, the notion of democracy could not be conceptualized in a way that it leads to or supports any sort of centralism. As the parliamentary system of democracy invariably slips towards centralism, it could not have been the best of models of government for India.

The notion of 'communitarian democracy' as advocated by JP carries a distinct set of political processes which is squarely different from the ones characterizing the nature of political processes in parliamentary democracy. For instance, the essence of the parliamentary democracy lies in intense competition among the political parties to seek power and establish their preponderance in the political system. On the contrary, JP suggested that the essence of the communitarian democracy lies in cooperation and co-sharing as such a system must afford due space to all the interests of the society to be articulated in the political decision-making of the country in a harmonious manner. Naturally, in such a conceptualization of democracy, the emphasis of JP was on the moral and

---

[2] Ibid., 26.
[3] Ibid., 66–68.

ethical moorings of democracy in utter contrast to the material and power-centred nature of the parliamentary system. To JP, therefore, the fundamental task of communitarian democracy is the moral regeneration to be brought about by example, service, sacrifice and love of scores of voluntary workers.[4]

In concrete terms, the plea of JP to reconstruct the Indian polity was principally based on the framework of a decentralized, participatory and grassroots-oriented political order as reflected in practical shape by the idea of Panchayati Raj as existing in the country since the ancient times. This would be an essentially pyramidal model of democracy with widest possible diffusion of powers at the grassroots level making it the real level of government which matters most to the people. Thus, JP's model gives a more decentralized base to the 'four-pillar model of government' as suggested by Ram Manohar Lohia. To put it differently, while Lohia suggested villages, district, state and centre as the levels of governments, JP tried to broaden the base of local level of government by including a middle level also in between the village and district levels so that the operational imperatives of the local government may be strengthened. Thus, what JP suggested was five levels of decentralized polity consisting of village, block, district, provincial and central levels.

In JP's scheme of things on reconstructing the Indian polity, an overwhelming emphasis was placed on reviving and reinvigorating the Panchayati Raj system or what he calls 'swaraj from below'.[5] Under this framework, the basic and lowest unit of political organization would be the 'gram sabha' (village assembly) consisting of all the adults of the village. Primarily, being a deliberative body to ensure the participation of all the adult residents of the village in the governance of their affairs, the gram sabha would elect, ordinarily by consensus, five or more members among themselves to constitute its executive committee which would be called gram panchayat. Thus, through these 'panchs' (members of the village panchayat) acting as

---

[4] Ibid., 107.
[5] See Jayaprakash Narayan, *Swaraj for the People* (Varanasi: Akhil Bharat Sarva Seva Sangh, n.d.), Chapter 2.

the functionaries to take care of the day-to-day functioning of the system, the gram sabha was supposed to act as the lynchpin of the grassroots democracy conceptualized by JP.

Establishing an organic link among the various units of the Panchayati Raj, JP suggested the creation of two more interlinked bodies within the system. The middle level of Panchayati Raj, therefore, would be located identically at the administrative unit of block and would be known as panchayat samiti. Consisting of the representatives of the constituent gram sabhas, the panchayat samiti's operational area would be identical to the areas of its constituent gram sabhas. Functionally, the panchayat samiti would be entrusted with the responsibility of guiding and coordinating the activities of the gram sabhas with particular focus on the formulation and execution of development projects. Finally, the apex of the Panchayati Raj was conceptualized in terms of district panchayat or zila parishad, constituted by the members elected by the panchayat samitis. The functional domain of the zila parishad would ordinarily remain focused on consolidating and fine-tuning the development projects initiated or approved by the panchayat samitis with a view to ensure their technical and economic viability. The common feature underpinning all the three levels of Panchayati Raj would be their endeavour to provide the people an opportunity to participate in the management of their own affairs and enjoy the spirit of true democracy.

Although the bodies of Panchayati Raj constituted the core of the communitarian democracy advocated by JP, he did not remain oblivious to the imperatives of the provincial and central levels of government. What was unique in his conceptualizations on these levels of government was that he wanted them to remain confined, functionally, to their stipulated domains and devoid of any temptation on their part to bulldoze over the lower levels of democratic institutions. JP, thus, argued for a democratic and federal structure of polity in India so that the true spirit of democratic governance might be infused and afforded to the masses. Moreover, for this, he wanted the political system to be free from party politics based on numerous primordial and sectarian motivations to serve the selfish interest of the dominant unscrupulous elements in society.

An important element of the plan of reconstruction of Indian polity, as suggested by JP, included the reconstruction of the economic system also.[6] Being dead against the exploitative and competitive economic system as prevailing in the capitalist societies, he argued for the reconstruction of the Indian economic system on the doctrines of cooperation, co-existence and co-sharing. He decried the element of centralism in the Indian planning system and argued for remodelling of the planning system by making it decentralized and non-political. On the pattern of the grassroots orientation in the political system of the country, JP advocated for the village-ward orientation in the planning process of the country as well. He argued that the formulation of development plans should be initiated at the level of village with its progressive integration and consolidation at the block and district levels. The planning processes at the state and national levels should confine themselves with only providing technical and logistical support for the formulation and execution of the plans at the local levels. JP also called for sectoral balance and harmony in bringing about rapid economic development of the country. Thus, the restructured political economy of the country, in JP's view, would result into realization of true swaraj for the common people.

Despite seeming sentimental and apparent logical consistency in the plea of JP for the reconstruction of the Indian polity, his scheme has been criticized by scholars as being utopian and set to be suitable for the wonderland of JP's imagination.[7] A common critique of JP's scheme has been its obvious focus at reviving and implanting an ancient Indian construct which might have outlived utility in the contemporary times. Moreover, the disproportionate focus on the Panchayati Raj as the nucleus of the post-Independence Indian polity appears absurd to the extent of its practical abstractness, among others. Thus, over the years, JP himself became quite weary of the practical utility of his plea for the reconstruction of the Indian polity and shifted his focus of attention to what is called as 'sarvodaya.'

[6] Ibid., Chapter 3.
[7] For a lucid and representative critique of JP's plan for reconstruction of Indian polity, see W. H. Morris-Jones, *Politics Mainly Indian* (Bombay: Orient Longman, 1978), 97–106.

Sarvodaya

Sarvodaya was a conceptual construct JP borrowed from Gandhi to cumulatively articulate his vision of a decentralized and participatory and egalitarian socio-economic and political order for the country. Delineating the core concerns of the idea of Sarvodaya, Vinoba Bhave wrote, 'Sarvodaya does not mean good government or majority rule, it means freedom from government, it means decentralization of power'.[8] Conceptualized so, sarvodaya, thus, becomes synonymous with a state of order where the bonds of being governed by a seemingly alien or outsider ruler are totally absent and the people are able to enjoy the vocations of their life without any extraneous considerations. Hence, the full realization of the ideal of sarvodaya necessitates the absence of government itself in the first place, yet even if the government remains in existence, the power relations ought to be so decentralized that nobody finds himself in any sort of subjugation with other. It is within this theoretical framework that JP outlined his vision of a sarvodaya social order.

In visualizing his sarvodaya social order, JP begins with explorations in the innate characteristics of human nature. Although acknowledging that evil spirits and motivations exist in individuals and society, he argued that they can be overcome by virtues of compassion and non-violence. Moreover, by inculcating the positive values of life such as cooperation, generosity, creativity and eternal joy, the good spirits and motivations of the people might be brought on the fore to make them realize the significance of such traits in securing a happy and peaceful life for them. Above all, if the examples of such a perspective of life become prominent and people were properly educated in this regard, they would definitely pursue the noble causes and follow good men.[9] Thus, at the root of the proposed sarvodaya order of JP lied his indomitable belief in the inherently noble and positive nature of the common people which

[8] Vinoba Bhave, *Democratic Values* (Varanasi: Sarva Seva Sangh Prakashan, 1964), 3.

[9] Jayaprakash Narayan, *A Picture of Sarvodaya Social Order* (Tanjore: Sarvodaya Prachuralaya, 1961), 6.

may be harnessed to secure a just, egalitarian and democratically decentralized order in India.

The social component of the sarvodaya order rests on an all-inclusive egalitarian social structure.[10] The social relations would be based on the principles of equality, justice and inclusiveness of the diverse stocks of people. As the society would seek the welfare of each and every individual, there would not be any place for socially degrading and discriminatory practices rooted in the primordial and sectarian motivations of any other individual. JP was quite specific about the role of various sections in society and argued for visionary mindset and missionary zeal among the youth whose selfless and untiring efforts would be the main vehicle through which the reconstruction of the society would be materialized. Democratic ethos and spirit would visit all the walks of social interactions and nobody would be persuaded to do anything against his will despite the plausibility of the task at hand. Voluntarism would be major plank to get people do their bit for the welfare of society.

The political dimension of sarvodaya, as explained earlier, would rest on the widest and effective system of decentralized and participatory system of democracy concretized in the form of Panchayati Raj. What, however, was refreshing in the sarvodaya political order was JP's insistence on revolving his scheme of things around what is called *lokniti* (politics of people) and *lokshakti* (power of people) in place of the existing dependence on *rajniti* (politics of power) and *rajshakti* (power of state). Despite appearing unconventional, such notions of people-centric and society-centric perspective of the Indian politics would have been quite obvious given JP's constant prodding for decentralized and participatory nature of the sarvodaya political order. In fact, in the later years when the governments in India were charged with numerous cases of corruption and high-handedness in dealing with political opponents, JP relied exclusively on the powers having their roots in the social and other non-governmental formations. Thus, JP conceptualized the sarvodaya social order as consisting of morally

---

[10] Jayaprakash Narayan, *From Socialism to Sarvodaya* (Varanasi: Akhil Bharat Sarva Seva Sangh Prakashan, 1959), 39–41.

upright individuals having courage to stand up for the ideals such as 'self-government, self-management, mutual cooperation and sharing, equality, freedom and brotherhood'.[11]

Economically, the framework of sarvodaya order would seek to establish a balanced and equitable economic set-up in the country. India being a predominantly agricultural country, JP was sure to afford the first place to agricultural activities in the economic life of the people. Hence, he argued for organizing numerous collectivist farms under the collective ownership and management of the whole village. Further, JP's deep faith in the Gandhian economic perspectives apparently influenced him to advocate a prime place to village and cottage industries organized at local and regional levels. However, the wave of heavy industrialization in various parts of the world made him to offer a place to heavy and large-scale industries also in the industrial outlook of the economy. Thus, in sarvodaya economy, a balanced approach in according due weightage to various sectors of economy would be followed. The net gains from the economic activities of the society would be so equitably distributed that it results in a decentralized, prosperous, distributive and participatory economic order.

Methods of Realizing the Sarvodaya Order

Having conceptualized the sarvodaya social order in very insightful and precise terms, JP also appeared quite categorical in suggesting the appropriate methods of implementing the plan for creating a sarvodaya social order in India. Quite evidently, JP's deep erudition and lived experiences in various methods and institutional arrangements in bringing about drastic transformations in society made him a rebel vis-à-vis numerous conventional methods of effecting desirable social change. For instance, his old fancies about the classical Marxian prescription of changing the society through revolutionary violence no more remained favourite with him. Castigating the violent methods of social change, he held that such methods did not take care of the veracity of objective in view and 'ensure the victory of party that is more

[11] Ibid., 40.

skilled in its use'. The victory ensured by such methods would invariably, as shown primarily by the Russian experiences, be authoritarian and undermine 'all attempts at democracy and the attainment of social justice or equality'.[12]

Significantly, JP was equally disillusioned with the liberal methods of social change which is sought to be achieved through the means of legal provisions and institutional arrangement to implement them. JP's basic critique of the parliamentary route of effecting social change was that it would not yield desirable results without mentally preparing people to accept and adapt such changes in their life styles. As he wrote eloquently, 'It is not institutions, not laws, not political system, not constitutions which create good people. For that you require a widespread process of education understood in the widest sense of the word. Education does not mean academic education; but the improving of human beings through service, love, examples, preaching, reasoning and argument'.[13] JP also argued for setting of concrete examples by the leaders and awakened citizens of the country so that the masses could emulate such examples and, equipped with proper education, would be able to become the harbinger of a new sarvodaya social order in the country.

The cumulative impact of the twin virtues of education and concrete examples, in JP's view, would be to ingrain an indelible mark of awakening in a person's mental and moral values, infusing some sort of voluntary perspective in him towards the prevailing problems of society and plausible solutions for them. The concrete exemplification of such a moralist theoretical construct was experienced in the 'Bhoodan' and 'Gramdaan' movements launched by Vinoba Bhave. JP was very impressed with the idea and practice of such voluntary sharing on the part of the people and argued for the extension and strengthening of such movements by way of 'sampattidaan' (sharing together of property) and the ultimate 'jeevandaan' (sharing together the entire life of an individual and dedicating it for the cause of welfare of others). JP anticipated that such voluntary sharing together of

---

[12] Narayan, *A Picture of Sarvodaya Social Order*, 4–5.
[13] Ibid., 151.

various prized possessions of life would ensure a non-violent, voluntary and democratic transformation of the Indian society on the lines of the sarvodaya order.

Total Revolution

Total revolution (sampurna kranti) was the last intellectual intervention of JP in his unending quest to seek and establish such a socio-economic and political order in the country which would turn India into a democratic, federal, participatory, equitable and prosperous nation in the world. The concept of total revolution was for the first time evolved by Vinoba Bhave during the 1960s to articulate his desire for the need of a comprehensive movement in the country which would transform all aspects of life in order to 'mould a new man ... to change human life and create a new world'.[14] The idea was picked up by JP to call upon the people in 1975 to work for total revolution in order to stem the rot creeping into all aspects of public life and create a whole new world encompassing the basic elements of socio-economic and political order JP had been advocating in the name of sarvodaya.

The context of JP calling for the total revolution[15] was provided by the growing authoritarianism in the functioning of the government machinery headed by Indira Gandhi. One of the nefarious repercussions of such governance was the spreading of corruption in all aspects of political life in India. Hence, on the declaration of Emergency in June 1975, JP found it compelling to call for the total revolution in the country aimed at transforming the whole gamut of social, economic, political, spiritual, educational and cultural life of the people. JP was convinced that piece-meal engineering would not suffice to bring about the desirable level and pace of holistic transformation in India, thereby necessitating the call for the total revolution. Through his call for total revolution, JP, therefore, not only appeared satisfied with having cosmetic changes in the outer set-up of the socio-economic

[14] Vinoba Bhave, *Revolutionary Sarvodaya* (Bombay: Bharatiya Vidya Bhavan, 1964), 1.

[15] See Jayaprakash Narayan, *Total Revolution* (Varanasi: Sarva Seva Sangh Prakashan, 1975).

and political structures of power but also called for effecting and deepening an informed consciousness of the masses for ensuring the holistic transformations of the entire system. The essence of all such transformations would lie in restoring the basic spiritual foundations of all the aspects of human life in the country.

The concept of total revolution of JP aimed at reversing the tide of rot taking place in the political and economic system of the country ostensibly due to the concentration of political and economic powers in few hands and restoring the sanctity of institutions and procedures in those spheres of life by decentralizing such powers in hands of the masses. In the sphere of the political system, JP noted the inherent fallacies of the prevailing parliamentary system of government as its basic characteristics such as electoral system, party-based political processes and increasing concentration of powers in the hand of one person, that is, the prime minister, are bound to convert the system into a corrupt, tyrannical and farcical one. Hence, in his conceptualization of total revolution, JP was firm on reforming the electoral system in such a way that the people can vote in an incorruptible manner and in accordance with their free conscience. Moreover, in such a system, there would be no place for political parties and the potential concentration of powers in few hands would be effectively curbed by having greatest possible diffusion of political powers to various levels of government.

Like political power, JP was also convinced of the perverse effects of the concentration of economic power in the hands of few in society. He, therefore, called for total recasting of the economic system of country as well. Arguing for a mixed economy framework for India, JP aspired that the economic dispensation of the country must be able to provide for the basic necessities of people such as food, cloth and shelter. His idea of sampattidaan was nothing but a call for sharing together of one's wealth and economic resources in such a way that their utilization benefits the larger sections of people rather than ensuring affluence for a few. JP visualized an economic order for the country where there would be progressive socialization of the means of resources by way of establishing cooperative societies and voluntary associations to manage the resources with a view to ensure prosperity for all. Thus, even in the sphere of economic activities, JP's diagnosis of cure for the ills appeared rooted in concentration and decentralization of the powers, respectively. And, therefore, he suggested that the first and foremost task of the sarvodaya worker would be to 'diffuse political and economic power and decentralize the politico-economic structure'.[16] Indeed, decentralization, along with people's participation was argued by JP as the panacea for all the rots which have become deep-rooted in the politico-economic system of the country.

JP's call for executing the idea of total revolution in 1975 was accompanied by some sort of blueprint for the volunteers to carry out the implementation of the scheme of holistic transformations of the Indian society. He exhorted the people to rise against the authoritarian and inimical policies and programmes of government of the day and persevere to push it back to its legitimate domain. He also called for the dissolution of the legislative bodies in the country as they had ceased to reflect the opinion of the people by going neck deep in all sorts of political and economic corruptions. JP also pointed out the problem of price rise as the target of total revolution since it had the potential of turning the life of people into virtual poverty and starvation keeping in view their inability to pay for the exorbitantly high prices of the essential commodities. At the same time, he was also forthright in eradicating the existing social inequality in the country by putting a full stop on the discrimination among the people on the basis of religion and caste. In a nutshell, thus, the operationalization of the idea of total revolution in 1975 encompassed within its fold almost all the major problems facing the people before embarking on the path of long-term revolutionary transformations aimed at establishing the sarvodaya social order in the country.

In its operationalization, however, the idea of total revolution, as advocated by JP, occasionally evoked misplaced perceptions in

---

[16] Jayaprakash Narayan, *Towards Total Revolution*, vol. 3 (Surrey: Richmond Publishing Co., 1978), 79.

the minds of its practitioners. For instance, undoubtedly, it proved electrifying for the people and gave birth to a mammoth students' movement in many parts of the country with particular formidability in Bihar in 1974. But the public perception of the notion of total revolution appeared ambivalent as many construed it to be total subduing of 'rajya shakti' or state power at the hands of the people. However, JP was quite categorical that he did not advocate the disappearance of all political power but, rather, the placement of it where it belongs, in the hands of the people.[17] Similarly, few people tried to take recourse to some sort of violent methods also in carrying out the movement for total revolution. But JP was firm in his conviction that the total revolution could be brought about only through the peaceful and non-violent voluntary actions on the part of the people.

As is evident, JP had launched a successful crusade against the internal Emergency which resulted in its revocation in 1977. The campaign was fair because it was against the efforts of a select political leadership to debase governance for its partisan mission. In other words, by challenging the authority that took away the constitutionally guaranteed democratic rights, JP had articulated a voice for re-establishing the republican spirit of the Constitution. It would not be an exaggeration to suggest that Emergency was a paradox of history since it was 'as much a constitutional response by Indira Gandhi to the constitutional means as the opposition parties had adopted, to unseat her'.[18] The Emergency thus provided us with an experience that brought out very clearly that 'the Constitution contained provisions in it that could both enhance the democratic rights of the people and be used to deny [them] even the [constitutionally endorsed] fundamental rights'.[19] Nonetheless, the proclamation of Emergency had created a context in which the issue of ethics in

[17] Dennis Dalton, 'The Ideology of Sarvodaya: Concepts of Politics and Power in Indian Political Thought', in *Political Thought in Modern India*, eds. Thomas Pantham and Kenneth L. Deutsch (New Delhi: SAGE Publications, 1986), 292.
[18] Ananth V. Krishna, *India since Independence: Making Sense of Indian Politics* (New Delhi: Pearson, 2011), 143.
[19] Ibid.

governance was not only raised but was also sought to be conclu-sively addressed. JP can thus be said to have set in motion processes whereby the importance of a moral code of conduct for the public personnel was forcefully reiterated.

The paradoxical nature of Emergency and JP's successful mobiliza-tion against the excesses raise an open-ended question if one seeks to comprehend those two tumultuous years in independent India's recent political history. The Emergency was a constitutional act, so was the challenge that the opposition parties had mounted on the prevalent political authority. If Emergency was a constitution-endorsed design of authoritarianism, it was not a deviation from the rule of law; and hence, those who proclaimed escaped condemnation. Similarly, the opposition parties were within the constitutional bounds when they protested by undertaking what the ruling authority had dubbed as unconstitutional means. A very piquant situation had emerged. Whether the governing elites indulged in unethical practices while declaring an Emergency following the constitutional provisions is definitely a question that cannot be answered conclusively. Likewise, the fact that the mass endeavour towards unseating the Congress party was drawn on fulfilling the basic constitutional rights further complicates the issue. In either of the cases, the rule of law was not grossly violated although its application, seeking to realize the whim-sical personal preferences of the leadership, was certainly contrary to the fundamental ethical values from which the Constitution of India derives its sustenance. As shown in Chapter 5, the 1977 Shah Commission illustrated how a majority of the public personnel never cared for the basic ethical values while executing instructions from above; not only did they personalize authority, they also indulged in activities which were contrary to their constitutional obligations. The Commission had expressed being alarmed at the number of instances of deliberate distortions of rules and regulations for supporting their 'misdeeds'. The government became a captive of elite interests ignoring public outcry against the deviant public personnel. JP gave a powerful voice to those who, regardless of consequences, agreed to fight for the restoration of constitutional governance which was legitimately sacrificed, as the perpetrators of Emergency justified, to save the country from being devastated due to the organized protest of the opposition parties that had begun in Bihar in 1974. The support that JP was able to generate for his anti-corruption campaign had 'more to do with the political and economic context than Narayan's demagoguery'.[20] Plagued by social and economic underdevelopment, population pressures and underemployment in the state, the ordinary Indians seemed to have been completely disillusioned with the prevalent state which led to growing hostility towards those in charge of political authority and to 'their self-serving mismanagement'.[21] The movement struck organic roots in a propitious milieu and it was therefore easier for JP to mobilize the masses with a purpose. His leadership was undoubtedly a rallying point in bringing together people with contrasting ideological inclinations when he exhorted them to join him in his opposition to the Emergency.

The anti-Emergency campaign was thus as much an ideological protest against a debasing government as it was an endeavour to establish a code of ethics for those holding public authority. A fight for restoring constitutional democracy, JP's crusade was, in other words, an effort towards creating and also consolidating a social climate for concerns for ethics to strike organic roots to avoid '[a]rbitrariness and reckless disregard of the rights of other and the consequent misery [which] ... terrorized citizens resulting in a complete loss of faith of the people in the fairness and objectivity of the Administration generally'.[22] By contributing to the rise of a context in which government machineries were utilized to the detriment of their public aim, the two-year Emergency was also an eye-opener in the sense that it had shown, rather virulently, how an ethically derailed public authority deviated from the basic code of conduct while discharging

---

[20] Mathew Jenkins, 'Anna Hazare, Liberalization and the Careers of Corruption in Modern India: 1974–2011', *Economic & Political Weekly* 49, no. 33 (August 16, 2014): 44.

[21] John R. Wood, 'Extra-parliamentary Opposition in India: An Analysis of Populist Agitations in Gujarat and Bihar', *Pacific Affairs* 48, no. 3 (1975): 319.

[22] Era Sezhiyan, comp. and ed., 'Third and Final Report', in *The Shah Commission Report: Lost and Regained* (Aazhi Publishers, Chennai, 2010), 228.

its role. Governance became highly personalized from top to bottom and authority was exercised in a tyrannical fashion violating, without qualms, the fundamental constitutional ethos supportive of democracy and individual rights.

Concluding Observations

The ideological milieu that the 1975 JP movement had created was translated in the repeal of a large number of Draconian laws (codified in the 1977 Forty-second Amendment Act) through the Forty-third and Forty-fourth Amendment Acts in 1978. In other words, the fact that the mounting public pressure resulted in the abrogation of laws supporting authoritarianism also confirms the critical role that social context plays in shaping a specific ideological stance. Similarly, the insistence on a strong Lokpal by those involved in the India against Corruption campaign of 2011 can also be said to have its roots in the movement that Hazare had launched against the debilitating impact of corruption in India's public life.

There is one fundamental conceptual point here: corruption and decline of ethics are dialectically inter-connected; while the former has had 'variegated incidence in different times at different places, with varying degrees of damaging consequences',[23] the latter also unfolds gradually and is thus contingent on specific mindsets which either remain indifferent or supportive of 'some sort of malfeasance for private enrichment'.[24] There can thus hardly be a universal explanatory model because this interrelationship is also context driven. For instance, in the erstwhile Licence-Quota-Permit Raj guaranteeing massive discretionary power to those holding public authority, corruption was considered to be 'the much-needed grease for squeaking wheels of rigid administration'.[25] Gradually, the idea seems to have

[23] Pranab Bardhan, 'Corruption and Development: A Review of Issues', *Journal of Economic Literature* XXXV (September, 1997): 1320.

[24] Ibid., 1321.

[25] Samuel P. Huntington, *Political Order in Changing Societies* (New Haven, CT: Yale University Press, 1968), 386.

lost steam. In the mid-1970s, the efforts towards utilizing government machineries for personal gains provoked mass consternation which was reflected in the 1975 JP movement. Challenging the ideological design of those in power, the campaign for JP's total revolution created, rather instantaneously, a constituency of support in the country presumably because of the abuse of authority by the powerful at the cost of the ordinary citizens. This was the main factor behind the massive campaign that JP had spearheaded in collaboration with political forces with incompatible ideological predilections.

CHAPTER 3

Consolidation of Dynastic Politics

One of the major side effects of electoral politics in almost all the major democratic countries in the world is the prevalence of political dynasties.[1] Taking advantage of the elector's sustained support and vote for longer periods of time, certain political families are indeed able to monopolize the political power in such a way that they become a formidable player and serious contender for power at all the times in a country. Although the phenomenon of dynastic politics is not uncommon even in the mature democracies, it attains alarming proportions in countries like India where the primordial affinities of people such as caste, religion and language remain a major determinant of voting behaviour of common electors. At the same time, the resilience of the dynastic politics is also maintained through the politics of patronage as well.[2] The roots of dynastic politics in the

---

[1] Although dynastic politics has not been a preferred subject of research among analysts, an important work on the subject is Kanchan Chandra, ed., *Democratic Dynasties: State, Party and Family in Contemporary Indian Politics* (New Delhi: Cambridge University Press, 2016).

[2] Editorial, 'Resilience of Dynastic Politics: Dynastic Politics Rules because It Is the Best of Way to Practice the Politics of Patronage', *Economic & Political Weekly* 47, no. 25 (June 23, 2012): 7.

country may be considered to have begun even before India attained Independence. But since the cause of joining politics during that period of time was as pious as fighting for the independence of one's motherland, nobody could question the veracity of generations after generations of a family joining the national movement. However, the perspective and scenario of dynastic politics underwent radical transformation after Independence when joining politics became a means of controlling the levers of political power in the country. Thus, while in the pre-Independence days, joining politics meant serving the cause of nation, in the post-Independence times, politics turned out to be a career for the young ladies and gentlemen of well-entrenched families who have already been holding control over the political power at different levels.

The first political dynasty in India is unarguably the Nehru–Gandhi family whose lineage goes back to the pre-Independence days. Carrying forward the political legacy of his father Motilal Nehru, Jawaharlal Nehru not only emerged as the towering personality of the national movement but also became the prime minister of India after Independence. However, Jawaharlal Nehru's emergence as the most powerful political personality in the post-Independence period has never been attributed to his being son of Motilal Nehru. Rather, Nehru played a critical role in the national movement and earned himself the unflinching faith of Mahatma Gandhi that eventually became the most significant determinant in getting him the position of the prime minister of the country. But the dynastic contours of his family became apparent with the emergence of his daughter Indira Gandhi as the prime minister banking on the lineage of her father and grandfather. Since then, the Congress party has turned into a pocket borough of that family. Later, taking cue from the first political family of the country, many more political dynasties have emerged in different parts of India converting the electoral arena of the Indian democracy, primarily if not totally, into a power struggle among just a few families. Bringing out this stark reality of the Indian politics, two analysts write so succinctly,

> while the Nehru–Gandhi family dominates the discourse about dynasty, this culture thrives across political parties and

regions—from the north to the south, the west to the east. Such is the extent of dynastic politics that some families have members who not only cut across political divide but also across state lines.[3]

Elections as Means of Legitimization of Dynastic Politics

In democratic political systems, more often than not, elections are used as a means of legitimization of dynastic politics.[4] As a matter of fact, creation of political dynasties in democratic political systems usually germinates from two patently undemocratic considerations on the part of well-entrenched political interests of certain individuals. First, on account of reasons ranging from participation in some movements including national movement to belonging to a royal family, when a person gets a chance to get elected and hold public office, there is much likelihood of that person getting re-elected and continuing in the office for a fairly long period of time, particularly in parliamentary democracies like India. Getting re-elected and holding a public office for longer periods of time eventually drive a sense of private ownership of the electoral process as well as public offices in the persons holding them. Not only the power and prestige coming with the public offices tend to make them habituated to them, the easy accessibility of these offices make them think in terms of making the public offices as their personal fiefs. Hence, when the holders of these offices are rendered incapable of continuing to hold them due to old age or any other incapacity including passing away, they tend to anoint their kith and kin as the natural inheritors of their political legacies in terms of electoral constituencies and public offices they used to hold.

Second, since the democratic and republican form of government does not allow space for hereditary or traditional holding of

[3] Ruhi Tiwari and Rohini Swamy, 'These Are India's 34 Most Powerful Political Families', *The Print*, 8 March 2019, accessed 8 March 2019, https://theprint.in/politics/these-are-indias-34-most-powerful-political-families/202724/

[4] An alternative argument is also advanced to take elections as democratization of power and not legitimization of dynastic rule. See Subrata K. Mitra, 'India: Dynastic Rule or Democratisation of Power?' *Third World Quarterly* 10, no. 1 (January 1988): 129–159.

power, the politically well-entrenched individuals seek to utilize the route of elections to transfer their political legacy to their kith and kin. In fact, elections are the only way for legitimization of transfer of political legacies of deep-rooted political interests to their next generations. Although the entire game of transferring one's political legacy to the next generation is well designed and planted, it remains legally unquestionable because there is nothing illegal in standing in elections and getting elected. Ethically, however, such unscrupulous designs are quite obvious and potentially dangerous for vibrant nature of the democratic polity. Thus, taking advantage of these functional deficiencies of democracy, well-entrenched selfish elements are able to perpetuate their dominance over the representative institutions of democracy. In this regard, India may be reckoned as one of the established democracies where the phenomenon of dynastic politics is found to be full blown. Not only at the national level, the breadth of dynastic politics gets widened as one goes down the line. No state in India is free from a few entrenched political families that continue to hold the levers of political power. Similarly, most, if not all, of the political parties are also afflicted by this phenomenon in varying degrees. While the personality-based political parties are nothing but pocket borough of their founders, even the parties that have long and glorious public standing are also not immune to domination by dynastic politics.

Nehru–Gandhi family is referred to as the first political family of the country. The epithet does not appear to be out of place given the stewardship of the oldest political party of India resting primarily with one or the other member of the family barring a few occasions. Similarly, with the exception of only P. V. Narasimha Rao and Manmohan Singh, whenever the Congress got a chance to form the government at the centre, a member of the family only has headed the government. The two non-family members of the party could occupy the position of prime minister only due to the fact that none of the family members was prepared to take up the position despite such a clamour from the party circles. In fact, the dynastic contours of the Congress party did not appear to be quite apparent during the times of Jawaharlal Nehru despite active role assumed by his daughter in the affairs of both party and government. Thus, Indira Gandhi was sufficiently groomed even from the pre-Independence times to take up responsibilities in public life at opportune times. But since the dynastic tendencies in the Indian politics had still not become very strong, Indira Gandhi could not stake her claim for the office of prime minister after the death of her father in 1964, paving way for Lal Bahadur Shastri to become prime minister.

The circumstantial turn of events within a short span of time led to the untimely death of Shastri which again left the office of prime minister an open-ended issue. Not to miss the opportunity for the second time, Indira Gandhi managed to become the prime minister. In her bid for the office of prime minister, apart from any other thing, what Indira Gandhi banked upon most was her quali-fication as daughter of Jawaharlal Nehru. Thus, a healthy political convention which had been put into shape by way of appointment of Shastri as prime minister instead of Indira Gandhi after the death of Nehru was nipped in the bud. In place of that what got established was that the most significant qualification of a person to hold any high public office was to be the son or daughter of the incumbent holder of office. In other words, since Indira Gandhi's selection as prime minister was clinched primarily on the basis of her lineage to her father, this heralded the convention of dynastic politics in India. However, her elevation to the position of prime minister was quite unwillingly accepted by the top leadership of the Congress party. Indira Gandhi was very well aware of such a state of things in her party and was looking for ways to not only establish her supremacy in the party but also get legitimization from the general populace of the country. She was convinced that only when she could secure the solid backing of the people that her claim to the office of prime minister of India could naturally be accepted over and above her lineage to her father. It was probably these considerations that eventually led to the split of the Congress party in 1969 affording her the opportunity to form the Congress (R).[5] Later, her party became the true inheritor of the legacy of the Congress party, thereby strengthening the move towards dynastic politics in India.

[5] Inder Malhotra, *Indira Gandhi: A Personal and Political Biography* (London: Hodder and Stoughton, 1989), 128.

In the parliamentary democracy, elections are considered as the final settler of any sort of political dispute or contestation. Once a person, issue or event becomes a subject of electoral battle and gets vote of majority of people, that usually becomes legal, legitimate and acceptable notwithstanding the moral or ethical deficiencies of that subject. Such an incontrovertible sanctity of electoral legitimization of an individual became quite alluring for her given the tight position in which she was pushed by the political dynamics of the time. Clearly, the inherent reluctance of the senior leaders of the Congress to accept Indira Gandhi as the prime minister started getting reflected in their raising objections to her style of functioning. Moreover, in the day-to-day working of the party, her say was almost negligible as the party stalwarts would not allow her to interfere in the affairs of the party in the capacity of the head of government. The chasm between the top leadership of the Congress party and Indira Gandhi became so intense that she was left with no option than to go for splitting the party. Although the majority of the party members of Lok Sabha were with her, her government was reduced to a minority, and therefore, for survival of her government she had to take support from the left parties, apart from certain other regional parties. But running such a minority government was not an easy proposition as she had to face unsavoury behaviour on the part of opposition parties on day-to-day basis. In fact, the opposition parties were at their best to undermine the legitimacy of the government by very frequently bringing no confidence motion on the floor of Lok Sabha. So much so that within a span of just one year (1969–1970), the opposition parties were able to introduce as many as three no-confidence motions in the lower house of the Indian parliament, which she survived anyhow.[6]

Despite managing the survival of her government after split in the party, Indira Gandhi faced the perpetual problem of being recognized as a leader in her own without being referred to as daughter of Nehru who had just been made prime minister on account of her lineage to him. As the prime minister, she probably did her best to prove her fitness for being the prime minister by taking a number of measures

[6] Meera Raghani, *India and Indira* (Varanasi: A. S. Mookherjee and L. D. Raghani, 1972), 3.

and initiating a host of policies and programmes that aimed at bringing about a turnaround in the social and economic status of the people. But the concerted opposition to her government's policies from both the judiciary and her political opponents left her with no option but to go to the larger court of people. In other words, after carrying on with running the government for some time, she thought it prudent to go for general elections in order to get the public approval for her claim to the office of prime minister and the actions and policies she initiated in that capacity. Thus, the 1971 general elections were portrayed by Indira Gandhi as a kind of plebiscite on her personality, lineage, policies and programmes. Through vigorous and strategic campaign along with pro-poor posturing during the elections, she could win a landslide in these elections. Although she could manage to get support from almost all sections of society, the groups that were said to have voted en masse in favour of Indira Gandhi consisted primarily, if not exclusively, of minorities, particularly Muslims, scheduled castes and women.[7] Apart from other things, the results of these elections legitimized Indira Gandhi's ambitions of dynastic politics and set an undesirable trend in the Indian politics.

Dynastic Context of 1984 General Elections

Dynastic orientations of 1984 general elections can probably be traced back to the previous general elections held in 1971 and 1980. The landslide victory of Indira Gandhi in 1971 Lok Sabha elections made her assume unparalleled powers in both party and government. It would, rather, not be incorrect to argue that she became synonym to party and government. With the old party organization remaining with the syndicates and getting smashed in the general elections, the electoral victory of 1971 was to be considered as a personal victory of Indira Gandhi who could mobilize the voters to vote for her even in the absence of any party organization or functionary at the booth level. So whatever party organization emerged in the post-election scenario was nothing but product of her vision and efforts. Thus, she became

[7] S. Nihal Singh, *Indira's India: A Political Notebook* (Bombay: Nachiketa Publications, 1978), 182.

the matriarch of the party for whom the party was subordinate to her, and she considered her over and above the party organization. Similar was to be the status of government and ministers. Since the formation of government was because of her landslide victory scripted single-handedly by her, all the ministers and functionaries of the government owed their power and position to the prime minister only. As a result, she virtually considered both the party and government as her personal fief which she created and owned by dint of her individual efforts and perseverance. Hence, on such personal fiefs, there could not have been claim of any other person than her own sons.

On the familial front, the two sons of Indira Gandhi—Rajiv and Sanjay—were of quite different nature and preferred to pursue divergent courses of life as their career options. While Rajiv preferred to live a non-political life remaining engaged in his career of a commercial pilot,[8] his younger brother was out-and-out a public figure who wished to get involved in each and every affair of party and government on behalf of his mother. Thus, Sanjay was perfectly groomed by his mother and her political cronies to take charge of the party and government at opportune time in future, leaving not even an iota of doubt in the minds of political analysts that the dynastic ambitions of Indira Gandhi would be carried forward by her younger son Sanjay in place of the elder one. Gradually, Sanjay was given greater responsibilities in the party organization in order to make him learn the nuances of party organization. But since his personal orientation was also for taking control of the reins of government, he started playing proactive role in running the affairs of the government wielding informal powers as son of the prime minister. In fact, the most significant political act of Sanjay that left indelible mark on the democratic polity of the country would be his role in pushing his mother for the imposition of Emergency in 1975 amidst the growing political crisis arising out of JP's nationwide massive anti-government movement.

But before Sanjay Gandhi could have formally taken over the political and governmental responsibilities of his mother, he met with

---

[8] Bhabani Sen Gupta, *Rajiv Gandhi: A Political Study* (New Delhi: Konark Publishers, 1990), 67.

an unfortunate death in an air crash in Delhi in 1980. Such a sudden and tragic death of her political heir apparent left Indira Gandhi shattered and caused a sort of vacuum in the inheritance of her political legacy. Given that Rajiv Gandhi was until then a complete apolitical person keeping himself engaged in his professional responsibilities with Indian Airlines, for a while, it seemed as if the Nehru–Gandhi political dynasty was not going to continue as the first political family of the country. Such an apprehension got more strength with Indira Gandhi leaving it upon Rajiv to decide the future course of life without any fear of or favour to his mother. But what Indira Gandhi could not do was got done by her loyal party men who appeared more disturbed than Indira Gandhi herself on the possibility of a break in the political lineage of Nehru–Gandhi dynasty as the born ruler of India. So they started making earnest appeals to the heir apparent to accept their requests to join politics and become the saviour of party, government and the country in the main. Although Rajiv Gandhi resisted such appeals for some time on the strength of the unflinching support of his wife Sonia for his stand of not joining politics, he could not put up with that formidable stand for long in face of repeated appeals and eventually agreed to join politics in the purported interest of the nation.

The thread of dynastic politics was retied with induction of Rajiv Gandhi in the whirlwind of the Indian politics. His grand entry began with his nomination as the Congress candidate for Amethi Lok Sabha election fallen vacant after death of his brother Sanjay. Predictably, Rajiv Gandhi won this election with comfortable majority and assumed the first formal political role as a Member of Parliament. At the same time, it was also decided by Indira Gandhi to bestow some organizational responsibilities to him in order to give him certain exposure to the structure and functioning of the party organization. Accordingly, he was made the general secretary of the party with the responsibility of revitalizing the frontal organizations of the party, particularly the youth Congress. Thus, the political and organizational grooming of Rajiv Gandhi began under the experienced hands of party stalwarts who were keen to make sure that the next line of familial lineage was to be ready to take up the reins of the party or government as and when required. With such a long-term perspective, the dynastic chain in the Congress party was again reconnected and kept in place to ensure seamless transfer of power from one generation to another at appropriate time. The anticipated time for transfer of power from one generation to another of the Nehru–Gandhi family unfortunately came earlier than expected when on 31 October 1984, Indira Gandhi was assassinated by her security guards at her New Delhi residence.[9]

While the entire nation was plunged into a pall of gloom over the tragic assassination of its prime minister, the party brass wasted no time in nominating Rajiv Gandhi as the leader of the Congress Parliamentary Party and, in turn, prime minister of India. Thus, the baton of government was passed on smoothly to the next generation of the family, thereby deep rooting the dynastic portents of the Indian politics for the years to come. Given that the newly appointed prime minister did not have any experience of holding any official position in the Government of India, his initial days as prime minister witnessed one of the most dastardly massacres of Sikhs in the capital city of Delhi. However, the situation was brought under control within a couple of days though the public sympathy was with the prime minister on the loss of his mother that absolved him of accountability for death of such a large number of innocent people. As had the trend been set by his mother Indira Gandhi, it was also suggested to Rajiv Gandhi to prove his legitimacy as the leader of the party and government by going for general elections sooner than due date. As the wave of sympathy on account of the death of his mother was sweeping all the nooks and corners of the country, Rajiv Gandhi was advised that sooner the general elections are held better that would be for the party. Accordingly, general elections were announced to be held in the second half of December 1984.

1984 General Elections

The general elections of 1984 might also be considered as a conscious attempt on the part of the proponents of dynastic politics to legitimize the transfer of power from one generation to another at the hands of

---

[9] Robert L. Hardgrave, 'India in 1984: Confrontation, Assassination and Succession', *Asian Survey* 25, no. 2 (February 1985): 133.

the common people of India. In comparing the circumstances and processes of transfer of power from one generation to another during 1965 and 1984, sharp differences could easily be made out. Since the dynastic politics had still not become part of political traditions in India in 1965, Indira Gandhi was not considered as the natural heir to the position of prime minister fallen vacant after the passing away of her father. As a result, Lal Bahadur Shastri was appointed the prime minister with Indira Gandhi remaining nowhere in the reckoning. As against that, by 1984, dynastic politics had been deeply ingrained in the political culture and public psyche of the Indian political class. As a result, no sooner than Indira Gandhi was assassinated, no time was wasted in nominating her son Rajiv as the prime minister as there was no question of anybody else staking claim to the position of leader of Congress Parliamentary Party that would have eventually landed him or her into the office of prime minister.[10] Thus, the trend of dynastic politics had already gained ground with the moral bankruptcy associated with it getting washed out by way of electoral mandate secured by the new generation of leadership in succeeding elections.

After announcement of the general elections, hectic political activities surrounded the Congress office at Akbar Road in New Delhi. Given that Rajiv Gandhi was a political novice, most, if not all, of the activities of managing the elections right from distribution of tickets through the campaigns and analysing the outcomes rested with the old guards of the party. However, two distinct patterns were evident throughout the proceedings of these elections. First, each and every activity of the party was attributed to Rajiv Gandhi with a view to projecting him as the supreme leader of the party irrespective of whosoever held the formal position of party president. Second, in the course of election campaigns, the issue that was highlighted more than anything else was that Indira Gandhi had attained the martyrdom for the cause of the nation, and it was time now for the nation to repay the debt to her son for her sacrifices. In other words, the whole electoral exercise was portrayed in the image of a grateful nation paying its debt

[10] Karen Kelly, 'A Gandhi Carries On', *Harvard International Review* (January–February 1985): 26.

Table 3.1 Results of 1984 General Elections[a]

All India (514)	INC	BJP	CPI	CPI (M)	ICS	JNP	LKD	Others	Independents
No. of Seats	404	02	06	22	04	10	03	58	5
Percentage of votes	49.10	7.74	2.71	5.87	1.52	6.89	5.97	11.56	7.92

Source: Computed from the *Statistical Report on General Elections, 1984 to the Eighth Lok Sabha*, vol. I (New Delhi: Election Commission of India, 1985), 78.
Note: [a] The table excludes the figures from Assam and Punjab as elections in these states could not be held along with the other states due to law and order problem in the two states.

to the departed leader by voting overwhelmingly to her son who had now been given the charge of carrying forward her political legacies. Rajiv Gandhi was projected as the natural successor to his mother, and the voters needed to vote for him to ensure that the dynastic rule of Nehru–Gandhi family continued in the country unhindered.[11] Undoubtedly, the sympathy wave led the Congress to sweep the polls and securing an unprecedented number of seats in the lower house of the Indian parliament.

Table 3.1 presents the summary of the results of the eighth general elections held in December 1984. Initially, the elections were held for only 514 Lok Sabha seats as the elections for Lok Sabha seats lying in Assam and Punjab could not be held due to challenges of social movements and terrorism, respectively, in the two states. The unprecedented impact of sympathy wave on the voting behaviour of people could be seen from the number of seats won and percentage of votes polled by the Congress party in these elections.[12] Both of these figures were historical for the party as it had never been polled such a high percentage of votes in any of the past general elections. The support base of

[11] James Manor, 'Rajiv Gandhi and Post-Election India: Opportunities and Risks', *The World Today* 41, no. 3 (March 1985): 53.
[12] Praveen Rai and Sanjay Kumar, 'The Decline of Congress Party in Indian Politics', *Economic & Political Weekly* 52, no. 12 (March 25, 2017): 46.

the Congress party extended to almost every state and union territory. All the social groups voted in favour of the party in such a concerted way that the opposition parties were swept away to their worst ever performances in any of the general elections. Such a stunning victory for the Congress party was anticipated neither by the Congress party nor the opposition.[13]

The historical victory of the Congress in these elections not only surprised its leadership including the prime minister but also upset the composition of the lower house in such a way that a regional party, the Telugu Desam Party (TDP), emerged as the largest opposition group with 30 seats in the Lok Sabha whose leader was to be appointed as the leader of opposition. In other words, the victorious march of the Congress party led to the decisive trouncing of most, if not all, of the opposition parties such as the Bharatiya Janata Party (BJP), the Janata Party and the Lok Dal. These powerful parties of the Indian politics were reduced to insignificance in the Lok Sabha. Among the left parties, the CPI (M) could succeed in keeping its support base intact to some extent in its traditional bastion of West Bengal by winning a respectable number of 22 seats. However, the other important left party, the CPI could not withstand the Congress wave and could manage to win only six seats with a meagre 2.6 per cent of votes polled. In this regard, an interesting trend had been the mismatch between the percentage of votes polled and the number of seats won by different opposition parties.[14] For instance, despite securing 7.74 per cent of votes polled, the BJP could win only 2 seats as compared to the Indian Congress (Socialist) (ICS) which won 4 seats despite securing only 1.52 per cent of total votes polled.

The sweep of the Congress party continued even after the conclusion of the general elections in December 1984. The deferred elections of Assam and Punjab were held later in early 1985, in which the winning streak of the Congress continued though not with the same

[13] Paul R. Brass, 'The 1984 Parliamentary Elections in Uttar Pradesh', *Asian Survey* 26, no. 6 (June 1986): 653.

[14] T. C. Bose, 'The Eighth General Elections and the Indian Polity', *Indian Journal of Political Science* 47, no. 1 (January–March, 1986): 142.

momentum in which it had won the main general elections held in December 1984.[15] Since both the states of Assam and Punjab were marred by social movements and terrorism, respectively, the parties spearheading and/or having sympathetic outlook towards these issues emerged as the major gainers of the elections. Thus, the major gainer of Lok Sabha polls in Assam had been the Asom Gana Parishad, the novice political party of college and university students of Assam whose nominees cornered majority of Lok Sabha seats in the state. Similarly, in Punjab, the Congress was taken as the spoiler of the cause of Sikh state, and, therefore, the Shiromani Akali Dal (SAD) that won majority of seats in the state emerged to be the star of the Lok Sabha elections in the state. Despite the adverse situations in the two states, the Congress was able to add 10 more seats to its swelling kitty of 404 seats in the Lok Sabha. Thus, in the final composition of the eighth Lok Sabha, the Congress commanded the unprecedented majority of 414 seats that made its leader Rajiv Gandhi the most formidable personality of the Indian politics of the time.[16]

Interestingly, the 1984 general elections were fought on the issue of national security. The Congress sought to present the assassination of Indira Gandhi as the gravest challenge to the national security of India given the prevalence of insurgency and terrorism in certain parts of the country. Since the terrorism in Punjab seemed to be at its peak at that time and the assassination of Indira Gandhi was directly related to the happenings in Punjab, it was argued that her assassination was a direct threat to the national security of the country on the part of the forces active to destabilize the country and undermine its democratic polity. As a natural corollary of such an argument, the voters were called upon to vote in favour of the Congress party under the leadership of Rajiv Gandhi to show their resolute resolve to thwart any challenge to the unity and integrity of the country. However, such arguments and exhortations of the Congress leaders appeared

---

[15] Vani Kant Barooah, 'Incumbency and Parliamentary Elections in India: An Analysis of the Congress Party's Electoral Performance, 1962–1999', *Economic & Political Weekly* 41, no. 8 (March 3, 2006): 744.

[16] Iqbal Narain, 'India in 1985: Triumph of Democracy', *Asian Survey* 26, no. 2 (February 1986): 258.

just as attempts to rationalize the sympathy wave that was sufficiently visible in all the nooks and corners of the country in support of the Congress party. Indira Gandhi's assassination was taken by people as an irreparable loss to the first family of the country, and therefore, the scion of that family, Rajiv Gandhi, must be given a landslide victory in order to prove the point that the country stood in solidarity with the family in safeguarding the unity and integrity and warding off all attempts at destabilizing the country. Amidst such a charged atmosphere, the unprecedented victory of the Congress party under Rajiv Gandhi appeared a foretold story that got translated in mammoth majority for him in the Lok Sabha.

Impact of 1984 General Elections on Indian Democracy

The outcome of the 1984 general elections set a number of powerful trends that left far reaching implications for the Indian democracy. One of such impacts had been the loss of importance of issues as the basis of contesting elections in a democracy. Theoretically, in a democratic polity, different political parties present themselves before the voters on basis of certain issues, policies and programmes embalmed in the ideological perspective that various parties stand to profess. Before the 1984 general elections, the significance of issues in electoral politics in India had also been well entrenched and parties always used to come out with distinct sets of issues and challenges that they would address once voted to power. Even during the times of Pandit Nehru and Indira Gandhi, when their towering personalities would lead to obliteration of issues from general elections, they would also proclaim their focus on certain vital aspects of life of people. If nothing else, they would present themselves only as the critical issue in the elections. In this context, Indira Gandhi's words are quite memorable. When asked about the issues of the 1971 general elections, she replied cryptically, 'I am the issue'.[17] But insofar as the 1984 general elections were concerned, Indira Gandhi's assassination had left such

[17] Cited in Katherine Frank, *Indira: The Life of Indira Nehru Gandhi* (London: Harper Collins Publishers, 2001), 323.

deep impact on the psyche of the Indian electorate that they tended to forget everything else and decided to vote for her party and son without probably expecting anything in return.

More than anything else, the unprecedented mark that these elections left on the Indian democracy was legitimization of dynastic rule in the country. Rajiv Gandhi's uncritical acceptance as the mass leader of India even without testing his political or administrative credentials at any level of government proved that Nehru–Gandhi family has now got firmly established as the first family of the country with its scions likely to inherit the informal right to rule over the country through democratic methods. Arguably, though the seeds of dynastic politics were sown with the anointment of Indira Gandhi as the prime minister after the death of Lal Bahadur Shastri, such a move was critically accepted, subdued in tone and came after a reasonable interregnum after the death of Nehru. Moreover, apart from being Nehru's daughter, Indira Gandhi had by that time emerged as a political personality on her own banking upon her role in the national movement, her proximity with the leading stars of Indian national movement, particularly Mahatma Gandhi, and her efforts in strengthening the party and hands of her father during the course of his tenure as prime minister of India. She did have sufficient administrative experience as a minister in the central government and was considered competent to take over the reins of the country at an appropriate time by the supporters of the Congress party. However, in case of Rajiv Gandhi, very few, if any, of the merits that made his mother one of the powerful contenders for the position of prime minister, were present at the time of his appointment as the prime minister. In fact, at that time, his only qualification for the position of prime minister was that he was the son of Indira Gandhi. So his credentials for the top office of the country could have been justified only on the logic of dynastic rule which the 1984 elections legitimized and turned him into a more mass leader than his mother and maternal grandfather.

These elections also probably irrevocably established the centrality of regional parties in the Indian democratic politics. As a matter of fact, though, the importance of regional parties had already been visible in a number of states, particularly the northern and southern states of India, they would one day overtake the so-called national parties to become the main opposition party in the Lok Sabha was not in anybody's reckoning. There were a number of mass-based regional parties in the Hindi heartland of Uttar Pradesh and Bihar along with many other states like Tamil Nadu in south. But the sympathy wave created in favour of the Congress party and Rajiv Gandhi in the aftermath of Indira Gandhi's assassination happened to be so unparalleled in the history of post-Independence India that very few of the political parties could hold on to their strongholds and paved way for deep inroads by the Congress in their traditional vote banks. As a result, TDP emerged as the dark horse of the 1984 electoral politics bagging the highest number of seats among the opposition parties. Since then, the formidability of regional parties in different states of India has consistently been rising so much so that they would soon make the nature of Indian party politics a coalitional one in place of one-party dominant system. Although the victory of the BJP in 2014 general elections as full majority party in Lok Sabha revived the days of single majority government at centre, the weight of regional parties in the Indian politics did not get diminished in any substantial way.

In a way, the eighth general elections may be considered as one of the paradoxical general elections in India. The paradox of the polls lay in the fact that while it produced one of the highest majorities for the Congress party in the Lok Sabha, such a brute majority was given to the youngest and one of the most inexperienced holders of the office of prime minister in the country. On account of the dynamics of dynastic politics, a superlative majority was given to a person not because of his unparalleled perseverance and superfine political and administrative credentials, but merely because of his lineage to a family that had already given two prime ministers to the country. What repercussions such an unconsidered voting behaviour towards an untested individual could have been were visible soon after Rajiv Gandhi took charge of the office of prime minster after constitution of the eighth Lok Sabha. His penchant for resolving various pending ethnic issues both within and outside the country not only brought consternations in the Indian foreign policy but also cost his life. His defence deals were questioned by his opponents with such deft and stridency that he lost the next general elections. Thus, the only positivity that the eighth Lok Sabha polls brought was to establish beyond any doubt the legitimacy of Rajiv Gandhi as the mass leader riding on the wave of dynastic politics.

Concluding Observations

Each of the general elections in India has been underlined by one or the other fundamental transformations that have impacted the nature of the Indian democracy in significant ways. That way, the 1984 general elections stand as the landmark election that helped in the consolidation of dynastic politics in the country. The most interesting part of the eighth general elections is the context in which they were announced and conducted on the part of the Congress party. Undoubtedly, after the tragic death of Sanjay Gandhi, Rajiv Gandhi was being projected as the heir apparent to his prime minister mother and for that, gradual responsibilities were being bestowed upon him in the party organization. But as far as governmental or administrative responsibilities were concerned, it was not anticipated that his mother would pass away so quickly that he would have to shoulder the responsibility of running the government even without having any experience on that front. The turn of events did not allow Rajiv Gandhi to wait for more and he had to be anointed as the head of the government in place of his mother. Thus, Rajiv Gandhi's appointment as prime minister did not surprise anybody though the apprehensions in the sane minds of the country remained lingering as to how his inexperience would cast a shadow on the democratic government of the country.

The timing and processes of the 1984 general elections were finely tuned to meet the requirements of legitimizing the dynastic rule in the country. Not much time had passed since the assassination of his mother that Rajiv Gandhi was advised to go for general elections. The public sorrow in the psyche of common people of India was very much fresh and intact by the time of the announcement of elections. The Congress party leaders were sure that that was the ripe time to go for the polls if the party was to cash in on the death of Indira Gandhi. If the elections were delayed, the public memory regarding Indira Gandhi's supreme sacrifice for the cause of the nation would start fading away. As a result, in the forthcoming general elections, the electorate would tend to look into the successes or failures of the Congress-led government in place of Indira Gandhi's assassination. So it might not be far from the truth to argue that the announcement of the eighth general elections was a conscious attempt on the part of the Congress party to run away from any objective assessment of the performance of the government during the last four years. In turn, what the party wished was to make the elections bereft of any other issue than the assassination of Indira Gandhi which would further be portrayed as the sacrificial tradition of the Nehru–Gandhi family for the larger cause of the nation.

The outcome of the elections very well served the purpose for which they were organized. The splendid majority of the Congress party was unhesitatingly argued to be a vote in support of the newly appointed Prime Minister Rajiv Gandhi who was supposed to carry forward the rule of the family. Given that the election was suggested to be contested on the issue of warding off all probable challenges to the national security of the country, and Indira Gandhi's assassination was the most formidable challenge so far, the verdict of these elections was explained on those lines as well. The election was taken as a celebration of dynastic politics in such a way that the common people of India were sought to be convinced that the vital national interests of the country could be protected only if the reins of the government were in the hands of a scion of the Nehru–Gandhi family. It was also acknowledged as the uncritical support of the Indian electorate to Rajiv Gandhi's carrying on the tradition of his family by becoming the prime minister even without any previous experience in running the government. Thus, the most significant impact the 1984 general elections left on the Indian democracy was in consolidating the dynastic portents of the Indian politics. It not only legitimized the dynastic rule in the country but also opened the doors for emergence of many more political families in which democratic politics was nothing but a tool of legitimizing the seamless transfer of power from one generation to another within a family.

CHAPTER 4

Anti-Congressism with Renewed Vigour

Concerted opposition to the Congress on the part of the other parties has been one of the significant characteristic of Indian politics. The hegemonic nature of the party that ruled over the country for a long period of time in the post-Independence period owing to its legacy of the national movement has created a kind of aversion among almost all the opposition parties irrespective of their areas of influence. Interestingly, there is no denying the fact that a majority, if not all, of the opposition parties as well as their leaders did have some kind of direct or indirect association with the Congress in the past. But they left the Congress party at different points of time for different reasons. For instance, no less than a leader like V. P. Singh, the person who replaced Rajiv Gandhi as the prime minister of the country after the 1989 general elections was one of the towering personalities of the Congress holding as important ministries in the Rajiv Gandhi government as that of defence and finance, decided to leave the party just before the ninth general elections. The primary reason for Singh to leave the party was probably his shrewd calculation to become the catalyst of the anti-Congress political forces in the country in the wake of the party and its leader Rajiv Gandhi facing serious allegations of corruption epitomized by Bofors kickback scandal. In other words, as the public opinion during that time appeared to be turning against the

Rajiv Gandhi government, Singh found that as the most opportune time to leave the party and become the public hero.

Clearly, a majority of the leaders who left the Congress at different points of time apparently took that step on account of their selfish motives, though they tried to portray their departure from the party as a step in the broader public interest. For instance, while a number of leaders left the Congress during the time of Indira Gandhi on the pretext of saving democratic ethos of the party from the dynastic portents, several leaders departed from the party during the time of Rajiv Gandhi to take the high moral ground of not being part of the corruption that was alleged to have marred the party and government at that point of time. In the meantime, a number of regional satraps had also left the Congress to form their regional parties as they did not see any future for them by being part of the grand old party of the country. Irrespective of the motivations for different leaders to leave the Congress, the fact of the matter has been that over the years they turned out to be bitter adversaries of the party they originally belonged to. Besides these former Congressmen, there have also been a large number of leaders and parties who have traditionally harboured antipathy to the Congress party on account of their ideological predilections. The prominent among them could be the BJP whose espousal of the cause of Hindutva has always kept it on a different pedestal than the Congress throughout the democratic political processes of the country.[1] The left parties whose leadership has at times been averse to the ideology, policies and programmes of the Congress have also taken a distinct stand with regard to the Congress, and, therefore, they have never been part of the party in their entire political career.

Notwithstanding their parental roots, over the years, these parties and leaders had become bitter critics of the Congress. But in the face of the hegemonic character of the party, these parties failed to take on the Congress individually. So, what they were presumably looking for was an opportunity to come together to form a formidable front against the Congress so that they could put up a strong fight against

---

[1] Christophe Jaffrelot, *The Hindu Nationalist Movement and Indian Politics* (New Delhi: Penguin, 1996), 379.

the party. Eventually, such an opportunity arose for many of these parties soon when Singh left the Congress and formed his own political platform called Jan Morcha as the front against the corruption of the Congress. Soon, a number of other parties and leaders also joined Singh in forming what ultimately came to be known as the Janata Dal. Thus, the stage was set for the ninth general elections in the country with the Congress under the leadership of allegedly tainted Rajiv Gandhi entering the fray to face the opposition parties who appeared to be riding high on the wave of anti-Congressism in the face of corruption charges against the prime minister. The present chapter attempts to analyse the major theoretical underpinnings of the ninth general elections that have gone to determine the broad contours of the democratic politics in the country.

Political Scenario

With the announcement of the election schedule for the ninth general elections, the political scenario of the country appeared to be in a state of flux. The leaders of the Congress who seemed to be in the dilemmatic situation with regard to the electoral fortunes of the party started deserting the party one by one. As Singh had already floated his front on the issue of anti-corruption, such leaders naturally found a refuge in that front to take on the corrupt Congress. But majority of desertions from the Congress party over the years had also taken place partly because of dynastic orientations of the party. Given that after the assassination of Indira Gandhi, Rajiv Gandhi was made the prime minister at the relatively younger age of just 40 years, it had become apparent for many of the senior leaders of the party that they could never dream of becoming the prime minister of the country if they continue to remain in the Congress party. The apprehensions of such leaders were indeed true in view of the past record of the party. So what they found appropriate was to leave the party and become part of the anti-Congress bandwagon so as to carve out a distinct space for them. The political scenario of the country, therefore, during the ninth general elections appeared to be quite muddied because of the prevalence of a large number of anti-Congress groups vying for the political space likely to be vacated by the Congress in the wake of its likely rejection by the citizens due to the charges of corruption marring the prospects of the party.

After the sacking of Singh from the cabinet and his subsequent resignation from the Congress party, the turn of events in the country took such a curious turn that he somehow emerged as the crusader against the corruption and maladministration of the Rajiv Gandhi government. However, the background for the departure of Singh from the government seemed to have been created much before the time of elections. In view of the absence of any charismatic leader in the country at that period of time who could have taken on the incumbent prime minister despite serious charges of corruption against him, Singh was convinced that there existed a chance for him to emerge as the hero of the masses in case he was able to present himself as the person who sacrificed his power and position for the sake of fighting against the corruption of the government. He, therefore, started initiating subtle moves that would by implication present a picture of him as worried about the state of affairs in the party as well as government. With his moves apparently getting public reception through the favourable media and other means of public opinion shapers, he looked for an opportune time when he could make his final move from the government. Thus, Singh's cunning plan of emerging as the public hero to wage crusade against corruption materialized well as per his designs with his unceremonious removal from the cabinet by the prime minister.

The basic handle in the hands of the detractors of Rajiv Gandhi to beat him with was the Bofors scandal. As a matter of fact, when he had begun his stint as the prime minister of the country, Gandhi was seen as one of the unconventional politicians who did have an unblemished character and image. So much so that he was given the epitaph of Mr Clean owing to his uncharacteristic personality among the band of politicians who had one or other charges levelled against them. However, soon after his thumping electoral victory in the 1984 general elections, Gandhi began on a spree of not only taking head on different kinds of problems facing the country internally but also went to the extent of getting involved in resolving the long-standing issues of the neighbouring countries as well. While many of the forays of his government got success in resolving certain long-standing challenges facing the country, some of his decisions soon started becoming points of controversy and dispute attracting media attention and enquiry. One such issue was the purchase of Bofors guns from Sweden in which it was alleged that some of his close aides had received huge kickbacks. The allegations were accorded certain degree of credence with the media reports and the report of the Comptroller and Auditor General of India raising doubts about the transparency and integrity of the people involved in this deal. With the rising public perception against the image of the prime minister, persons like V. P. Singh obviously got a chance to make hay when the sun shined.[2]

The public perception within the country with regard to the prime ministerial stint of Rajiv Gandhi also got a beating with a number of other policy failures specifically attributed to him. In this regard, two issues stood out prominently. One, while Gandhi tried to resolve a number of long-standing challenges facing the unity and integrity of the country such as Assam and Mizoram, the part success of his moves in Punjab was presented by the opposition as his major policy failure. During his prime ministerial tenure, terrorism in the state had almost reached its crescendo with probably no day passing off without scores of people getting killed at the hands of the terrorists in the state. Although Rajiv Gandhi tried to sign a peace accord with the leaders of Punjab as well, his strategy in the state could not prove to be as successful as they had been in the other parts of the country. Thus, terrorism in Punjab remained one of the major unresolved issues that blemished the successful stint of his government. Two, in his urge to go beyond the territorial boundaries of the country and meddle in the resolution of the problems facing the neighbouring countries, Rajiv Gandhi also signed a peace accord with the Sri Lankan government towards the resolution of that country's ethnic problem involving the Tamils. As part of the peace accord, the Government of India sent the Indian Peace Keeping Forces (IPKF) to Sri Lanka to help Sri Lankan

[2] For a critical analysis of the tenure of Rajiv Gandhi as prime minister, see Atul Kohli, 'India's Democracy Under Rajiv Gandhi (1985–9)', in *India's Democracy: An Analysis of Changing State-Society Relations*, ed. Atul Kohli (New Delhi: Orient Longman, 1991), 321–337.

government put down the rebellion mounted by the Sri Lankan Tamils. While his moves were not able to resolve the Sri Lankan conundrum fully and finally, they, nonetheless, earned the public ire both in India and Sri Lanka that eventually cost his life.

During this period, the political churning in the country was also taking curious turns with different national and regional political parties desperate to expand base in their respective areas of influence. In their electoral pursuits, the most formidable challenge was undoubtedly the pan-India presence of the Congress party that had just in the previous election been able to corner most of the Lok Sabha seats. Moreover, the apparently ideologically rival parties such as the BJP and the left parties were also trying to augment their seats in the lower house of Indian parliament by riding on the anti-government wave in different parts of the country. Amidst such a climate of political flux, the most shrewd and subtle moves came from V. P. Singh who successfully tried to align his Jan Morcha with a number of regional parties such as the Telugu Desam Party in Andhra Pradesh, the DMK in Tamil Nadu and the Asom Gana Parishad in Assam, among others. These electoral alliances of the disparate parties in different parts of the country clearly provided them an edge over their rivals, particularly the Congress in the electoral fray. Subsequently, in the ninth general elections, the opposition parties had indeed been able to make good fortunes at the cost of the Congress as a result of which the party in power lost the elections with a hung verdict being delivered by the people to constitute the parliament.

Throughout the course of the ninth general elections, the most significant phenomenon that seemed to have characterized the political scenario in the country could be seen in the form of anti-Congressism. Looking at the political spectrum of the country, it could well be said that there was not much among the opposition parties to share among themselves as issues of common concern apart from their animosity for the Congress. In such a scenario, while the ideologically diametrically opposite parties such as the BJP and the left parties remained confined to their traditional bastions, the opposition space in the other parts of the country was augmented by the moral high ground provided by V. P. Singh to the regional parties who had already raised the electoral bars in their respective states against the Congress. In other words, though the incongruence of their ideological as well as political visions and perspective on different issues including ideology did not permit various political parties to come on a common platform in order to wage a combined fight against the Congress, their common enemy nevertheless remained the Congress which each of them tried to defeat albeit in their own distinct ways and regions. Thus, anti-Congressism had profoundly emerged as the most significant electoral plank upon which each and every opposition party tried to ride and make rich electoral dividends.

Given the wider divergence among the different political parties on a number of counts, though they could not arrive at any concerted and coordinated electoral adjustment, there did exist an undercurrent of sorts in which the urge for combined challenge to the Congress was in the air. Such kind of hidden desire of almost all the major opposition parties found expression in two distinct ways. First, there seemed a tacit understanding among these parties to focus on their traditional strongholds rather than spreading their wings to all the nooks and corners of the country in such a way that they eat into the votes of the other opposition parties that would have benefitted the Congress. Second, in the areas where the other opposition parties desisted from fielding their candidates just for the sake of making their presence felt, there appeared some kind of passive pointers to the cadres of these parties to vote for the winnable candidate likely to defeat the Congress nominee. That way, there ran a widespread sentiment among the opposition parties to take on the Congress in the most powerful manner, though all of them could not come together for obvious reasons of ideology or long-term political stakes. Resultantly, in majority, if not all, of the parliamentary constituencies stage was set for a straight fight between the Congress and one of the redoubt-able opposition candidates. The votes of the fringe opposition parties subtly got transferred to the winnable opposition candidate in such a concerted and coordinated manner that the defeat of the Congress candidates became quite probable. The net result of this wave of anti-Congressism was that the ruling party was defeated comprehensively though the opposition victory was also as fragmented as could have been possible.

An interesting phenomenon of the ninth general elections could also be discerned in terms of the electioneering undertaken by different political parties in various parts of the country. In view of the distinct ideological and programmatic standpoints of different political parties, it was obvious for each of them to focus on their core concerns as part of the positive denouement of their campaign strategies. But for almost all the opposition parties, proportional emphasis on the Bofors scandal as the dominant marker of the corruption and maladministration existing during the reign of the incumbent government had been the hallmark of their election strategies. They had usually desisted from making scathing attacks on their ideological adversaries from among the other opposition parties. Such a campaign strategy had a positive impact on the opposition parties in that the cadres and sympathizers of other opposition parties did not take the electoral appeal of the opposition candidates in negative form. In other words, the opposition parties in these elections had tried their best to shy away from mud-slinging on each in order to not break their tacit understanding in targeting the Congress party as the common enemy for each one of them whose defeat became their prime objective rather than any of the opposition parties trying to augment their seat share in the Lok Sabha to such an extent so as to be able form the government at the centre on their own.

Electoral Outcome

Except the Congress, the outcome of the ninth general elections had a lot of surprises for almost all the stakeholders vying to maximize their gains in the wake of the fluid situations prevailing in the country. The fragmentation of the polity on the lines of caste, class, religion, region and ethnicity had probably been so intense and widespread that it appeared improbable for any of the political parties to secure even a working majority in the lower house of the parliament. The existence of distinct pockets of influence of different opposition parties did allow all of them to make big gains for them at the cost of the Congress. But such gains could not translate into sufficient number of seats for any of them to be in a position to form the government on their own. Moreover, the major winners in these elections belonged

Table 4.1 *Major Winners in 1989 Lok Sabha Elections*

Political Party	Seats	Vote %
Congress	197	39.53
Janata Dal	143	17.89
BJP	85	11.36
Left Front	52	10.16

Source: Computed from the *Statistical Report on 1989 General Elections* (New Delhi: Election Commission of India, 1989), accessed 1 June 2019, https://eci.gov.in/statistical-report/statistical-reports/

to such divergent ideological stocks that they would never have had any kind of relationship with one another in normal situations. But the feelings of anti-Congressism had been so strong in each of the opposition parties that they could not resist the temptation of keeping the Congress at bay even at the cost of making compromises with their declared stands vis-à-vis their ideological adversaries.

As expected, the major loser in these elections had been the Congress party. As Table 4.1 indicates, the party that had the commanding position in the previous Lok Sabha with 416 seats was reduced to well below even half of that mark. In other words, the tally of seats for the Congress came drastically down to just 197 in comparison to the 416 that the party could corner in the eighth Lok Sabha elections. Its vote share also came down from 49.10 by around 10 percentage points to stand at just 39.53. The basic reasons for such a drastic decline in both the percentage and the seat tally of the party could be attributed to the concerted efforts of the opposition parties on two counts. First, they had indeed been successful in demonizing the Congress party and its top leader in the name of corruption and price rise to such an extent that it had started looking like a liability on the country. At the same time, the opposition parties also tried to work in tacit tandem with each other in such a way that they were able to mount a concerted and coordinated fight against the party. As a result, the party failed to repeat its spectacular performance of the eighth general elections, especially in the Hindi heartland states and got its seat tally reduced to even less than 200 in the ninth Lok Sabha.

In turn, the BJP entered the mainstream arena of the Hindi heartland as the viable alternative to the Congress.[3]

Interestingly, despite emerging as the kingpin of the anti-Congressism in the wake of his ouster from Rajiv Gandhi government, V. P. Singh could not command universal acceptability in all parts of the country alike. His political conglomerate in the name of the Janata Dal consisted of the major stakeholders of only a few of the states coming mainly from the Hindi heartland. As a result, the honours of both seats and vote percentage in the aftermath of decline of the Congress were shared by a number of parties, the most significant gainer of which had been the BJP.[4] Yet the Janata Dal emerged as the second largest party in the Lok Sabha with 143 seats. What could be seen as the turning point of these elections had been the mobilization of the middle range castes to vote for the Janata Dal who had emerged as the most ardent advocate of the social justice in the country. Moreover, the strategic voting of these people had helped the party pocket 143 seats despite securing just 17.89 per cent votes in all. But the vote for party in these elections had indeed been a positive vote of the Other Backward Classes (OBCs) as a reward for implementation of the Mandal Commission recommendations.

Among all the political parties, the most significant gainer of these elections had been the BJP. Ever since its formation, the party had been trying to gain somewhat respectful, if not formidable, foothold in the electoral landscape of the country. But the hegemonic influence of the Congress party across the country did not permit any leg space for the BJP for the simple reason that the probable voters of the BJP could have been the ones that had also been the ardent supporters of the Congress. So BJP's earnest efforts in creating a distinct wedge in the core voter base of the Congress through its unique ideology-driven emphasis on Hindutva had reached its probable target in the aftermath

[3] Y. K. Malik and V. B. Singh, 'Bharatiya Janata Party: An Alternative to the Congress (I), *Asian Survey* 32, no. 4 (1992): 330–331.

[4] Geeta Puri, 'An Exhilarating Electoral Experience: The BJP Overcomes Its Identity Crisis', in *Lok Sabha Elections 1989*, ed. M. P. Singh (New Delhi: Kalinga Publications, 1992), 138.

of the Rath Yatra of the party stalwart L. K. Advani.[5] Moreover, the clever move of the BJP had also polarized a large section of the Indian electorate particularly the upper-caste Hindus on the issues of Hindutva and Ram temple.[6] Thus, the political landscape during these elections had become so complex that the established discourses got decisively shattered allowing the BJP a widespread acceptance across the different castes and regions of the country. Consequently, the party was able to improve its seat tally remarkably from just 2 in the previous house to that of 85 in the ninth Lok Sabha that afforded it the critical position of king maker. The vote share of the party had also increased substantially to the tune of 11.36 per cent that had surpassed the combined vote share of the left parties which had been in the mainstay of the political scenario of a number of states.[7]

Admittedly, the march of the left parties in these elections could not be said to be as astonishing as that of the BJP or the Janata Dal. The political stakes of the left parties tended to be further compromised with the sudden rise of the forces of social justice in different parts of the country based on sectarian mobilization.[8] As a matter of fact, given the ideological and programmatic similarities between the proponents of social justice and the left parties, the rise of the former was undoubtedly likely to cost the left parties as the voters who would have been voting for the left parties had now got another political alternative to vote for. In such situations, the left parties appeared to be placed in a quandary with regard to their strategy during these

---

[5] For a critical examination of Rath Yatra as a path-breaking event in the democratic process of the country, see Bidyut Chakrabarty, ed., 'Introduction', in *Whither India's Democracy?* (Calcutta: K. P. Bagchi & Co. 1993), 1–28.

[6] Y. K. Malik and V. B. Singh, *Hindu Nationalist in India: The Rise of Bharatiya Janata Party* (New Delhi: Vistaar, 1994), 189.

[7] For a lucid account of how the decline of the Congress has proportionally facilitated the rise of the BJP in different states, see V. B. Singh, 'Rise of the BJP and Decline of the Congress: An Appraisal', in *Indian Democracy: Meaning and Practices*, eds. Rajendra Vora and Suhas Palshikar (New Delhi: SAGE Publications, 2004), 304.

[8] The dynamics of sectarian mobilization in Gujarat has been ably analysed by P. Patel in his 'Sectarian Mobilisation, Factionalism and Voting in Gujarat', *Economic & Political Weekly* 34, no. 34–35 (1999): 2425.

elections. Nevertheless, the seemingly unassailable presence of the left parties in the states such as West Bengal, Kerala and Tripura did help them secure a respectable number of seats in the house despite their perceptible losses in the Hindi heartland with the rise of the forces of social justice. Thus, the left parties, combinedly, were able to secure a vote share of 10.16 per cent winning 52 seats in all, thereby guaranteeing a crucial role for them in the case of hung house as was expected.

One of the less impressive performers in the ninth general elections could be seen in the form of the host of regional parties that could barely hang on to mark their presence in the new house. In fact, the losses of the Congress did not seem to convert into gains for the regional parties. Moreover, in a number of states where the stakes of the regional parties could have been higher, the Congress party did not perform as badly as it did in the Hindi heartland. As a result, barring the All India Anna Dravida Munnetra Kazhagam (AIADMK) from the deeper south, no other regional party could secure even a double digit seat in the Lok Sabha. This was a striking phenomenon given the fact that in the previous house when all the mainstream political parties and forces were made to bite the dust in the electoral fray in the wake of the sympathy wave for Rajiv Gandhi, it was the TDP that had defied that wave and emerged as the main opposition party in the eighth Lok Sabha. But in these elections, the party had to contend with just two seats. Furthermore, the powerful regional parties such as the Shiv Sena, the Akali Dal and the DMK failed to capitalize on the failures of the incumbent government to improve their tally in the new house ostensibly because of the socio-political dynamics of different states (Table 4.2).[9]

The creation of a hung house in the wake of the ninth general elections in fact represented the fragmentation of the Indian electorate with the weakening of the Congress as the hegemonic party that could hold on to all the social groups and economic interests. The unleashing of the different kinds of political interests and inescapable social churning taking place in the country had imparted distinct shades of orientations among the voters whose reflection in the ninth

[9] Kumar, 'The National Parties and Regional Allies', 302.

Table 4.2 *Performance of Regional Parties*

Political Party	Seats	Vote %
AIADMK	11	1.5
National Conference	03	0.2
TDP	02	3.29
BSP	03	2.07
JMM	03	0.34
Shiv Sena	01	0.11

Source: Computed from the *Statistical Report on 1989 General Elections* (New Delhi: Election Commission of India, 1989, accessed 1 June 2019, https://eci.gov.in/statistical-report/statistical-reports/

general elections resulted in a number of parties sharing the majority of seats in the Lok Sabha. But the outcome of these elections also set the tone for the future of Indian political process given the sharp divisions produced by voters through their support for different political parties. The centrist space of the Indian politics that had hitherto been occupied by the Congress seemed to be up for grab in these elections and the parties that could succeed in grabbing that space emerged as the new political force. In this regard, while the victory march of the BJP had been more enduring, the non-cohesive nature of the Janata Dal had primarily been responsible for making it a disintegrated force sooner than later.[10]

Anti-Congressism as New Ideology

The ninth general elections facilitated the emergence of the anti-Congressism with renewed vigour in the Indian politics. In other words, the host of opposition parties that could not secure clear mandate from the electorate to form a non-Congress government did not wish to miss the opportunity to oust the Congress from the power at the centre despite their not forming the government by themselves. This has

[10] E. Sridharan, 'Coalition Strategies and the BJP's Expansion, 1989–2004', *Commonwealth & Comparative Politics* 43, no. 2 (2005): 199.

indeed been the trait of the democratic politics in the country that the political stakeholders espousing the cause of anti-Congress has always clamoured to oust the grand old party of India and replace it with the non-Congress government. But none of these parties has ever been in a position to form the government on their own. As a result, whenever the opposition parties got a chance to form the government at the centre as in 1977, such a government would inevitably be a coalition of disparate political forces that would otherwise detest one another just as they do for the Congress.

The situation unfolding after the results of the ninth general elections were announced proved the long-standing belief of the analysts that for the opposition parties to come together for any meaningful purpose would only be to oust the Congress from power. But their ability to form and run a government at the centre consisting of the host of parties has always been in doubt. Interestingly, that has also been the saving grace for the Congress in that after every non-Congress government's fall, in the subsequent general elections, the party has been able to make a comeback as it did in the time of first Janata government. Nevertheless, it is quite startling to see the anxiety of the opposition parties to ensure the exit of the Congress from power by all means. The situation had been more interesting in the aftermath of the ninth general elections because of the system and mechanism through which the government was formed and allowed to run for whatsoever term it remained in office. Moreover, the internal bickering of the opposition coalition has also provided the Congress a chance to ensure that more than one prime minister enters the fray to run the opposition governments.

As in the case of the first Janata experiment, when the government of Morarji Desai fell, the Congress did not prefer to go for the outright elections. Rather, it prodded the desperate Charan Singh to stake his claim to form the government that the Congress would support from outside. It would then try to discredit the opposition conglomerate in such a way that in the ensuing general elections the electorate could be convinced that only the Congress party could give a stable government that would be able to last the full term of office. The turn of events in the aftermath of the ninth general elections was a kind of action replay of the first Janata experiment with the same script and subtext of the political drama. That way, the Congress has always retained its relevance as the focal point of political process in the country whether it remains in government or in the opposition. In a way, the Congress exploits the sheer selfish interests of the opposition leaders as per its own calculations so as to make most of the political drama enacted by the opposition leaders whenever they get a chance to form the government at the centre.

The political scenario emerging out of these elections also demonstrated the need and acceptability of political expediency even on the part of the ideology-based parties whose avowed declarations are torn apart once it comes to join hands for the sake of anti-Congress government at the centre. Clearly, after the failure of the Janata Dal to secure a working majority in the Lok Sabha to form a government, there was also the possibility before the president to invite the leader of the biggest party in the house to form the government. Given that the Congress had emerged as the biggest party in the house, the opposition feared that if they did not cobble up the numbers, the ball might be rolled out in the court of the Congress. Therefore, the ideologically diametrically opposite parties such as the BJP and the left combine wasted no time in making up their mind to prop up the government of V. P. Singh from outside. This was a unique proposition in the Indian democracy when the ideologies of the parties were given a go by just to make sure that the Congress remained out of power at the centre.

While the trend of extending outside support to a government has been in vogue at the state levels for quite a long period of time, this phenomenon has generally been uncommon at the centre. Only on few occasions in the past had the governments been formed at the centre with the outside support of other parties. Even in those cases also, the support to the governments was strategic and could not last long. In other words, such outside supports to the minority governments were not part of any long-drawn strategy of the parties and appeared to be contingent in nature. But in case of the ninth Lok Sabha, the two ideologically opposed political parties took the deliberate and well-considered decision of supporting the V. P. Singh government from outside that could actually survive for a fairly long period of time.

When this government fell, the Congress wasted no time in coming up with its deceitful plan of supporting the Chandra Shekhar government from outside so as to gain time for strategizing its electoral plan as and when the elections take place.[11] Thus, the phenomenon of minority governments being supported from outside by a host of parties became the established norm of the Indian democracy.

The deep rooting of the phenomenon of minority governments forming and surviving with the outside support of a number of parties indeed betrayed the opportunistic characteristics of almost all the political parties in the country. Ordinarily, it is quite often that a party or all the parties fail to secure a working majority in the lower house of parliament. In that case, formation of the government becomes a challenge, to overcome which the concerned parties need to evolve certain consistent position in consonance with their ideological and programmatic orientations. But evolution of such a normative trait in the country has obviously been sacrificed on the altar of the opportunistic desires and aspirations of almost all the political parties as they take such occasions to reorder their electoral strategies so as to face the upcoming electoral challenge in a more systematic manner. These opportunistic moves on the part of the different parties are also conditioned by the fact that the production of a hung house in the aftermath of an election would in most probability be followed by the announcement of fresh general elections as the government of the day would not be able to complete its full term.

The formation of the governments led by opposition parties at the centre beginning with the ninth general elections has been taken as the maturing of the Indian democracy. The established norms of the older democracies have been that the governments or the ruling echelons of a country need to rotate among the competing claims to the political power. So much so that in many countries there has been made a constitutional provision prohibiting a single individual from even contesting elections for more than two terms for a particular

[11] For an interesting account of the politics of the time, see Dipankar Sinha, 'V. P. Singh, Chandra Shekhar and "Nowhere Politics" in India', *Asian Survey* 31, no. 7 (1991): 598–612.

political office. Although no such provision exists in the country, it has been felt desirable that the rotation of governments need to take place in such a way that no party is able to hold the power at the centre for more than two consecutive terms. So the reversal of the fortunes of the grand old party in the general elections at periodic intervals has been a positive signal for the vibrancy of the Indian democracy. That way, results of the ninth general elections had indeed been a pointer in the right direction as it provided the opposition parties a chance to form the government albeit for a short span of time.

Concluding Observations

The democratic dynamics in the country since Independence has ordained such circumstances in which the Congress party has remained in power for a long period of time. The legacies of the national movement have in fact helped the party penetrate into the bottom of heart of the general masses in such a way that majority, if not all, of them have become an avowed Congressmen. Cashing upon this goodwill of the people, the Congress could remain in power even after the departure of the leaders who really had taken part in the national movement and could be considered as the true inheritors of the nationalist legacy of the Congress. This however does not mean that there did not exist any kind of opposition to the Congress ideology and programmes. Rather, several streams of social, religious as well as political movements have been in vogue in the country that espoused exactly the opposite cause articulated by the Congress. But none of the anti-Congress forces have been formidable enough to take on the Congress in an effective manner. As a result, they did not seem to be left with any other alternative than to join hands together to put up a combined fight against the Congress. Thus, anti-Congressism has been a constant factor in the Indian politics right from the 1960s. While its first meaningful articulation could be seen in the first Janata experiment of 1977, the ninth general elections have also witnessed the reiteration of the same sentiments in a different form.

Anti-Congressism as the cementing factor of the opposition unity in the democratic process of the country has, however, never been proved to be strong enough to entail any kind of durability in the opposition unity. Such a strange phenomenon could probably be explained with two interrelated factors. At the outset, anti-Congressism becomes the cementing factor of opposition unity only as long as they are separate from one another but clamour for removing the Congress from the position of power at the centre. In other words, as long as the opposition parties are in the opposition, it becomes almost intolerable for them to live with the Congress government at the centre. Hence, they do not hesitate in going to any extent for removal of the Congress from power even by compromising with their foundational values and traits. But once their common objective of ousting the Congress from power is achieved and the time comes for them to form the government of unity consisting of the mosaic of opposition parties, their internal differences come to the fore. This naturally gives birth to the phenomenon like outside support or not opposing the government and abstaining from the house whenever the floor test takes place for the government. However, such ploys are only momentary reliefs for the government in power, with the parties resting outside looking for the opportune time to pull the government down. It is a rude reminder that anti-Congressism can never be the sustainable foundation for opposition unity in the country.

CHAPTER 5

Primordialization of Democratic Process

The elections to form the 10th Lok Sabha could be said to be one of the most complex general elections in India where the shape of things to come was just beyond the speculation and forecasting of the psephologists and pollsters. The turn of events leading to the declaration of the 10th general elections had been full of such intriguing moves and malicious countermoves that they could not have led to any other scenario but the primordialization of the democratic processes in the country. The announcement of the V. P. Singh government's decision to implement the Mandal Commission recommendations with regard to the reservation of 27.5 per cent of seats for the candidates belonging to the social and educationally OBCs had revolutionizing impact on the majority middle rung classes of the Indian society. This announcement apparently re-energized the political stakes of the people belonging to these intermediary castes to such an extent that they clamoured to corner the prime place in the electoral democracy of the country. In order to counter this artful dodging of V. P. Singh, the BJP also raised the bogey of Ram temple in Ayodhya as its main electoral plank in the ensuing general elections. The resultant social and political landscape of the country became so complex that the fragmentation of the democratic process on the lines of the primordial affinities became a distinct reality.

The decline of the Congress as the dominant political party in the country had unleashed various kinds of social forces that sought to claim the political space vacated by the grand old party of India.[1] But the ideological and programmatic fault lines among the different social and political groups had been so many and so profound that they could not think of evolving a common strategy or platform to take on the Congress. Hence, during the ninth general elections while the different non-Congress parties appeared united in their resolve to dislodge the Congress from the seat of power at the centre, they could not agree on whom to anoint as the prime minister once the Congress was defeated in the battle of votes. Consequently, when the final results of the ninth general elections were declared, the scenario of a hung Lok Sabha had put the opposition parties in such a quandary that they could imagine and actually did what they had not been able to do in the past. Leader of a minority political party was made the prime minister with the left and right parties extending their support to him from outside. But the political bickering among the major players of the electoral politics in the country continued unabated during this period that eventually not only led to the downfall of the government but also unleashing of new trends in the Indian politics whose primary focus remained embedded in arousing the primordial affinities of the people and reap the electoral dividends like never before in the electoral history of the country.

Mandal and Mandir

The contextual premise of the 10th general elections revolved around the two primordial goalposts of caste and religion that were sought to be made the determining factor of electoral politics in the country. Given that the government led by V. P. Singh was a minority government surviving on the crutches of support provided by the ideologically diametrically opposite political parties such as the BJP and the left, the durability of the government was anybody's guess. But the perplexing political scenario prevailing at that point of time was further muddied

[1] M. L. Ahuja and Sharda Paul, *1989–1991 General Elections in India: Including November 1991 By-elections* (New Delhi: Associated Publishing House, 1992), 63.

with the concerted efforts of different political parties, particularly the BJP. In the meantime, a subtext of the national politics had also been unfolding at Delhi and its neighbourhood Haryana. In order to mount the pressure on Prime Minister V. P. Singh to yield to a variety of demands, his deputy and Haryana Jaat leader Devi Lal had called for a mammoth rally at his stronghold in the state to show his political prowess to his boss. Thus, various kinds of political games and artful dodging had been taking place in Delhi and its neighbourhood. Irrespective of the long-term implications of the moves and counter-moves of that time, the immediate target of most of those political tactics had been Prime Minister V. P. Singh. Eventually pushed to a corner from all-round intimidations and assault on his authority, Singh had apparently felt so nervous that he had started looking for some matching sticks with which he could beat his political detractors. Given the numerical clout of the OBCs in the political landscape of the country, Singh tried to upset the political calculations of the different political parties and leaders by positioning him as the messiah of the OBCs through his decision to implement the recommendation of the reservation of seats for them.

Alongside the internal bickering within the Janata Dal, the BJP had been trying to expand its support base in the country by taking advantage of its support to the government at the centre. For that, the party stalwart L. K. Advani had embarked upon his ambitious tour of different parts of the country on his chariot in the name of seeking public support for the construction of a Ram temple at Ayodhya in place of the Babri Masjid standing at the birthplace of Lord Ram.[2] But in anticipation of the potential spectacular political mileage likely to be drawn out of this march, the proponents of social justice could simply not tolerate this march. As a result, on the tacit support of the central government, the chariot of Advani was stopped in Bihar on the instructions of the state chief minister, Lalu Prasad. This move of the Bihar chief minister was inspired not only by his wish to stop the onward march of the Hindutva forces but also to portray him as the saviour of the Muslims in the state. That way, he eyed the solid vote

[2] See Thomas Blom Hansen and Christophe Jaffrelot, eds., *The BJP and the Compulsions of Politics in India* (New Delhi: Oxford University Press, 1998).

bank of the people of his own Yadav caste in conjunction with the substantial population of Muslims, thereby creating his long enduring Muslim–Yadav vote bank in the state. But Advani was also probably looking for such a state of things to unfold in order to push his claim that the caste-based parties along with the left and the Congress were obstructing the construction of a Ram temple in Ayodhya.[3]

Consequent upon the arrest of Advani in Bihar, the BJP withdrew support to the V. P. Singh government at the centre reducing it to minority. The subsequent fall of the government had in fact unleashed a variety of social and political forces in the country that acted vehemently to consolidate their political base in different regions on the basis of arousing the primordial affinities of the people belonging to different castes, religions, languages, among others. Although the political stakes of Prime Minister Singh no longer remained vital in the prevailing situations, his strategic move of implementing the recommendations of the Mandal Commission surely went to unleash the latent political force of the OBCs whose articulation had been varying from state to state depending on the political space vacated by the Congress in different states.

Based upon the numerical preponderance of the OBCs, the most spectacular impact of the primordialization of the democratic process in the country had been felt in the populous and key Hindi heartland states of Uttar Pradesh and Bihar. Interestingly, for a long period of time after Independence, these two states had been the bastions of the Congress as long as the party was able to keep intact its strategic balance among the different caste groups of these states. But with the gradual erosion in the universal support base of the party, the political space vacated by it started getting occupied by the proponents of social justice and Hindutva. The proponents of the social justice had virtually got a shot in their arm with the plank of OBCs' reservation. The latent political and social ambitions of the OBCs got aroused by the state-level leadership of these caste groups that eventually transformed into a number of regional political outfits in different states. After the

[3] Oliver Heath, 'Anatomy of BJP's Rise to Power: Social, Regional and Political Expansion in 1990s', *Economic & Political Weekly* 34, no. 34–35 (1999): 2515.

disintegration of the Janata Dal at the national level, these regional parties emerged as the formidable political forces in Uttar Pradesh and Bihar upstaging the well-entrenched political parties like the Congress.

With the political vacuum getting widened in different states, particularly in the Hindi heartland, by the dwindling support base of the Congress, the party that eyed to step into the footsteps of the Congress had primarily been the BJP.[4] Amidst the ideological landscape of the country getting mired into the competing claims of the left parties, the Congress as well as the parties standing for social justice to occupy the leftist space, the BJP was obviously left with no other option than to go for consolidation of its rightist ideology enmeshed into its long-standing demand for the construction of Ram temple in Ayodhya. As a matter of fact, the key ideological premise of Hindutva that had been a sort of article of faith for the party had virtually got crystallized at that time into its campaign for the construction of Ram temple at the birthplace of Lord Ram. Thus, amidst the powerful thrust of the proponents of social justice for awakening the latent political and social power of the OBCs, the BJP sought to counterbalance these forces with its renewed and vigorous thrust towards bringing the issue of Ram temple at the centre stage of democratic politics in the country sooner than later.

Insofar as the democratic churning in other parts of the country was concerned, the forces of social justice could not magnify their presence to the extent they had been able to do in Uttar Pradesh and Bihar. But the hegemony of the Congress party was surely getting shattered in the states such as Madhya Pradesh, Rajasthan, Himachal Pradesh, Haryana, Maharashtra and Gujarat and getting replaced by the hegemonic presence of other parties. For instance, in Gujarat, the BJP had emerged as the chief claimant of the electoral space vacated by the Congress and had made good fortunes in the 10th general elections.[5] In other words, the political space vacated by the Congress in these states was up for grab on the part of the opposition

---

[4] See Malik and Singh, *Hindu Nationalist in India*, 1995.
[5] Ghanshyam Shah, 'Tenth Lok Sabha Elections: BJP's Victory in Gujarat', *Economic & Political Weekly* 26, no. 51 (1991): 2923.

parties. However, for reasons of varying caste combinations as well as the limited spheres of influence of the erstwhile Janata Dal in these states, the forces of social justice could not attain as formidable position in these states as they could do in the two major states of the Hindi heartland. Thus, the democratic space in these states fell into the share of the BJP that had always registered its presence in these states in varying measures. Hence, in the ensuing general elections, the electoral battle in these states set out to be between the Congress and the BJP, though several fringe political outfits remained in the fray with sporadic pockets of influence.

On the eve of the 10th general elections, therefore, the political scenario in the country had been in a state of instability. The incumbent ruling party at the centre had been in shambles with most, if not all, of its important leaders opting for splitting the party to form their own regional outfits to optimize their gains in the upcoming elections. The sagging fortunes of the Congress party in the Hindi heartland had almost made the region an open battleground among the various aspiring political forces seeking support of the electorate on different grounds. Thus, while the regional parties springing out of the Janata Dal exhorted the voters, particularly the OBCs, to vote for them to enable them complete the unfinished task of social justice, the BJP unhesitatingly espoused the cause of Hindutva as the mainstay of its electoral strategy. Among these situations, the Congress came up with the plea of a stable government which, it argued, had been the forte of the grand old party only. Thus, the political landscape of the country during these elections had become so complex that it indeed became difficult for the voters to make up their mind to vote for one party or the other.

Electoral Strategies and Outcomes

The 10th general elections were held in the atmosphere of both hope and desperation. The failure of the government to complete its full term and internal ruptures that had kept the government busy with its in-house management had provided the Congress the conventional argument to put before the voters that the opposition parties could never learn the art of running the government for a full term of five years. As a result, the party was buoyed to join the electoral bandwagon and aimed at bloating the charges made against it during the previous general elections. The top leadership of the party including the prime ministerial candidate Rajiv Gandhi embarked upon the whirlwind tour of different parts of the country on the plank of providing a stable government at the centre, if the party is voted back to power. However, the party did face the stupendous task of convincing the voters who had already been oriented towards the issues of Mandal and Mandir.

Riding on the wave of Mandal, the disparate parties forming the Janata Dal at that point of time began the electoral campaign with the renewed vigour by taking credit for making the vast majority of OBCs realize their long-cherished dream of joining the government jobs on the basis of reservations granted to them. This electoral argument of the Janata Dal was really able to cut much ice with the OBCs, particularly in the states of Uttar Pradesh and Bihar, where the long traditions of socialist movement had already awakened a large mass of middle classes to claim their dues in the political and administrative cake. The Mandal issue in fact was taken by them as some sort of unprecedented empowerment through which a golden future would be looking at them. The leaders such as Lalu Prasad in Bihar and Mulayam Singh Yadav in Uttar Pradesh tried to maximize the gains arising out of this historic decision of the V. P. Singh government. Thus, for the first time, the Janata Dal looked at replacing the Congress as the most significant gainer of the social churning taking place in the two critical states in the arithmetic calculations of the general elections.

Amidst these buoyancies of the two important stakeholders in the 10th general elections, the BJP naturally decided to consolidate its previous gains by re-emphasizing the Hindutva as the mainstay of its electoral strategy. The party was sure of expanding its electoral base in the Hindi heartland by countering the Mandal wave by raising the Mandir issue with much more vigour than before. At the same time, the BJP tried to play down the caste-based appeal of the proponents of social justice in the name of calling for Hindu unity so as to regain the prestige and glory of the past. Thus, the bogie of cultural nationalism came as the readymade campaign strategy for the party to not only counter its opponents but also make a positive appeal to the voters to make their choice for the party. However, during these elections, like the previous ones, the parties, including both the BJP and the Janata Dal focused only upon the areas that had traditionally been their bastions from the past. In the meantime, apart from the Hindi heartland, the BJP extended its areas of influence to the western part of the country particularly in the states of Gujarat and Maharashtra. Indeed, despite its best efforts, south still remained the region where the party could not extend its reach beyond a limit.[6]

The main battlefield for the 10th general elections though was thought to be the Hindi heartland, yet the decisive factor in the eventual outcome of the elections had been the voters of the southern and eastern parts of the country. As a matter of fact, the fragmentation of the voters in the northern states had been so intense that there could not have been any escape from the multi-polar contest in most, if not all, of the constituencies in these states. But the situation was markedly different in the southern and eastern states, where the lack of appeal of both the proponents of Mandal and Mandir did not entice them to try their luck in these states. As a result, the contest in these areas remained traditionally poised between the rival regional parties with only the Congress making its presence felt in these states. Moreover, in many of the southern states, the regional parties were apparently having edge over the Congress as the previous negative perception of the party had not disappeared to the desirable extent. As a result, in the final reckoning, a number of regional parties had put up great shows in these elections.

The most significant turnaround in the course of the 10th general elections came just before the second phase of polling. On a campaign trail in the deep southern state of Tamil Nadu, Congress leader Rajiv Gandhi was assassinated by a suicide bomber belonging to a Tamil terrorist group of Sri Lanka at Sriperumbudur. This tragic incident came as a bolt from the blue for the people in the country who were busy readying themselves for casting their valuable vote in the remaining

---

[6] James Manor, 'BJP in the South India: 1991 General Election', *Economic & Political Weekly* 27, no. 24–25 (1992): 1269.

phases of the elections. So, in the following phases, not only the intensity of the electoral campaign became subdued, there appeared widespread feeling that the death of the Congress leader had been a great loss to the country. Although the death of Rajiv Gandhi had left the Congress in a state of mourning, the incident nevertheless had sent a subtle wave of sympathy in favour of the party in all parts of the country including the deep south in Tamil Nadu.[7] The people conceded the death of the Congress leader as part of the legacy of the family to lay down their lives for the sake of the country as had been done by his mother and it needed to be honoured with the positive vote for the party.

The 10th general elections would have turned into the greatest fight between the proponents of the Mandal and Mandir but the tragic assassination of the Congress leader impacted it. The emotive appeal of the non-Congress parties in the name of the Mandal and Mandir had really impacted the voting behaviour of a large number of people voting in the first phase of these elections. But the tide of their appeal became bloated in the aftermath of the death of Rajiv Gandhi. The subsequent voting in different parts of the country had gone in favour of the Congress party in a substantive manner. As a result, the party which was considered to have been pushed to a corner by the forces seeking votes in the name of the emotive issues of caste and religion bounced back magnificently. In the final reckoning, the party was able to improve its seat tally to the tune of 244 in comparison to the seats of the other parties that had remained way behind the tally of the Congress (Table 5.1). Yet the party was short of a clear majority staring at the scenario of a minority government at the centre with support of other parties.

Apart from the Congress, the party that had improved its seat tally in the Lok Sabha in the aftermath of the 10th general elections had been the BJP. The onward march of the BJP in the electoral arena had quite significantly been propelled by the spade work done for the party by its parental organization, the Rashtriya Swayamsevak Sangh

---

[7] R. Manivannan, '1991 Tamil Nadu Elections: Issues, Strategies and Performance', *Economic & Political Weekly* 27, no. 4 (1992): 169.

Table 5.1 *Major Winners in 1991 Lok Sabha Elections*

Political Party	Seats	Vote %
Congress	244	35.66
BJP	120	20.04
Janata Dal	69	11.77
Left parties	57	9.66

Source: Computed from the *Statistical Report on 1991 General Elections* (New Delhi: Election Commission of India, 1991), accessed 21 May 2019, https://eci.gov.in/statistical-report/statistical-reports/

(RSS). At the same time, the party had positioned its emotional appeal to the people in such a way that the upper-caste voters did not find any other avenue to go than the BJP. In other words, the increasing stridency of the middle castes along with the open appeal of the Janata Dal to these castes even at the cost of the upper-caste voters, in fact, pushed the non-OBC voters to the fold of the BJP. These voters, who had traditionally been the vote bank of the Congress, had presumably shifted their loyalty to the BJP in the wake of the discrediting of the Congress government headed by Rajiv Gandhi. Since then, the turn of events in the country had been such that they could not find any other alternative than to vote for the BJP as the saviour of the interests of the Hindus.

The party for which the 10th general elections were likely to prove a matter of life and death was none other than the Janata Dal.[8] The basic reasons for such high stakes of the party in these elections were three. One, it consisted of such sporadic group of regional satraps who would have remained part of the party only in case the party would become part of any ruling dispensation so that they could enjoy the power for longer periods of time. Next, the party had played its most valuable card of social justice in the name of Mandal Commission recommendations, and the failure of this card to produce desirable results for the party would have reduced them to where they used to

[8] Lewis P. Fickett Jr., 'The Rise and Fall of the Janata Dal', *Asian Survey* 33, no. 12 (December, 1993): 1153.

exist decades ago. In the end, the party also wanted to put forward the argument that the fall of the government was for the valuable cause of protecting the secular fabric and interests of the minorities for which the minorities needed to support the party en masse. But the grand plans of the party fell flat in the face of the sympathy wave in favour of the Congress and it remained confined to just 69 seats as compared to the handsome victories of both the Congress and the BJP.

The left parties did not experience much variation in their electoral fortunes as they did not yield much space for other parties including the Congress in their traditional bastions. Fighting the elections on the combined strength of one another, the left parties in fact maintained their consistent performance by securing the respectable number of 57 seats in the Lok Sabha. Interestingly, there did not seem to be much at stake for the left parties in these elections as they neither had been part of the gamble in pulling down the government nor did they join the poll battle on any creative interpretation of the existing Indian realities. The renewed thrust on the plank of social justice by the Janata Dal was in fact a part of the left agenda who had been calling for the empowerment of the marginalized sections of society through the constitutionally ordained methods. Hence, in the 10th general elections also the left parties stood afloat in the face of the triple challenges emanating from the sympathy wave of the Congress, Hindutva of the BJP and the social justice of the Janata Dal.

Apart from the national parties, the regional parties also had a lot of stakes in the 10th general elections, particularly for those whose fortune had dipped remarkably in the previous general elections (Table 5.2). In this context, the case of the TDP and Shiv Sena stood out prominently. In other words, in the elections for the ninth Lok Sabha, the two parties had failed to perform as per their prowess in their respective strongholds of Andhra Pradesh and Maharashtra. But these parties had indeed been able to make a spectacular comeback in the 10th general elections improving upon their previous tally. Besides them, the two other parties that had been able to maintain consistency in their performance were the Bahujan Samaj Party (BSP) in Uttar Pradesh and the AIADMK in Tamil Nadu. The tally of six seats of Jharkhand Mukti Morcha (JMM) had later become the

Table 5.2 *Status of Regional Parties in 1991 Lok Sabha Elections*

Political Party	Seats	Vote %
TDP	13	2.96
AIADMK	11	1.61
BSP	03	1.8
JMM	06	0.53
Shiv Sena	04	0.79
AGP	01	0.54

Source: Computed from the *Statistical Report on 1991 General Elections* (New Delhi: Election Commission of India, 1991), accessed 21 May 2019 https:// eci.gov.in/statistical-report/statistical-reports/

saving grace for the government of the Congress at the time of the trust vote that the party faced on the floor of the Lok Sabha. The good performance of these parties showed their resilience to put up a grand show irrespective of the directions the national politics was likely to take.

Primordialization of Democratic Process

The nature and dynamics of the 10th general elections left a deep mark on the democratic process of the country. This impact can be explained in various interrelated ways. The turn of events taking place both before and during the elections had unleashed a number of unconventional social forces in the country. For instance, caste has always been a very important factor in determining the electoral processes and outcomes in the country. Right from the days of the first general elections, there has been consistent efforts on the part of all the political parties to make sure that all the castes, regions, religions and other primordial affinities of the people get adequate representation in the political configuration of the party. That way, caste could not become an element of division and cleavage in the society which can be further widened in order to secure greater political gains for certain groups or sections of society. But in the course of the 10th general elections, a fundamental change was brought about in the role caste played in the democratic discourse of the country.

During the 10th general elections, the parties claiming to work for social justice tended to use caste for blatant selfish interests even at the cost of disturbing the social fabric of the country. Now, with the declaration for implementation of Mandal Commission recommendations, the proponents of social justice started using the caste in such a way as to put the different sections of society in a position of animosity to each other. In other words, their aggressive advocacy of the assertion of the new-found rights of the OBCs even at the cost of the other sections of society would patently put the different groups of society face to face with each other. Although such a public posturing of the Janata Dal and its constituent parties would surely be for the sake of consolidating their crucial vote bank in order to seek and obtain their votes en bloc, it did not give right message in the society. This eventually tended to make the overt play of caste politics in the states such as Uttar Pradesh and Bihar in such a way that one caste felt agitated against the stridency of others.

On the political front, the greater consolidation of the OBC votes on the part of the Janata Dal made the other claimants of their votes shaky resulting into the initiation of countermoves by the latter to galvanize the voters in their support. In this context, the most significant counter moves came from the side of the BJP which felt threatened to lose its core vote bank if the different constituents of Hindu society started looking at each other with suspicion and disbelief. It therefore went on sharpening its Hindutva ideology so as to put it as the uniting force of the Hindu society in the face of the divisive politics of the rival opposition parties. That way, the entire electoral process during the course of the 10th general elections revolved around the issues of Mandal and Mandir with the other issues of national importance getting pushed into insignificance. Such polarization of the votes went to the extent of creating violent wedges among different sections of society resulting in killings of one section of people by another and outbreak of communal riots in different parts of the country, thereby vitiating the peaceful atmosphere in which the entire electoral exercise had to be completed.

The fragmentation of the Indian society for the sake of votes could, thus, be said to be the most significant transformation that the 10th general elections brought about in the democratic process of India. However, amidst the claims and the counterclaims of different political parties as standing for the cause of the people of their own castes or religions, certain sections of people remained committed to their traditional patrons and leaders irrespective of the political manoeuvring by other political parties. In this context, the performance of the BSP in these elections could be said to be remarkable as the core cadres of the party consisted mainly of the persons belonging to the Scheduled Castes and that too of certain sub-groups even among them. In other words, the social churning that had apparently started with the implementation of the Mandal Commission recommendations apparently failed to have any impact on the core vote bank of the BSP that had stood with the party making it win a number of seats in Uttar Pradesh. That way, the parties like BSP had tended to act as the stumbling block in the way of the proponents of social justice because they thought of retaining their independent identity in the social and political arenas of the country.

During the course of the 10th general elections, the tragic assassination of Rajiv Gandhi came as the saddest news for the people of the country. He was not only the youngest prime minister of India but also a very malleable and accommodative politician who was gradually maturing into the seasoned statesman having a very long innings to play in the democratic process of the country. His death plunged the entire country into a pall gloom with his family sternly refusing to join the political space falling vacant after his death. However, his death stirred a very strong sympathy wave in favour of his party for the remaining phases of the elections. This unfortunate incident has amply proved that Indian electorate is a very emotional lot who get carried away into sympathizing with a person or party losing its important leaders. As a matter of fact, the landslide victory of Rajiv Gandhi in the 1984 general elections had also been ordained by the sympathy wave arising in his favour after the assassination of his mother at the hands of her bodyguards. The same story had now got repeated in the case of the Congress as the sagging fortunes of the party were turned around by the unexpected turn of events. As a result of the sympathy wave in favour of the Congress in the remaining phases of the 10th general elections, the process of the primordialization of the democratic process was halted to a large extent. The Congress was able to make electoral gains even in the areas where it would not have achieved much given the shift of its core vote bank to the parties espousing the causes of social justice.

Sudden turnaround in the electoral fortunes of the Congress notwithstanding, the party could not secure a working majority in the Lok Sabha. It had fallen short of a substantive number of seats to be able to form the government on its own. This had again presented the scenario of a coalition government at the centre. However, no other party was near to the tally of the Congress that could have posed a challenge to it in the formation of the government. But the moot question before the party was the election of its parliamentary party leader whom the president could invite to form the government. Eventually after much confabulations, the party was able to elect party veteran Narasimha Rao as its leader. Later he was able to muster sufficient numbers by drawing on the support of certain likeminded parties. Although the coalition formed at this time was not a pre-poll alliance, it nevertheless was able to last the full term of five years barring a few hiccups that the government was able to survive by hook or by crook. For instance, on one of the occasions of trust vote in the house, the government was charged with bribing the members of parliament belonging to the JMM for their crucial support in helping the government win the vote of confidence in the house. That way, while horse trading had been reported in a number of states on the occasion of trust vote of a government, this was probably for the first time that votes were being bought to secure the stability of the government at the centre.

Concluding Observations

The elections for the 10th Lok Sabha offered a number of creative inputs in the conceptualization of democratic experience in the country. The prelude events of the elections were of great significance in the reinvention of the Indian democracy. Before these elections, the vital national interests of the country were considered as something sacrosanct. But during these elections, in the game of one-upmanship the political parties went to the extent of causing subtle harms to the vital interests of the society. During much of the campaigning for these elections, the resort to primordial affinities of the people turned out to be norm of the electioneering for almost all the political parties. As a result, the democratic process had entered into a phase of competitive populism in which one party was ever ready to counter the moves of another party by evolving matching contexts and pretexts to win the votes of the masses. In such a scenario, the parties that held on to the developmental and programmatic discourses appeared to be at the receiving end. Further, the regionalization of the political process also engenders the challenge of stability and durability of the government at the centre as the possibility of one party securing a working majority in the Lok Sabha becomes a remote possibility. Anyway, these elections did experience the greater primordialization of the democratic process in the country that set the terms of democratic upsurge in the times to come. Interestingly, the caste-based electoral mobilization did yield good results for the parties like the Janata Dal. But in the later years, the growing appetite of the caste-based mobilizers for greater political clout in the system had eventually led to the undoing of the parent party itself. Consequently, the party system of the country got regionalized and federalized with the regional satraps taking the centre stage in the government formation at the central level. The impact of the caste-based mobilization was in fact more vigorous and yielding at the levels of the state. For instance, in the states like Bihar, the caste-based parties like the Rashtriya Janata Dal (RJD) were able to win three consecutive elections for the state assembly and remain in power for an interrupted span of 15 years. But at the central level such politics reached the points of saturation sooner than the states.

CHAPTER 6

Radical Churning in Indian Politics

In the second half of the 1990s, the democratic polity of India experienced a number of unprecedented social and political churning that virtually set the tone of the electoral politics in the times to come. The progressive weakening of the Congress had unleashed all kinds of social forces to show their prowess in carving out a distinct space for them in the political landscape of the country. In this regard, the democratic processes showed varying traits in different parts of India. For instance, while in the northern states that constituted the core of the Hindi heartland, the juggernaut of social justice had rolled in such a way that a number of parties sprung up drawing their lineage from the Janata experimentation to become the exclusive claimant of the sizeable votes of their particular castes. When they found that their own caste votes were proving insufficient to help them secure a majority in the state legislative assemblies or propel their national dreams to arrive at the centre stage of the national politics, they sought and succeeded in forging a formidable alliance with the floating groups like Muslims, thereby replacing the Congress as the ruling party in the states.

The progressive strengthening of the hold of caste-based parties in the core states of the Hindi heartland has been sought to be countered by the BJP through its increasing and consistent thrust on the ideology of Hindutva as the hallmark of its appeal to the voters. In fact, in order to present an alternative vision to the Congress's ideological and programmatic reach in the country, the party insisted on taking up a number of such issues and concerns that went to strengthen its image of a Hindu nationalist party. The party argued for the adoption of cultural nationalism as the founding principle of the Indian polity in such a way that the traditional Hindu way of life is blended with modernity. During this period, the party sought to symbolize its thrust on the ideology of Hindutva and cultural nationalism by calling for the construction of a grand Ram temple at the site of his birthplace by removing the disputed structure standing at that place as the Babri mosque. Thus, the stridency of the party on the issue of Ram temple apparently provided it a long following among the upper-caste Hindus who identified themselves with the traditional glory of the country.

Amidst the fast pacing of the social and political churnings in the north, the southern and eastern parts of the country remained engrossed with the regional orientation of the democratic politics. Majority, if not all, of these states had by now witnessed the rise of formidable regional parties that thrived on the anti-northern sentiments on the one hand and the politics of the clientele on the other. Given that the configuration of the Lok Sabha seats in these states would not allow them much stake to become the power holder at the centre, they surely tried to extract as much political mileage out of their electoral strength in the Lok Sabha as possible. Thus, this period of democratic politics in the country also offered a distinct space to the southern states that acted to decide the fate of the governments at the centre. During this period, the domineering nature of the northern states in the political landscape of India appeared to be shaky given the fragmented nature of votes in the key northern states. As part of the game of one-upmanship, the country witnessed so many persons becoming the prime minister within such a short span of time. This chapter seeks to analyse the nature and impact of the 11th and 12th Lok Sabha elections on the nature of the democratic polity of the country.

Circumstantial Complexities

Democratic processes in the country during the four tumultuous years from 1996 to 1999 took such curious turns that a number of unconventional tendencies appeared to become the defining features of Indian democracy. For instance, the economic backwardness of the country at the time of Independence had tended to make the economic and developmental issues as the core concerns of different political parties in the succeeding elections for a long period of time. Even the ideological skirmishes between the competing ideologies during that period of time revolved around the issues of the economic policies apart from the policies and programmes that could be visualized to ameliorate the social and economic conditions of the toiling masses. Sectarian and primordial affinities of the people were considered by the mainstream parties as some sort of taboos that need not be raked up lest that might create social cleavages and magnify the divisive tendencies in the society. Even if the opposition parties were to raise the issues of the public concern, these basically related to the issues such as price rise, cases of corruption and non-availability of the basic goods for the people which were considered as the failure of the government for which it needed to be voted out at the time of elections.

But the decade of the 1990s witnessed the radical transformation in the democratic discourse in the country that also impacted the electoral politics in a big way.[1] As the Congress party's position in the democratic politics of India weakened, the rise of opposition parties was the obvious outcome. But what turned out to be the astonishing feature of the political discourse of the time was that the opposition parties could not secure a foothold among the psyche of the general public on the bases of common concerns and issues of governance and economic development. Their long drawn discomfitures in the electoral politics had virtually compelled them to opt for certain unconventional methods of political or democratic discourse that might help them to attract the attention of the common people and

[1] Sudha Pai, 'Transformation of the Indian Party System: The 1996 Lok Sabha Elections', *Asian Survey* 33, no. 12 (December, 1997): 1178.

provide them the much desired space in the electoral arena. However, such space could not have been provided by the conventional tools of political mobilization and therefore certain emotive issues and concerns of the people had to be invented so as to strike at their emotional chord to arouse their affinity with a particular party. Thus, politics during this period turned out to be the theatre of invention of catchy emotional issues and raking up the controversial subject that would earn greater political dividends for a party. These resulted in widening of the electoral participation of the different sections of society.[2]

Exploitation of the social issues and concerns of the people for sheer political benefits has taken alarming proportions since the times of the Janata Dal government headed by V. P. Singh. There could not be denying the fact that the reservations for the socially and education-ally backward classes of the Indian society have been visualized in the Indian Constitution and the same should have been implemented in the due course of time. Moreover, the reservations for the Scheduled Castes and Scheduled Tribes have already been implemented right since the adoption of the Constitution and the scheme has been working successfully since then. But such constitutional stipulations were ingrained in the Constitution as sacrosanct ideals that need not be exploited for selfish and motivated gains for a particular individual or political party. Such a silent spirit of the Constitutional provisions was blatantly sought to be shattered during this period of time in such a way that the politics of that time turned out to be competitive moves and countermoves among the different stakeholders to gain greater political or electoral mileage than their adversaries. Since then, the circumstantial dynamics of the political process in the country turned vicious with all sorts of manoeuvring becoming acceptable towards securing votes during the elections.

The ruling period of Prime Minister V. P. Singh was undoubtedly full of ups and downs from the very beginning. Although he tried to

---

[2] Yogendra Yadav, 'Electoral Politics in the Time of Change: India's Third Electoral System, 1989–1999', *Economic & Political Weekly* 34, no. 34–35 (1999): 2397.

ride on the wave of anti-Congressism by raking up the cases of corruption and maladministration of the Rajiv Gandhi government, he could not secure as strong mandate from the people as he had expected. Moreover, since his political base had traditionally been rooted in the core constituencies of the Congress party, he could simply not go beyond that traditional voter base once he left the government and the Congress to create a distinct political space for himself. His Jan Morcha virtually consisted of the former Congressmen who also were dissatisfied with the working of the Rajiv Gandhi government. So, what V. P. Singh had to depend on was the disparate groups of the former Janata Party that were also looking for some sort of sheet anchor which could help them expand their electoral base beyond their select pockets of influence. Thus, the party they formed in the name of Janata Dal was nothing but a conglomerate of disparate politicians having their own pocket parties seeking to attain certain degree of formidability in the political landscape of the country which would never have been possible on their own.

So when the Janata Dal government was formed under the stewardship of V. P. Singh, the disparate political groups had been anxious from the day one to secure as much political space in the government as possible. Well aware of such latent desires and aspirations of different leaders and their parties, the prime minister himself had tried to accommodate as much of these leaders as possible in the key positions of the government. For instance, in recognition of the key role played by the Haryana stalwart Devi Lal, he was made the deputy prime minister. But the major hurdle in the smooth running of the government was probably the hidden desire of a number of leaders of the Janata Dal to become the prime minister in place of the incumbent prime minister. As a result, they could not tolerate the smooth running of the government and tried to create such hurdles that would unseat the incumbent prime minister and would allow them to take his place. The first of such attempt was made by Devi Lal through a massive rally organized in his pocket borough of Jind in Haryana. Such a political manoeuvring of Devi Lal was sought to be countered by the prime minister through his misuse of Constitutional mandate for political gains by declaring his government's decision of implementing the Mandal Commission's recommendations straightaway.[3]

The decision of the government naturally took all the political parties off guard as they were not prepared to face such a potentially stirring decision on the part of the government. The decision immediately started polarizing the mass of Indian society into two distinct groups of those supporting and opposing the decision. But the tricky question in this regard was that no political party or individual could openly challenge the veracity or need for implementing the constitutional provisions envisaging reservations for the socially and educationally backward classes in government jobs. But at the same time, they also could not take the situation as it is because that could have spelled political doom for them. It was in this context, therefore, that the different political parties started their own creative investigations into the primordial cleavages of the Indian society that could have been exploited to gain political mileage in both short and long terms. The decision of the government was taken enthusiastically by the forces of social justice who took it as their overdue that the previous governments denied them. So in the celebratory mood for securing their long-drawn desire to have reservations in the government jobs, these forces started galvanizing the beneficiaries of the OBC reservations so that they could be used as a solid vote bank in the elections. But the other parties, particularly the BJP could also not be left behind in rivalling with the forces of social justice and started sharpening its Hindutva agenda to put before the masses as an alternative vision of politics where the vision of Hindutva would prevail over all other considerations of the people.

Shifting Loyalties

The 11th and 12th general elections had been underpinned by the fast pace of the shifting loyalties of different political parties. This phenomenon had been conditioned by two interrelated factors.

[3] M. P. Singh, 'Whither Indian Party System? The Electoral and Legislative Dimensions', *Indian Social Science Review* 3, no. 1 (2001): 85.

One, the weakening of the Congress as well as the Janata Dal had precipitated a kind of tremor in these parties in such a way that a number of fence sitters in these parties looked for opportunities to quit the party and either form their own political party or join any other party. But the tendency of joining the other parties was less visible for a simple reason that there were not many parties at that time that they could have joined after leaving their parental party. Hence, what most, if not all, of the leaders did was to leave their parental party to form their own parties and create a distinct support base for them. Two, the selfish interests of some of the leaders of both the parties had become so pronounced that they appeared to be left with no other option than to leave their original party and set up their own political party.[4]

While this tendency had been relatively less in the case of the Congress, this proved to be the nemesis of the Janata Dal which by the 1998 general elections had almost lost its existence with almost all the major constituents of the party preferring to leave the party and form their own party. The residue of the party though continued to be called as Janata Dal, its electoral performance in the general elections proved to be dismal and the party eventually was driven out of existence. On the other hand, the prominent leaders of the Janata party went ahead with leaving the party and came up with their own parties having distinct nomenclatures as per the basic thrust with which the party had been formed. For instance, in Uttar Pradesh, Mulayam Singh Yadav left the Janata Dal to form his own Samajwadi Party (SP) which eventually emerged as one of the most formidable parties in the state. However, most of the parties springing from the Janata Dal came up in Bihar. So, while Lalu Prasad parted ways with the Janata Party to form his pocket borough in the name of RJD, Nitish Kumar ditched his original party to form the Janata Dal (United). Apart from that, Samata Party was also formed under the leadership of George Fernandes and Jaya Jaitley. Similarly, various offshoots of Janata Dal also came in Haryana and Karnataka, apart from others.

---

[4] Robert L. Hardgrave, *1996 Indian Parliamentary Elections: What Happened? What Next?* (Austin, TX: University of Texas, 1997): 16.

The Congress had traditionally been enjoying the support of the different sections of society in almost all parts of the country given the nationalist legacy of the Gandhi–Nehru family.[5] During this period, in the absence of any Gandhi–Nehru patriarch at the helm of affairs, the party also suffered a number of splits with many of its prominent leaders leaving the party and forming their own parties. In this regard, two cases of departures from the party left deep mark on the electoral performances of the party in these elections. One of the major departures from the party might be seen in the form of G. K. Moopanar leaving the party and forming his Tamil Maanila Congress. Moopanar was one of the pillars of the party in Tamil Nadu and had worked for a number of years as party general secretary. He was considered as the representative of the southern state of Tamil Nadu and the party used to be recognized in that state through his persona only. His departure therefore left a deep dent in the electoral prospects of the party in the state from which it could never recover during the subsequent 2–3 general elections. Another notable departure from the party had been that of a number of leaders to form a new party in the name of Indian National Congress (Tiwari) after the party veteran N. D. Tiwari. This incident also compromised with the electoral prospects of the party in the states such as Uttar Pradesh and Madhya Pradesh. Thus, the sagging fortunes of the party tended to dip further with a number of its prominent leaders leaving the party.

Amidst the splits and departures from the mainstream parties, the BJP was busy looking for dependable allies in different parts of the country. The party's performance in different general elections since its formation had convinced the leadership of the party that the party's restrictive social support base and confinement of its areas of influence to only the Hindi heartland states, and that too with less influence in the populous states of Uttar Pradesh and Bihar, would not allow the party to secure as much success as it desired. But the party also felt constrained by a number of factors to increase its area of influence to

---

[5] For an insightful analysis of the social profile of the Congress voters, see Anthony Heath and Yogendra Yadav, 'The United Colours of the Congress: Social Profile of Congress Voters, 1996 and 1998', *Economic & Political Weekly* 34, no. 34–35 (1999): 2518–2528.

other parts of the country.[6] In such a situation, the only option left for the party was to hunt for more and more alliance partners who could be roped in to act as the prelude to party's entry in those states. So keeping the support of its traditional allies such as the Shiv Sena and the SAD intact, the party did succeed in garnering the support of as varied parties as that of the Samata Party from Bihar to that of the Haryana Vikas Party from Haryana. Although the party also extended overtures to a number of other parties as well, many of these parties refused to respond to the overtures of the party. Nevertheless, the party was indeed able to expand its social and political base in the country by riding on the back of different regional parties.[7]

Amidst the shifting loyalties of different parties and individuals, the plight of the splintered groups of the Janata Dal seemed quite interesting. Given the large number of parties formed out of the splintered groups of the party, these parties had a multiple number of choices to determine their future courses of action. For instance, in view of the ally hunting of the BJP, a few of the parties did respond positively to the overtures of the BJP and formally became part of the NDA. On the contrary, certain parties found it comfortable to cosy up with the grand old party of the country, and therefore entered into strategic partnership with the Congress. The most important and durable partner of the Congress party has indeed been the RJD of Lalu Prasad Yadav. At the same time, a number of parties such as the SP under the leadership of Mulayam Singh Yadav decided to become partner of the Third Front spearheaded by the left parties, especially CPI (M). The decision of the SP to join the bandwagon of the left parties had been dictated by their ideological affinities. Finally, some of the splintered parties of the Janata Parivar decided to keep their identity intact by not joining any of the available options. Thus, the electoral scenario during the two general elections had been so complex that it was not easily known as to which party had been with which alliance at a given period of time. For instance, a

[6] Pradeep K. Chhibber, 'Who Voted for the Bharatiya Janata Party', *British Journal of Political Science* 27, no. 4 (1997): 637.

[7] M. P. Singh and Rekha Saxena, *India at the Polls: Parliamentary Elections in the Federal Phase* (New Delhi: Orient Longman, 2003): 187.

number of parties that had been with the NDA in the 1996 general elections had quickly switched sides to leave the NDA by the time of the 1998 general elections.

Electoral Configurations

The electoral outcomes of the two general elections held in quick succession with each other might be reckoned as marker of the political uncertainties prevailing in the country. Moreover, the deepening of democracy in the country had been taking such curious turns that the established norms and conventions of the democratic system of India were getting shattered one by one. The situation got further complicated with the arrival of a number of actors and competing claims on the votes of the similar groups of people. In place of the developmental and governmental issues and promises, the transformed democratic discourse had been underlined by overt appeal to the people of distinct castes and religions to vote for their so-called custodians. Along with these, the ideological and programmatic rivalries as well as animosities among different parties had been increasing so much that certain parties had turned out to be pyrrhic in the political spectrum. In such a complex scenario, the outcomes of the two general elections presented very interesting picture that cast distinct impact on the process of formation of government as well as the longevity of the government. India, during this period, was thrown in the vortex of extreme instability not seen before in the political history of the country.

The social and political churning had become the hallmark of this phase of electoral politics of India, the most significant gainer of which in terms of seats had definitely been the BJP. In fact, this phase might be seen as the reinvention of the BJP from being a fringe element of Indian politics to become the nucleus of the political system. However, certain significant pointers of the time could be seen as important terms of discourse of BJP's rise to the top of the system. With the appeal of the cultural nationalism cutting ice with the different social groups particularly the upper castes people who once constituted the core support base of the Congress, the party had consistently been improving its

Table 6.1 *Position of the BJP and Its Allies in 1996 and 1998 General Elections*

Parties	Seats (1996)	Seats (1998)
BJP	161	182
Samata Party	08	12
Shiv Sena	15	06
Haryana Vikas Party	03	01
AIADMK	00	18
Others	–	46

Source: Computed from the *Statistical Report on 1996 and 1998 General Elections* (New Delhi: Election Commission of India, 1996 and 1998), accessed 19 July 2019, https://eci.gov.in/statistical-report/statistical-reports/

tally of seats in the Lok Sabha. As the figures in Table 6.1 indicate, the party had improved its seat tally from 161 in 1996 to 182 in the 1998 general elections. But the growing acceptability of the BJP on the part of the people did not go well with other political parties who stood in clear competition with the BJP in cornering the benefits arising out of the social and political churning in the country. For instance, in the beginning, the parties that came into open alliance with the BJP had been just a few excepting its traditional ally, Shiv Sena. The parties based on social justice tried to portray the BJP as some sort of untouchable but the electors of the country had something else in mind.

For the Congress, the period of 11th and 12th general elections could be said to be a period of decline and stagnation. As a matter of fact, left without any formidable sheet anchor in the form of a Gandhi–Nehru scion taking charge of the party, the Congress almost became nobody's baby during this period. The bad phase of the party had further been complicated with two unsavoury incidents that took place around this time. One, after the ouster of the Narasimha Rao government, the political credit of the party seemed to be at its nadir on account of a number of factors. For instance, his government's perceived clandestine collusion in the demolition of the Babri Masjid had extremely angered the Muslims. Consequently,

Table 6.2 *Position of the Congress in 1996 and 1998 General Elections*

Party	Seats (1996)	Seats (1998)
Congress	140	141

Source: Computed from the *Statistical Report on 1996 and 1998 General Elections* (New Delhi: Election Commission of India, 1996 and 1998), accessed 19 July 2019, https://eci.gov.in/statistical-report/statistical-reports/

they shifted their loyalty to the regional parties who were seen bracing to take on the BJP. Similarly, the allegations of corruption and scandals during his tenure had also dented the image of the party in the eyes of the common electorate and they became reluctant to vote for the party in the coming elections. Two, unleashing of the forces of caste and religion during the time of the Janata Dal government had reached their crescendo by now leaving very less scope for parties like the Congress that still persisted with the issues such as development and governance. As a result, the electoral performance of the party remained stagnant during this period as shown in Table 6.2.

The left of the centre space vacated by the Congress since the inauguration of the structural adjustment programmes by the Narasimha Rao government had been sought to be occupied by the National Front. Such kinds of fronts have become the frequent creations in the democratic politics of the country since the rise of the BJP. The proponents of these fronts take the BJP and the Congress as two untouchable poles of the political spectrum. So what they needed to do was to evolve an alternative to both of them calling it the Third Front or the National Front. The nucleus of the National Front had been constituted initially by the SP at the behest of the CPI (M). Later the CPI (M) had also joined this front along with its other left allies. As regards the other participants in this front, they kept on changing from time to time. For instance, while TDP became part of the front during the 1996 general elections, it changed sides later on and became a supporter of the BJP government. Accordingly, the electoral performance of the National Front had also varied from election to

Table 6.3 *Position of the National Front Constituents in 1996 and 1998 General Elections*

Parties	Seats (1996)	Seats (1998)
Janata Dal	46	06
SP	17	20
TDP	16	12

Source: Computed from the *Statistical Report on 1996 and 1998 General Elections* (New Delhi: Election Commission of India, 1996 and 1998), accessed 19 July 2019, https://eci.gov.in/statistical-report/statistical-reports/

election (Table 6.3). But because of the growing strength of the BJP, the front could never become a powerful political platform with even its primary membership varying at different points of time. During the 11th and 12th general elections, the National Front had become the catalyst of many of the parties fighting against both the BJP and the Congress.

Alongside the major players of the electoral games during the 11th and 12th general elections, a number of parties continued to have their sway over the voters in an independent manner. While some of these parties had been formed as a reaction to the departure of their leaders from their parental party, a few of them had really maintained the consistency of their electoral performance based on the unflinching support of their cadres. In this regard, as has been shown in Table 6.4, the case of the Tamil Maanila Congress stood out so strikingly. Formed under the leadership of the veteran Tamil Congressman G. K. Moopanar after his departure from his parent organization, the electoral performance of the party in the 1996 general elections had been an eye-opener for the political analysts. Within a short span of its formation, the party had been able to win as many as 20 seats in the state though the tally of seats came down drastically to just 3 in the 12th general elections taking place just after two years. On the contrary, the electoral performance of the BSP could also be seen as a new trendsetter in the electoral politics of the country. Interestingly, BSP, over the years, had desisted from aligning with any of the political groupings and had preferred to go alone in the

Table 6.4 Position of Other Major Parties in 1996 and 1998 General Elections

Parties	Seats (1996)	Seats (1998)
Left Parties	52	48
Tamil Maanila Congress	20	03
DMK	17	06
BSP	11	05

Source: Computed from the *Statistical Report on 1996 and 1998 General Elections* (New Delhi: Election Commission of India, 1996 and 1998), accessed 19 July 2019 https://eci.gov.in/statistical-report/statistical-reports/

elections in Uttar Pradesh. Yet the cadre-based support for the party had been so strong that its performance over the years had by and large remained consistent.

On the whole, the 11th and 12th general elections were reflection of the changing paradigms of the democratic politics of India. The old idioms and values of the party system, electors, political alliances and voting behaviour of the common electorates had undergone subtle transformations during these elections. The grand old party of the country had silently given space to the parties that had been almost unknown or out of existence just a few years back. But gradually they had come up as the main actors in the political matrix of the country. In this regard, the cases of both the caste-based parties and religion-based parties had been striking. What was more interesting was the fact that these two sets of parties initially emerged out of the anti-Congressism that had been the underlying theme of democratic politics of the country for a long period of time. But once they were able to oust the Congress from the mainstream of the democratic politics, they themselves became staunch rivals and the subsequent elections had become the fight between these two sets of parties. However, in their sustained rivalry, the BJP had definitely marched much ahead of the caste-based parties. The 11th and 12th general elections had in fact been the launching pads for the BJP which got ample opportunities during these elections to test the waters in order to ready itself for bigger strides in the times to come.

Implications for Democracy

The 11th and 12th general elections were held in the period of extreme political instability in the country. With the production of hung parliament in both the elections, no party stood the chance of forming government that could last long. Thus, these elections introduced the element of sustained instability in the political system of India. Such a state of things could be understood as an aberration given the long track record of the country for having stable and strong governments.[8] But the circumstances prevailing after the 11th and 12th general elections in fact did not permit the formation of strong and stable governments for two distinct reasons. One, the politicking during this period had reached its peak. All the parties were busy in undermining the position of the other in such a way that they were becoming culprits in the public perception for making the government unstable. Two, the selfish interests of a number of leaders had become so pronounced during this time that they had started exploring the possibilities of occupying the chair of the prime minister. In such situations, nobody was ready to help the other in becoming the prime minister unless the reciprocal gesture was also offered to him. In the absence of such reciprocity, the government formation remained a very difficult proposition with the major contenders of power remaining outside the power games to buy time for entering the poll arena once again.

With the fall of the successive governments, a number of parties had started taking the fluid situation of the time as the opportune time for them to reposition their electoral strategies, while others remained busy in the game of government formation. In this regard, the perspective of the BJP had been quite different from others. Undoubtedly, the successive efforts of the party to form government at the centre had been sabotaged by opposition parties. In other words, all the times the BJP was able to form the government, the opposition parties had always joined hands with one another to ensure the downfall of the government. Thus, the government formation experiences of the BJP in the previous times had been very unpleasant. So, the party was now left with no option than to buy time out of the skirmishes taking place

---

[8] Chandan Mitra, 'Unholy Alliances', *Seminar* 454 (June, 1996): 17.

among different Janata offshoots and evolve a concerted strategy that could catapult it to power at the centre. In this move, the party was greatly assisted by the formation of governments at the centre with the support of either the regional parties or the Congress. Thus, the rise and fall of different governments did take place but the blame game among the different stakeholders did not affect the BJP and it busied itself in going for the fresh elections.

The role of the Congress during this period had been quite unstable and aimed at taking advantage of the situation in order to maintain its hold over the government. Right from the declaration of results after both the elections, an anxious BJP did try its luck in forming the government. But given the political scenario and the party position in the Lok Sabha, it was sure from the very beginning that the party would not be able to form a stable government. Yet when the party failed to understand the writings on the wall, the rest of the things were done by the regional parties on whose support the BJP was banking to prove the majority in Lok Sabha. But once the BJP was out of the scene, the scenario was quite open for the regional parties as well as the Congress to evolve their concerted strategies on the formation of the government. However, in these situations, the Congress was in the dilemma of staking its own claim to form the government or to go for supporting the leaders of the regional parties. Eventually, the Congress arrived at the conclusion in desisting from forming government on its own and extending outside support to other parties. But such experiments of the party could not last long as the desperation of the party with the governments that it was supporting grew sooner than expected. As a result, the party did not shy away from pulling the governments down. Thus, the Congress machination to enjoy the power without being held accountable to the parliament and the people did not continue for long and the bluff of such a strategy was called very soon.

Concluding Observations

The period of the 11th and 12th elections had been the period of the rise of the hitherto latent sections of the India society for whom voting in the general elections was more a ritual than a thoughtful decision.

But with the caste-based mobilization by the parties propounding the cause of social justice getting increased stridency in the electoral system these castes became aware of the value of votes and what their votes could do for them. That had indeed been the turning point which made the electoral politics in the country substantive rather than ritualistic. While the deepening of democracy had already been showing a good track record in the southern parts of the country, the new churning that had been introduced by unleashing of the forces of social justice had its electrifying impact on the intermediary castes in the Hindi heartland. In this process, almost the entire system of politics and the electoral dynamics underwent radical transformations. Not only the established patterns of voting, voter mobilization and identifying the vote with the caste identity of an individual were highlighted, but this also resulted in the formation of a number of new political parties. As these parties sought to expand their social and political base rapidly among the masses of their caste along with the strategic alliance with other pliable castes, this gave birth to an unconventional band of leaders who hitherto had remained oblivious of political forays. That way, the deepening of democracy introduced a pattern of electoral politics that had radically been altogether different from the traditional format of politics being practised by the parties like the Congress. This period therefore resulted in the greater strengthening of the position of the caste-based parties and proportional reduction in the strength of the Congress.

CHAPTER 7

Rise of the Right

Indian political landscape from the very beginning has been a mosaic of various ideologies and competing claims and counterclaims of varying interests of the society. However, the formidability of a particular ideology or interest in order to become the authoritative value of the society has always depended on the circumstances prevailing at a particular period of time as well as the imperatives of general interests of the nation and its people. For instance, during the national movement, the most important objective of all the major political groups, irrespective of their ideology, and the general interest of the nation and its people revolved around the country getting complete independence from the colonial rule. So all the political formations used to work among the people to awaken them for the cause of waging a sustained struggle against the colonial rulers so that the independence of the country could be hastened. But given that the Congress was in the forefront of the national movement, it became the political formation to attract the mass support of people drawing on the active participation of almost all sections of the people. This does not mean that other ideological groups did not remain actively engaged in waging struggle against the colonial rule. What is being argued here is that the presence of all other groups in the national movement remained marginal only in the face of the formidability with which the Congress was able to carry the cross of the national movement. But in the course of time as the other ideological groups got opportunities to prove their worth among the people, they started getting wider public support and later became countervailing forces to the hegemonic presence of the Congress.

The same analogy could probably be drawn with regard to the rise of the right on the political horizon of the country. The people with ideological persuasions rooted in the right have always remained active in the political life of India. But their presence in the country could not become significant for the obvious reason that the political mainstream in India has always been tilted towards the left given the infatuations of a large number of Indian politicians with the left ideology. At the same time, a distinct approach towards the issues and challenges facing the country could be discerned between the left and the right since the days of Independence. For instance, on the vital issues of national importance, the left has always been strident in pushing forward their point of view in comparison to the right that has preferred the incremental approach. The situation after the Independence took the curious turn ordaining prominence of the left with the coronation of Jawaharlal Nehru as the prime minister of the country. An ardent supporter of the left ideology, Nehru from day one did not conceal his predilections towards the left in both his words and deeds. It was therefore not surprising that soon the left ideology-driven plans and programmes began to roll out in the country. But amidst all such fast pacing of the policies and programmes towards the socialistic pattern of society, the rightist elements in the Indian politics remained committed to their ideology and kept working silently to convince the larger masses of the veracity of alternative perspective or vision for the country. Although the ideology of right has been articulated by a number of political parties, the most effective articulation of this ideology in the country has been put forward by the erstwhile Jana Sangh, the predecessor of the BJP. Despite remaining the marginal force in the political spectrum of India for a long period of time, the formidable rise of the right could be seen in the aftermath of the 1999 general elections. The present chapter seeks to analytically articulate the circumstances leading to the rise of the BJP as the ruling party and its implications for the democratic discourse of the country.

Overcoming the Short-lived Tenures

The rise of the BJP as the ruling party of the country has not been as smooth and universally acceptable as for other parties including the Congress and the Janata outfits in their different incarnations. It is quite interesting to look at the circumstances in which the party reached to the seat of power at Delhi but was not allowed to stay there for long in view of the numerous inhibitions harboured by others with regard to the BJP becoming the ruling party at the centre. As such, the different tenures of the party in office at the central level are indicative of the difficulties with which the rise of the right could be taken as the acceptable norm of the democratic discourse in the country. For instance, in its first tryst with power at the centre, the party remained in office for less than two weeks as suspicious attitude of the rest of the political spectrum did not allow any of them to support or join hands with the party to ensure the longevity of the government. As a result, the government led by Atal Bihari Vajpayee fell unceremoniously within the shortest period of time for any government in the country. This experience reminded the party of the abhorrence that the mainstream political class nurtured against it.

Learning the hard lessons from its first tryst with the power at the centre, the BJP re-strategized its political arithmetic in such a way that its acceptability among the mainstream political parties was endorsed. The party could very well realize that the major difficulty with other political parties had not been with the rightist approach of the party on economic issues but with its enmeshing the rightist ideology with the ideology of Hindutva along with its discordant views on a number of controversial issues facing the country. The fear of other parties thus did not emanate from their distrust in the rightist ideology but with the Hindutva and other controversial positions taken by the BJP on different issues including the Ram temple, status of Jammu and Kashmir within the Indian Union, the uniform civil code, among others. Even on these issues, other parties did not seem to be uncomfortable with the BJP for the sake of any other concern but fear of the desertion of Muslim voters who had been key to their electoral performances in both state and national elections. Thus, the basic mantra left for the BJP was to tone down its insistence on the controversial issues and find a common ground to gel with other political parties.

The political scenario of the country during the last few years had been such that the political disintegration of different social groups had become almost complete between the competing political claims such as the proponents of social justice, the Hindutva-based parties and the political formations thriving on the basis of local or regional issues and concerns, especially in the southern and eastern parts of the country. During this churning, the BJP had indeed been able to arouse the Hindutva orientations of a large section of the society and its monopoly on this emotive issue had been so complete that it did not leave any scope for any other political party to eye the votes likely to be cast on the basis of the Hindutva persuasions. On this count, the only exception could be seen in the form of Shiv Sena which has been able to maintain its vibrancy in the Maharashtra politics despite playing the same electoral tune as that of the BJP. But for other opposition parties, Hindutva became as alien ideology as that of staking claim for the Nehruvian socialism as their own preserve.

The BJP, in order to expand its social and political acceptance, on the one hand, and earn more and more allies, on the other, embarked upon the twin strategy of keeping its hard line political stances such as Hindutva and the Ram temple, and its perspectives on other controversial issues facing the country as its long-term guiding principles, but remaining ready to present a liberal or accommodative face to its allies and to the general masses on the practical pedestal. In other words, the party performed a very delicate task in a wonderful way by retaining its strident approach to its foundational issues but on the ground remained a pliable, accommodative and liberal political party with which the liberal, centrist and rightist political forces can align with in the short term. Personality wise, while L. K. Advani represented the hard face of the party in a seemingly uncompromising manner, the soft face of the party was put forward in the shape of Vajpayee as a malleable and sweet personality ready to mix and work with any political party falling within the broad ideological spectrum of rightist orientation. With this strategy, the party could win a number of allies and partners that eventually made the party head the ruling alliance after 1999 general elections to complete the full term in office.

Political Scenario on the Eve of Elections

The 13th general elections were called in the wake of the previous government led by Vajpayee failing to win the vote of confidence in the Lok Sabha. The fall of the government was meditated by with-drawal of support to the government by AIADMK leader Jayalalithaa on the rejection of her demand from the central government for dismissal of the Tamil Nadu state government headed by her arch-rival Karunanidhi of the DMK. Although the demand for dismissal of the DMK government appeared totally illogical, unconstitutional and uncalled for, the AIADMK still insisted on the demand. It in fact tried to exploit the situation as the blackmailing ploy with the central government given the vulnerability of the government depending on the support extended by her party. Taking it as the best opportunity to sacrifice the government on the altar of unjustified demands of the allies, the BJP decided to go for the mid-term polls after the Congress declined the presidential invitation to form the government after the resignation of the Vajpayee government. Thus, the prelude situations before the convening of the 13th general elections were taken by the BJP leadership as the opportunity for them to seek fresh mandate from the public for a better majority to the party in the ensuing general elections.

The BJP's preparedness for the 13th general elections could be gauged as preordained in view of the way the party agreed for the sacrifice of the government. With the exception of only the Tamil Nadu politics, the other things for the coalition government were running as per the script barring few occasional hiccups now and then. But on the whole, the allies of the party in the NDA remained firmly standing with the party in its decision to quit and go for fresh elections. Thus, the party looked at bright electoral fortunes in the 13th general elections in view of its appeal to the voters to give it a fresh and convincing mandate to complete the unfinished agenda of nation-building and leading the country into the 21st century. The moderate and accommodative face of the party helped it not only retain its old allies in the NDA but also kept the alliance open for others to join as and when the need arose. The party also looked at increasing its formidable strength in the Hindi heartland along with getting more and more electoral mileage in companionship of its other alliance partners in the states where the party did not have any formidable presence.[1] In this context, it was quite fruitful for the party to become the keystone of the anti-Congress political formation so that the regional and other parties opposed to the Congress could join hands with the BJP either as part of the NDA or extending outside support to the party.

While the BJP along with its NDA partners was getting ready for the 13th general elections, the main opposition party, the Congress, was in shambles in view of the multiple challenges besetting the party. At the very outset, the party which had been habituated to be patronized by a member of the Gandhi–Nehru family felt somewhat orphaned after the death of Rajiv Gandhi and refusal of any of his family members taking charge of the party. As a result, the party had participated in the previous general elections in somewhat half-hearted manner and therefore it was not expected to reap rich electoral dividends even on the failure of the previous short-lived governments headed by different parties and leaders. Next, sensing the pathetic condition of the party, when the wife of Rajiv Gandhi, Sonia Gandhi, made up her mind to head the party as its president, formidable internal dissensions emerged within the party with the Maharashtra strongman Sharad Pawar raising the issue of her foreign origin. Subsequently, he along with a number of other prominent leaders of the party resigned from the party, thereby compromising with the electoral prospects of the party in the potentially fertile states like Maharashtra. Moreover, Sonia Gandhi's recent forays in the political landscape of the country did not probably afford her sufficient experience and political acumen to take insightful decisions as had been taken by her mother-in-law after sensing the pulse of the electors. The Congress entered the fray in

---

[1] For a persuasive analysis of the ideological consolidation of the right, see Pradeep K. Chhibber and Rahul Verma, *Ideology and Identity: The Changing Party System in India* (New Delhi: Oxford University Press, 2018): 249.

the 13th general elections as a reluctant participant with the intention of accepting whatever verdict coming out of the polls.

During the time of the Congress redundancy in the course of its lesser activity, the role of opposition to the government was played by the so-called Third Front consisting of a mosaic of left parties along with the various splinter groups of the erstwhile Janata Dal that had now taken shape of a number of regional parties active in different states such as Uttar Pradesh, Bihar and Haryana. After the disintegration of the second Janata experiment in the form of the Janata Dal, now the splinter groups coming out of this party attained different names resembling the core values that defined their ideological perspectives as well as the historical legacies with which they carried forward their political activities.[2] But in the absence of any of their leaders having an important role in the national politics, the primary focus of these parties had now become confined to the politics of the states in which they remained relevant. In such a situation, the basic responsibility of putting forward a formidable fight against the NDA, in general, and the BJP, in particular, lay on the shoulders of the left parties. However, these parties already had a constricted support base in just a few states and therefore the possibility of any pan-India opposition group emerging against the NDA seemed to be improbable, and the 13th general elections therefore witnessed the BJP entering the fray with an upper hand in comparison to its rivals and opposition parties.

There also existed a lot of variation in the campaign strategies of different political parties during the 13th general elections. The BJP tried to enter the electoral fray with the twin strategy of containing any negative campaign against the party or the coalition by proving its innocence in the name of not getting ample opportunity to do much for the welfare of the people. But on the positive side, the party did not shy to capitalize on the Kargil War that the NDA government had fought against the Pakistani aggression in the hill tops of Kargil

[2] E. Sridharan, 'The Fragmentation of the Indian Party System: 1952–1999, Seven Competing Explanations', in *Parties and Party Politics in India*, ed. Zoya Hasan (New Delhi: Oxford University Press, 2002): 489.

well within the Indian territory. Admittedly, the Kargil War might be seen as the god-sent opportunity for the BJP to show its resoluteness in taking on the challenges facing the unity and integrity of the nation. In fact, over the years, BJP had been strident in putting forward its argument for a resolute and firm handling of the issues posing any threat to the unity and integrity of the nation. But the party never got a chance to show to the people how capable was the party to put its words in action whenever an occasion arose to this effect. Thus, much of the election strategy of the BJP during the 13th general elections depended on the showcasing of the Kargil War as the proof of the determinate behaviour of the party in times of crisis facing the nation either from within or outside.

The electoral scenario therefore appeared distinctly poised in favour of the BJP and the NDA in comparison to the opposition parties including the Congress and the Third Front. The only formidable challenge likely to be arising before the ruling party was from the strong regional parties that had also stood their ground all through these years as the BJP had done. So, throughout the campaign trail, the BJP had tried to tread a cautious path in such a way that it could put forward its views and appeals to the electorate without casting any aspersion, especially on the regional parties that could become the probable ally of the party in case it became short of majority in the Lok Sabha.[3] Moreover, the party focused on its core vote banks in the Hindi heartland states along with its areas of influence in the western parts of the country. In the rest of India, the party banked on its allies to make most of these elections and augment the tally of seats in the Lok Sabha. For the opposition, while the Congress appeared in doldrums given the novice moves of the party president, the other parties remained engaged in their pocket boroughs at provincial levels. Thus, these elections appeared as the best possible chance for the BJP to maximize its gains and help its allies all over the country to come up with handsome electoral results so that the NDA could emerge as the coalition with at least working majority in the Lok Sabha.

[3] Yogendra Yadav, Sanjay Kumar, and Oliver Heath, 'The BJP's New Social Bloc', *Frontline* 16, no. 23 (1999): 14.

Electoral Outcome

The electoral outcome of the 1999 general elections has been described as the defining moment in India's recent political history.[4] It is for the first time the right had come so close to forming a stable government at the centre. Interestingly, the results of the 13th general elections presented a complex picture in which no party or coalition could get a majority, though the NDA came much closer to the magical number of 272. As the figures in Table 7.1 show, the BJP could not even reach the 200 mark despite the best efforts of its leaders as well as adoption of the multipronged strategy by the party. Nevertheless, the loss of the party could indeed be made up by the formidable regional satraps whose influence in their respective states had helped them reach rich dividends even in the 13th general elections. The major loss of the BJP could be seen in the states of Uttar Pradesh and Bihar where the

Table 7.1 *Seats Won by NDA Constituents*

NDA Constituents	Seats
BJP	182
JD (U)	21
Shiv Sena	15
DMK	12
BJD	10
Trinamool Congress	08
PMK	05
INLD	05
MDMK	04
National Conference	04
SAD	02
RLD	02

Source: Computed from the *Statistical Report on 1999 General Elections* (New Delhi: Election Commission of India, 1999), accessed 21 June 2019, https://eci.gov.in/statistical-report/statistical-reports/

[4] Bidyut Chakrabarty, *Forging Power: Coalition Politics in India* (New Delhi: Oxford University Press, 2006), 171.

forces of social justice continued to maintain their sway over different social groups that had been sufficiently mobilized during the heyday of the Janata Dal rule at the centre.[5] Insofar as the formation of the government was concerned, the NDA could not conjure up the requisite number on its own. But during this time, the alliance got the strong backing of the Andhra strongman Chandrababu Naidu whose TDP had come out with flying colours in these elections winning as many as 29 seats. Thus, the NDA with the solid backing of the TDP was able to form the first non-Congress government that lasted its full term in office.

Given that the Congress had entered the poll arena during the 13th general elections with a subdued mindset due to both the internal dissensions within the party leading to the resignation of a number of leaders and the political immaturity of its President Sonia Gandhi, the party in fact did not seem to expect grand show in these elections. At the same time, the party could not enter into such broad-based alliance with the regional parties as had been done by the BJP. Its electoral understanding remained confined to only those parties that had either major differences with the BJP such as the AIADMK and the RJD or its traditional allies like the Muslim League in Kerala. But the party's traditional vote bank in different parts of the country came to the much-wanted rescue of the party enabling it to win 114 seats even in the ambience of gloom and hopelessness (Table 7.2). That way, the party remained in the political reckoning of the time to emerge as the lynchpin of the opposition unity in the Lok Sabha. Thus, the party was afforded the role of the main opposition party through which it could mount formidable opposition to the government and prepare the groundwork for the next parliamentary elections.

The loss of the BJP and the Congress in the 13th general elections had gone in favour of the regional parties both in the Hindi heartland and other parts of the country. But the most fragmented electoral outcome could be seen in the state of Uttar Pradesh where the whopping

[5] Phillip Oldenburg, 'The Thirteenth Election of India's Lok Sabha', accessed 12 July 2019, https://web.archive.org/web/20080604152951/http://www.asiasociety.org/publications/indian_elections.13.a.html

Table 7.2 *Seats Won by the Congress and Its Allies*

Congress and Its Allies	Seats
Congress	114
AIADMK	10
RJD	07
Others	04

Source: Computed from the *Statistical Report on 1999 General Elections* (New Delhi: Election Commission of India, 1999), accessed 21 June 2019, https://eci.gov.in/statistical-report/statistical-reports/

number of seats for the Lok Sabha was shared majorly by different stakeholders. In other words, the electorate of Uttar Pradesh even by now could not overcome the primordialization of their political affinities and continued to vote as per their caste calculations or loyalties. Thus, the two important regional parties of the state came out with good show in the 13th general elections. While the SP rode on the support of its traditional vote bank of Yadavs, the other important party, the BSP, won as many as 14 seats riding on the support of the Scheduled Castes. In view of the soft Hindutva exhibited by the Congress during the reign of P. V. Narasimha Rao, the Muslims in the state had deserted the party to vote for the SP and the BSP depending upon the winning capability of the candidate. The performance of the left parties had traditionally been confined to their strongholds in West Bengal and a few other states while the splinter group of the Congress, the Nationalist Congress Party (NCP) headed by Sharad Pawar also put up an impressive show by winning eight seats in these elections (Table 7.3).

The outcome of the 13th general elections had indeed been reflective of the mindset prevailing in the country since the implementation of the Mandal Commission recommendations. The social and political churning that had been carried out at that period of time had by and large subsisted until the 13th general elections. Further, the voting pattern and winning trends of different political parties also reflected the fragmented voting behaviour of the electors. As a result, the hope of the NDA and the BJP to sweep these elections got dashed and the

Table 7.3 *Seats Won by Left and Other Major Parties*

Parties	Seats
CPI (M)	33
SP	26
BSP	14
NCP	08
CPI	04
RSP	03

Source: Computed from the *Statistical Report on 1999 General Elections* (New Delhi: Election Commission of India, 1999), accessed 21 June 2019, https://eci.gov.in/statistical-report/statistical-reports/

alliance failed to get even the working majority in the Lok Sabha. At the same time, the Congress also could not bring about any turnaround in its electoral fortunes and banked upon its traditional voters and areas for maintaining a respectable winning streak in these elections. The loss of the national parties in turn was made most by the regional parties who did not allow the wave of Mandal or Mandir to upset their traditional support base in their respective states. The shortfall in the seats of the NDA to reach the mark of majority in the Lok Sabha to be able to form the government was eventually compensated by the support of the TDP. Thus, the 13th general elections threw up a mandate that allowed the NDA form the government with relatively comfortable majority based on which it could run the government for the full term of five years.

Implications for Democracy

The outcome of the 13th general elections had a number of serious implications for Indian democracy. At the outset, the most formidable phenomenon established by these elections had been that the time for the rise of the right had arrived in the country. The vision with which the BJP was set up in 1980 had more or less now been accepted by a large majority of the population. Although the BJP did have a number of such foundational beliefs and value premises which would not have made it acceptable to its electoral allies, the party had indeed been able to retrofit its short term as well as long term agenda in such a way that its acceptability across the political spectrum of the country increased manifold, thereby allowing it a foothold even in those areas that had previously been a no-entry zone for the party. Interestingly, the party did not abjure its basic resolves and values such as Hindutva, the Ram temple, abrogation of Article 370 and adoption of the uniform civil code. What it actually did was to put them on the backburner so as to present its liberal face before both, the electorate as well as its NDA allies and outside supporters. This strategic retreat of the party had played the pivotal role in helping it manage a comfortable majority in the Lok Sabha and form the government with a firm resolve and resolute mindset of governing the country.[6]

The confidence with which the BJP had been able to form the government at the centre by cobbling up a comfortable majority, thanks to the unconditional support of the TDP, was striking.[7] No other non-Congress party or alliance had earlier been able to form the government with such exuberance and clear vision as the BJP did in 1999. This was reflective of the growing confidence of the party not only in its abilities to meet the challenges of running a coalition government through its deft handling of its allies but also exhibited its belief in the veracity of the commitment with which its allies and partners had joined hands with it in forming the government. The obvious result of such a resolve produced the unprecedented distinction of the NDA government being the first non-Congress government to last its full term in office. This distinction has imparted a new vibrancy and flexibility to the Indian democracy which has generally been observed as the bastion of the Congress party. The successful running of the NDA government for its full term proved that the Indian democracy has matured enough to experience the rule of non-Congress parties and alliances with the same degree of commitment to the constitutional

---

[6] Paul Wallace and Ramashray Roy, *India's 1999 Elections and 20th Century Politics* (New Delhi: SAGE Publications, 2003): 187.

[7] Bob Hardgrave, 'The 1999 Indian Parliamentary Elections and the New BJP-led Coalition Government', accessed 19 July 2019, https://web.archive.org/web/20081011235012/http://asnic.utexas.edu/asnic/hardgrave/Elections1999.html

values and norms that need to be followed in order to maintain the sanctity of the democratic institutions and processes in the country. Thus, with the NDA government, the Indian democracy seemed to have entered into a new phase of maturity and vibrancy.

Democratic experience of the country over the years has somewhat given the impression that the social and political texture of India might have made it unfit to be ruled by the coalitions or alliances. In other words, for a long period of time, the system of government of the country was such that a single party in the form of the Congress used to govern the country and lasted its full term in office without any difficulty. But whenever the nature of government took the form of coalition or alliance of a number of parties, such governments did not last long and had to meet an untimely demise leading to calling of the mid-term polls. This had particularly been true in the case of the coalition experiences carried out by the Janata governments in their different incarnations. This had also given the impression that the idea of stable and strong government was the forte of the Congress only and the opposition parties could never be able to provide a stable and strong government at the centre. The formation of the NDA government in the aftermath of the 13th general elections had acted to shatter the myth regarding the stability of governments and the abilities of the non-Congress political parties to come together or singlehandedly form stable governments. That way, these elections had been the trendsetting ones that were able to set new traditions and beliefs in the democratic politics of the country.

The Indian democracy since its inception has been marked by certain degree of homogeneity in terms of the political culture as well as electoral behaviour of the people. In other words, the elections had never been the basis of social and political fragmentation of the Indian people. But the turn of events since the formation of the Janata Dal government under the leadership of V. P. Singh had tried to drive such a wedge in the minds of the Indian electorate that there emerged total fragmentation of the voters. The subsequent game of one-upmanship had stirred the social and political landscape of the country producing a number of political parties based on their primordial affinities. By the time of the 13th general elections, such fragmentation of the Indian voting behaviour seemed to have become complete with a number of regional parties based on caste, religion, language, region etc. making rich dividends out of the 13th general elections. The consolidation of the gains of the regional parties had proportionally resulted in the decline of support base of traditional parties like the Congress. The impact of this fragmentation had been taken both ways by the political analysts. While this has famously been argued as the deepening of democracy in the country, such a tendency could also be perceived as destruction of the social and political cohesion of the country with ominous portents for the long-term interests of both the people and the nation.

Concluding Observations

The wheel of the Indian electoral politics turned full circle in 1999 with the clamour of the BJP getting fulfilled to form a stable government at the centre. It had truly been a historic moment for the party as it had got itself catapulted to top of the political power from being a fringe element since the inauguration of parliamentary democracy in the country. The rise of the right also attains greater significance in India for three distinct reasons. One, the mainstream political ethos of the country from the very beginning has been underpinned by the stridency of the socialist values and operational mechanisms. Although the formidability of socialism in the political value premise of the country has been confirmed even from the pre-Independence times, its practical articulation in terms of the concerted policies and programmes looked as if the country has been oriented towards the socialistic pattern of society and there would be no possibility of going back on that promise. As a matter of fact, the influence of the social-istic values has been so powerful on the thinking and working of the top leaders of the country including Nehru that there did not seem to exist any space for the rightist ideology. Even the parties that used to profess the rightist ideology like the Swatantra Party had been reduced to insignificance in the electoral arena in such a way that there was no chance for the party to rise again and seek to establish the rightist ideology as the mainstream perspective of politics in the country. Even the predecessor of the BJP, the BJS, was also not in the position at that time to offer any worthwhile challenge to the hegemonic way in which socialism had its sweep in all walks of life of the people in India.

Next, the rise of the right through the efforts of the BJP appeared doubly difficult in view of the party seeking to blend the rightist perspective with the ideology of Hindutva. Significantly, over the years, the rightist ideology had not been abhorred but given a space with the intention that the same would be spun out of the system through the electoral dynamics of the Indian democracy in due course of time. But insofar as Hindutva is concerned, it has been a strict no-no for the powerful secular politicians and activists. So, when the BJP sought to conjoin its rightist ideology with its loftier vision of Hindutva, the political commentators did not have any hesitation in professing the worthlessness of the political endeavours of the party because they would never be able to break much ground with the general electorate of the country. In fact, the peripheral performance of the BJS over the years in the successive general elections came as the boastful solace for the socialists and secularists that the Indian electorate has already rejected the party and it would always remain a fringe element in the Indian political system in case it survives for some longer period of time. But something else was in store for this ideology in the times to come.

In the end, even before the BJP could emerge as the hegemonic party in the Indian political system as the Congress has been for a long period of time, it has already been declared as some sort of untouchable entity by the mainstream parties ranging from as wide spectrum as that of the Congress, left parties, caste-based parties and many other. A kind of perception was sought to be created in the minds of the general electorate that any sort of poll alliance with the party could be struck only by the parties that are dabbling with religion and politics like the BJP. It was in accordance with that impression that almost all major political parties declined to share power with the BJP and become part of the government when the party had tried to form short-lived governments. As a result, despite deserving a chance to form and run the government at the centre in accordance with the mandate of the people, the party was denied the opportunity on one pretext or the other. But the machinations of the opposition parties could not move the general electorate away from the party and it was able to increase its influence and appeal with the people step by step. The 1999 verdict could be seen as the decisive mandate for the party to become the ruling party of the country irrespective of the remorseful cry of the opposition parties.

CHAPTER 8

Clientelism as the Norm of Democratic Politics

The 14th and 15th general elections have been important landmarks in the democratic process of the country for they helped in
the consolidation of a number of tendencies that have previously
been practised as marginal activities. For instance, the Congress
has been shying away from entering into any electoral alliance with
any of the major political parties until the 13th general elections.
But when its best efforts to secure even a working majority in the
Lok Sabha after the 14th general elections could not yield desirable
results, the party was forced to accept coalition as the fait accompli
of not only the party but the country as well. Since that time, coalitional nature of the democratic politics in the country has come to
become the underlying phenomenon in such a way that even the
parties that are able to secure majority in the respective houses are
finding it difficult to eschew the coalition and feel duty-bound to
carry on with the alliance partners. Had this not been the case, the
two successive governments formed by the NDA at the centre under
Narendra Modi as prime minister would patently have been called
the BJP governments as the party has indeed been able to secure a
comfortable majority on its own in the lower house of parliament and
would not need support of any of its coalition partners for formation
of the government.

The 14th general elections took place in 2004 in the backdrop of the overconfidence of incumbent Vajpayee government deciding to go for snap poll even before it completed its term in office. The overdose of publicity and inflationary portrayal of successes of the government by a few of the party functionaries as well as government officials had presumably made the Prime Minister Vajpayee to go for renewal of the public mandate to rule the country for another term of five years. But this gamble of the Prime Minister proved counterproductive because the BJP as the dominant partner of the coalition along with other coalition partners suffered massive defeats in the elections. Although no party or coalition could secure even a working majority in the lower house of parliament, the centrist and left of the centrist parties did join hands together with the Congress to oust the NDA government from power. Subsequently, a new political alliance was formed in the name of UPA under chairpersonship of the Congress President Sonia Gandhi to cobble up a working majority in the Lok Sabha and stake claim to form government. In the wake of Sonia Gandhi refusing to become prime minister, her nominee Dr Manmohan Singh was elected leader of the UPA conglomerate and became the prime minister. Later, in the 15th general elections held in 2009, the UPA was again able to win the mandate to rule over the country for another five years. Thus, the 10-year rule of the UPA in the wake of the 14th and 15th general elections imparted distinct features to the democratic processes of the country. The present chapter seeks to critically examine the major transformations brought about by these two general elections in the Indian democratic experiences.

Consolidation of Coalition Politics

The period of the UPA rule could be seen as the phase of consolidation of coalition politics in the country.[1] The social and religious churning taking place during the decade of 1990s had tended to rupture the established norms of democratic politics in terms of caste, class and religious groups acting as conventional vote banks of different political parties.

[1] For a lucid account of the coalition politics in India, see Chakrabarty, *Forging Power*.

The obvious outcome of this churning had been in terms of massive disintegration of traditional social support base of the Congress party with a large section of almost all the social groups such as upper castes, OBCs, Dalits, Adivasis and even the urban middle class deserting the party. As a result, riding on the support of their distinct castes along with contingent voters like the Muslims, a number of regional parties, particularly in the Hindi heartland, emerged as formidable political force in various states. The BJP also took advantage of subtle disintegration in the traditional Congress vote bank. Consequently, it not only improved its seat tally in the Lok Sabha from 2 to 200 but was also able to enter into strategic political alliances with a number of regional parties to augment its seats. The formation of the Vajpayee government in the aftermath of the 13th general elections was the distinct electoral gain the BJP could secure by strategic positioning of its fixtures in different parts of the country.[2]

But the Congress could neither discern the gradual disintegration in its traditional vote bank so minutely nor was it able to come out of the hangover of its hegemonic presence in all parts of the country over a long period of time. In such a circumstance, it was simply out of place for the party to enter into any sort of electoral alliance with the regional parties in different states to make up for the deficiency in its vote share after the departure of a number of preponderant social groups from the fold of the party. Hence, the stage was set for the 14th general elections with different opposition parties readying themselves to take on the incumbent BJP and its alliance partners in various states on their own. Resultantly, the 14th general elections were a multi-cornered contest in which apart from the BJP and the Congress, the regional parties or left parties also entered the fray with formidable candidates. The outcome of these elections came as a shock for the BJP-led NDA as the incumbent government failed to secure a majority in the Lok Sabha. This presented the golden opportunity before the opposition parties to leave no stone unturned in keeping the NDA out of power. But the moot question before them was to arrive at a consensus leader whom they could present as their prime ministerial nominee.

[2] Mukulika Banerjee, 'Sacred Elections', *Economic & Political Weekly* 42, no. 17 (2007, 28 April): 1558.

Table 8.1 *Seats Won by the Congress and Its Pre-poll Partners in 2004*

Parties	Seats
Congress	145
RJD	21
DMK	16
NCP	09
PMK	06
TRS	05
JMM	05
MDMK	04
LJSP	04
Others	04
Total	219

Source: Computed from the *Statistical Report on 2004 General Elections* (New Delhi: Election Commission of India, 2004), accessed 22 July 2019, https://eci.gov.in/statistical-report/statistical-reports/

The choice of a leader to become the prime minister obviously centred on the top leadership of the Congress as the party in pre-poll alliance with its partners had been able to win an impressive 219 seats in the Lok Sabha. In fact, in order to take on the BJP-led NDA, the Congress had entered into electoral adjustment with a number of regional parties in the states such as Bihar, Tamil Nadu and Maharashtra (Table 8.1). Although the combined seat tally of this pre-poll seat adjustment could not go beyond 219, it made this group the formidable claimant to form the government at the centre. Moreover, as the other opposition parties including the left parties were not in a position to afford the return of the NDA to power by default, they readily agreed to extend outside support to the Congress-led UPA to stake claim for forming government.[3] Thus, as a plausible alternative to the BJP-led NDA, Congress reconciled itself to the idea

[3] Paranjoy Guha Thakurta and Shankar Raghuraman, *Divided We Stand: A New Time of Coalitions* (New Delhi: SAGE, 2004), 157.

of the UPA acting as the conglomerate of likeminded parties to form the government with common minimum programme for governance. The democratic polity of India, therefore, now definitively turned into somewhat bipolar mode with two contending political alliances vying for the electoral dividends in the country.

During the 14th and 15th general elections, the political scenario of the country was characterized by the NDA, particularly the BJP emerging as the new reference point of the electoral politics. Barring a few of its traditional allies such as the SAD and the Shiv Sena, almost all the political parties, both national and regional, cutting across ideological divide, posited themselves against the incumbent party in power. Although the ground realities and the imperative of keeping their traditional electoral bastions intact made these parties keep their independent forays in these elections, it was always in their mind to keep the NDA out of power in all probabilities. Hence, when in the aftermath of the 14th general elections, the non-NDA parties decided to come together to enable the Congress-led UPA form government at the centre, the moot question before them was the evolution of common minimum programmes for the government. Getting an opportunity to make their voices heard in the governance of the country, these parties argued for the framing of clientele-based developmental programmes that would not only cater to the needs of different sections of society but would also become the vote bank of the contending parties in the long run.[4] Such a strategy of development appeared in stark contrast to the sectoral developmental policies and programmes that have been the mainstay of the different five-year plans in the country since the drafting of the first five-year plan in 1950.

A remarkable feature of the general elections in 2004 and 2009 was the decisive leadership of Sonia Gandhi to steer both the Congress and the UPA to electoral victories that helped them form two consecutive governments at the centre. The specialty of Sonia Gandhi's leadership of Congress lay in the fact that she helped the party reinvent itself to claim power at the centre again. During the

[4] Kanchan Chandra, 'Elections as Auctions', *Seminar* 539 (2004): 39.

period when the Congress party was bereft of leadership of any of the Gandhi–Nehru scions, it apparently found itself in tatters with the cadres losing their enthusiasm for working for the victory of the party in the general elections. But Sonia Gandhi's arrival on the forefront helped it regain its lost vigour and stirred the passions of the cadres to go wholeheartedly for the victory of the party. Further, Gandhi's leadership of the UPA also imparted distinct weight to this somewhat amorphous political conglomerate with a number of quarrelsome alliance partners keeping low within the UPA in acquiescence with the sombre and composed personality of the Congress president. Moreover, the public perception of the sacrificial character of her personality had also helped her establish a unique rapport with the common electorate which could easily be converted into votes for the party. Thus, in both the 2004 and 2009 general elections, the personality of Gandhi as the leader of the Congress and the UPA must be credited with playing a critical role in putting back the party to power for two consecutive terms. Yet there existed a lot of constraints in the electoral mobilization of the people for the party to secure the desirable result.[5]

The democratic experience of the country during the first decade of the 21st century might be seen as the consolidation of the coalitional nature of politics.[6] This also signified the fact that the era of single party holding a majority in the Lok Sabha had gone. Now the governments at the centre had to be coalitional in nature with likeminded parties coming together to form the government. Interestingly, while for the NDA the coming together of different parties seemed to be guided by their ideological proximity, apart from the electoral imperatives, in case of the UPA, a varied range of parties came together more in opposition to the NDA forming the government than their ideological proximity with each other. Nevertheless, both the general elections, particularly the 15th general elections, were fought between the two coalitions rather than the parties in the Hindi heartland, with

[5] Pratap Bhanu Mehta, 'Constraints on Electoral Mobilisation', *Economic & Political Weekly* 39, no. 51 (December 18, 2004): 5404.

[6] E. Sridharan, 'Electoral Coalitions in 2004 General Elections: Theory and Evidence', *Economic & Political Weekly* 39, no. 51 (December 18, 2004): 5418.

the regional parties also joining the fray in the states where they had been in powerful position. As a result, the contours of the democratic polity in the country seemed inching towards multi polarity with the UPA and the NDA taking the pole positions in these elections. During both the elections, the regional parties along with the left parties made rich dividends though they remained allergic to the NDA, particularly the BJP, that obviously created a natural synergy between these parties and the UPA. It was this cementing factor that had helped both the UPA governments last their full term in office despite not having a convincing majority in the Lok Sabha on their own.

Outcomes of the Elections

The outcomes of the 2004 general elections had been momentous for a number of reasons. First, the hopes of the BJP that had been riding on the wave of the 'shining India' to return to power with even a better or independent majority had decisively been dashed as the party was reduced to the tally of seats that was well behind the Congress. In fact, the aspirations and the convictions of the party had been so high that it had decided in favour of preponing the elections taking the prevailing situation as quite opportune for the party to go to the electorate to get their mandate for governance of the country for a term of five more years renewed. However, that had not to be the case as the electorate had something else in their mind which the BJP surely could not read well before deciding in favour of advancing the general elections by a few months.

Next, the loss of the BJP had unmistakably been the gain of the Congress. Ever since the departure of the government of P. V. Narasimha Rao, the Congress party appeared to be in doldrums in the absence of the party leadership by a scion of the Nehru–Gandhi family. The reclusive stand of Sonia Gandhi in the wake of the assassination of her husband presumably in order to keep her children as well as herself safe from the hazards of political animosity had left the party in the hands of the non-Nehru–Gandhi member of the party. But for whatsoever reasons, such a stewardship of the party could not prove to be a beneficial step. As a result, the party kept on sliding down the ladder of its importance in the national politics in such a way that people had started writing off the party from the political reckoning of the country. It was during such a delicate juncture that she decided to take up leadership of the party into her own hands and readied the party machinery for the electoral battle likely to ensue very soon. In these elections the acceptance of her leadership of the party had very well been taken by the general electorate and the Congress indeed was able to beat the BJP in the battle of ballots.[7] This revived the political fortunes of the party in such a way that it eventually turned out to be the ruling party of the country for the next 10 years.

The relatively less number of seats won by the two claimants of the central power, the Congress and the BJP, had ultimately turned into the gains of the other national parties as well as the regional parties. This is clearly indicative of the deepening of democracy in India so much so that the gravity of power had probably shifted from the national parties to that of the regional parties. Moreover, the performance of the left combine had been stupendous in these elections as they had been able to put up a marvellous show. The combine had been able to win a whopping number of 59 seats in which the share of the CPI (M) itself was 43. The regional parties such as the RJD in Bihar, the SP and the BSP in Uttar Pradesh, the DMK in Tamil Nadu, the Biju Janata Dal (BJD) in Odisha and the NCP in Maharashtra had emerged as the formidable forces to leave their mark on the political scene even at the central level. Such kind of a result had proved that the era of single majority party rule at the centre had by and large been over as the regional and the other national parties could not be overlooked in shaping the nature of government at the centre by the two major national parties, the Congress and the BJP. Thus, these results laid the background for drastic restructuring of the nature of government formation at the centre with the Congress emerging as the nucleus of the new system (Table 8.2).

The winning streak of the Congress continued even during the 2009 general elections with even improved tally of seats. A number

---

[7] Yogendra Yadav, 'The Elusive Mandate of 2004', *Economic & Political Weekly* 39, no. 51 (December 18, 2004): 5385.

Table 8.2 *Performance of Major Parties and Groups in 2004 General Elections*

Parties	Seats	Vote Share (%)
Congress	145	26.53
BJP	138	22.16
Regional parties	174	32.86
Others	86	18.45
Total	543	100.00

Source: Computed from the *Statistical Report on 2004 General Elections* (New Delhi: Election Commission of India, 2004), accessed 22 July 2019, https://eci.gov.in/statistical-report/statistical-reports/

of factors might be discerned that had contributed to the rise in the electoral fortunes of the party. As for the case of the 2004 general elections, the party leadership resting in the hands of a member of the Nehru–Gandhi family had reassured the cadres and leaders of the party that the party was now well on track and they needed to work hard to make the electoral performance better than the previous one. This was accompanied by the sacrificial image of the party president, Sonia Gandhi, who earlier had refused to take charge of the government as the prime minister and appointed a seasoned Congressman Dr Manmohan Singh as the prime minister. This master stroke of the party president had indeed been able to establish an image of sacrifice and integrity in the minds of common people with regard to the personality of Sonia Gandhi. Most of all, what seemed to have gone in favour of the party had been the clientele approach that the government had adopted as the basic strategy of governance as well as underlying principle through which the government wanted to take care of the well-being of the people. Such an approach had helped in the creation of a dedicated vote bank for the party that had credited their economic upliftment to the policies and programmes of the UPA government. As a result, the Congress's score in the 2009 general elections had soared dramatically to cross the 200 mark and stood at 206.

In comparison to the upward movement of the Congress tally in the 2009 general elections, the BJP suffered the loss of substantive number of seats as well as percentage of votes. The party's electoral performance during this election took a backward march to reach the levels of the early 1990s when the party was looking helpless in the face of the formidable performances by the parties standing for social justice. The loss of the BJP in these elections could be explained with reference to two interrelated factors. One, as the clientele-based approach of the UPA government had created a wider base of supporters and sympathizers for the party, the BJP could not find much leg space among such groups of people to expand its base and augment the number of seats. Second, the party had been able to reach at the centre stage of electoral politics in the country, thanks to its emotive appeal to the people in the name of cultural national-ism and Hindutva. For instance, the party had steadfastly called for the construction of Ram temple which could never be done despite the party remaining in power for almost full term of office. So, the general electorate of the country had by now understood the hol-lowness of such emotive issues and therefore did not get motivated by the renewed appeal of the BJP to vote for it in the name of its ideological baggage.

Although the onward march of the Congress in these general elections had acted to stem the tide of the rise of regional and other national parties as important players in the national politics on the strength of their position in the Lok Sabha, these parties in fact con-tinued with good performances they had been showing for a number of years. The basic reason for them to put up good shows in these elections had been their deep penetration among the distinct social groups nurtured by them as their core vote bank. Such a turnaround in the electoral dynamics of the county had undoubtedly been brought about by the deepening of democracy in the wake of the unleash-ing of the forces of social justice since the early 1990s. Moreover, a number of regional and national parties had also been able to create particular spheres of influence in different states on the strength of which they were successful in reaping good electoral harvest year after year. Yet the electoral performance of the communist parties had seen drastic dip in the 2009 general elections on account of the Trinamool Congress (TMC) emerging as a powerful challenge to the communist monopoly over the Lok Sabha seats from West Bengal.

Table 8.3 *Performance of Major Parties and Groups in 2009 General Elections*

Parties	Seats	Vote Share (%)
Congress	206	28.55
BJP	116	18.80
Regional parties	159	31.01
Others	62	21.6
Total	543	100.00

Source: Computed from the *Statistical Report on 2009 General Elections* (New Delhi: Election Commission of India, 2009), accessed 22 July 2019, https://eci.gov.in/statistical-report/statistical-reports/

Similar dip could also be seen in the number of seats of the regional parties coming from Uttar Pradesh and Bihar. The non-Congress, non-BJP parties were therefore poised for a reduced number of seats in the Lok Sabha in the wake of the changed political scenario in different states (Table 8.3).

A comparative study of the outcomes of the two general elections reveals a number of interesting trends with regard to the democratic process of the country. The Congress which had been looked upon as the worn out force in the Indian politics had made a remarkable comeback riding on the back of the re-energized party under the leadership of Sonia Gandhi. Thanks to the governmental policy thrust on the clientelism as the hallmark of the public policy, the party was able to make deep impact on the lives of the poor and marginalized sections of society that readily became the supporter of the party. It was probably on the support of these voters that the party could substantially improve its tally in the Lok Sabha in the 2009 general elections. The electoral fortunes of the BJP had gone down in the two general elections making the party realize that only emotive issues are not enough to win the votes consistently. The party was therefore shattered out of its complacency to relook at its electoral strategy if it had to return to power at the centre in the near future. In these two elections, the major gainers had been the regional and other national parties well entrenched in their islands of support. The nurturing of a core support base had helped these parties to maintain their winning streak in both the general elections and remained the key players in the national politics.[8]

Democratic Implications

The two general elections held in 2004 and 2009, respectively, had brought about a number of fundamental transformations in the democratic polity of the country. They proved the dynamic nature of the Indian democracy by showing that the electoral fortunes of a party could never be written off despite the successive discomfitures of the party over a long period of time. Otherwise, during the last many years, the continuous dismal performances of the Congress party would have reduced the party to existential issues. But the way party was able to make a dramatic comeback in the political arena of the country had been quite striking. The continuous losses of the party could not dent the enthusiasm of its core cadre to work hard for the victory of the party in the general elections. Moreover, the traditional vote bank of the party had also come to its rescue when they could foresee that the party had overcome the hiccups of the previous years and was poised for a comeback. Thus, the political landscape of the country had experienced a subtle turnaround with the emergence of the Congress from the doldrums to take charge of the government at the centre. The dramatic comeback of the party had been accompanied by such turn of events in the later years that after a very long time, the party was able to repeat its spectacular performance in the two general elections back to back and run the government at the centre for full two terms of office.

Notwithstanding the return of the Congress to the centre stage of the democratic process in the country, a number of important pointers could be discerned about the party from its electoral performances over the years. For example, the changing electoral fortunes of the

---

[8] Ajay K. Mehra, 'India's Fifteenth General Election: Realities, Implications and Prospects', *Heidelberg Papers in South Asia and Comparative Politics* 56 (2010): 39.

party over the years had amply proved the perception that the party had moulded it into a pocket borough of the Nehru–Gandhi family. In the absence of any member of the family at the helm of affairs, it would be almost impossible for the party to remain a formidable force in the democratic process of the country. As could be seen, after the assassination of Rajiv Gandhi when the family had decided against getting involved in politics, the fortunes of the party had started dipping like anything. Although the party was able to form the government after assassination of Rajiv Gandhi, the electoral turnaround in the fortunes of the party could well be credited to death of its leader that ultimately created a sort of sympathy wave for the party and it was able to win a sizeable number of seats in the remaining phases of the elections. But after that the party could never recover from the handicap that it suffered due to the absence of the family members to guide and encourage the workers to work for the party in a tireless manner. The bad run of the party was reversed only after the arrival of Sonia Gandhi as the party president.

Entry of the coalition system of government in the lexicon of the Congress could also be taken as the important contribution of the two general elections. While the BJP had from day one accepted the fact that its inability to reach the different parts of the country could be compensated by entering into strategic alliances with a number of regional parties so as to not only augment its tally of seats in the Lok Sabha but also create an environment of positivity for the party in the hitherto unreached areas of the country. But for the Congress such a state of things appeared improbable given the habit of the party to run the governments enjoying comfortable majorities in the Lok Sabha. As a result, as late as 1999, the party was averse to the idea of forging any kind of alliance with any party. Its electoral alliance with the regional parties in Kerala could be taken as an exception given the coalitional nature of politics in the state. The coalitional inhibitions of the party could be warded off only after the arrival of Sonia Gandhi at the helm of affairs of the party. But once the party accepted the possibility of forming and running the government in coalition with the likeminded parties, it indeed was able to not only become the lynchpin of the UPA but was also credited with running two consecutive coalition governments despite various kinds of pushes and pulls from the coalition partners and other allies.[9]

The repetitive nature of the Indian politics could also be seen in the wake of the 14th and 15th general elections. There have been phases in the Indian politics when the anti-Congressism emerged as the defining feature of the democratic politics in the country. During such times, parties of all hues and ideologies cutting across all sort of differences, divergences and variations in their perspectives on different aspects of public life in the country did join hands together to keep the Congress away from the power at the centre. During the two general elections, the same story was repeated in the Indian politics. The only difference was that this time in place of the Congress it was the BJP. In other words, anti-BJPism had also become the prominent trait of the Indian politics during the 14th and 15th general elections. Interestingly, during these elections, a number of parties could put up formidable electoral shows in different parts of the country. As a result, neither the BJP nor the Congress could secure sufficient number of seats to form the government. But on both the occasions the disparate parties and leaders did not waste even a minute in declaring their intention of aligning with the UPA to help it form the government at the centre. Such kind of untouchable parties or ideologies could be seen as an old feature of Indian politics and its repetitive character is likely to be experienced in the democratic processes of the country from time to time.

At the conceptual level, what the 14th and 15th general elections had established was the idea of clientelism as the core principle around which the democratic politics in the country might move. As part of such clientelism, what usually the governments do is to identify certain substantive sections of society and evolve such plans and policies as part of the development strategy that most, if not all, of the governmental developmental interventions go to those sections only. Resultantly,

[9] For an analytical overview of the coalitional complexities in India, see K. K. Kailash, 'The Emerging Politics of Cohabitation: New Challenges', in *Emerging Trends in Indian Politics, The 15th General Election*, ed. Ajay K. Mehra (New Delhi: Routledge, 2010), 86–113.

such sections started acknowledging the role of the particular party or government in ameliorating their pathetic conditions and in turn became solid support base for that party. As a matter of fact, policies aimed at improving the social and economic conditions of the people had also been evolved in the past. But such policies have been general in nature and consisted of a diverse set of activities. But in the case of clientelism, the target groups are usually particular and the activities aimed at their welfare are designed in such a way that they look like designed for them only. A large section of people are generally left out of the clientele-oriented policies. Thus, after coming to power in the aftermath of the 2004 general elections, the UPA government concentrated on the formulation of clientele-oriented policies whose political ramifications had been much serious than anticipated. The repeat victory of the UPA in the 2009 general elections was credited to this clientelism of the party to a large extent.

In the course of the two general elections, the process of the deepening of democracy in the country could also be said to have reached its completion or saturation. The social and political fragmentation of the people had begun in the country in order to provide each of the social groups a distinct identity and space in the democratic process. In order, therefore, to channelize the votes of different social groups in concrete seats, a wide range of parties and groups were formed in different parts of the country over the years. Such a proliferation of the parties and political formations had been facilitated to a great extent by the disintegration of the Janata Dal that had been created to provide a plausible alternative to the Congress. But soon after its formation, the party could not maintain its cohesiveness and resulted in its leaders deserting the party one after another and going for forming their own parties in various states. These parties have basically been formed keeping in mind the particular caste, class, region, language or other such primordial affinities of the people that would allow them a distinct identity apart from their Indian identity. As a result, voting becomes a complex issue in the democratic process of India.[10] Vigorous identity politics in the later years proved very beneficial for these parties and they went to the extent of upstaging the established

---

[10] Mukulika Banerjee, *Why India Votes?* (New Delhi: Routledge, 2014, 163.

national parties like the Congress from holding much influence in certain states. The classic cases in this regard are the states of Uttar Pradesh and Bihar where the caste-based parties almost made the politics of the Congress redundant.

A natural corollary of the deepening of democracy in the country has been the regionalization of the party system in India. As a result, a number of regional parties appeared well placed to perform very well in these elections.[11] The march of the forces of social justice in different parts of the country has played out in such a way that the primordial affinities of the people started becoming more pronounced than their nationalistic and Indian identity. In many cases, certain regional parties tried to overplay these primordial affinities by seeking to put up certain categories of people as enemy of the native or certain other group of people in order to gain extra mileage in the elections. The sectarian politics of the Shiv Sena in Maharashtra and linguistic politics of the Dravid parties in Tamil Nadu are important illustrations of such overplay of the primordial affinities. But the net result of all such moves has been that many aspects of the nature of national politics including the political parties started losing their sheen. In their place, the regional parties emerged as the formidable custodians of the political interests of the particular groups of people. Such a regionalization of the democratic process in the country could well be seen in the results of the 2004 general elections in particular. The national parties in these elections turned pale in face of the formidable show of the regional parties. In such a situation, the formation of any government at the centre could not have been possible in any other form than a coalition of several parties.

Concluding Observations

The Indian democracy entered into a new phase of experimentation with the declaration of the results of the 14th general elections in 2004. While the most important claimant of the power in the aftermath of these elections the BJP was up for a stunning surprise, no other party

[11] Suhas Palshikar, 'Revisiting State Level Parties', *Economic & Political Weekly* 39, no. 14–15 (April 3, 2004): 1478.

could secure a majority in the lower house of the parliament. But by now anti-BJPism had already emerged as the new defining characteristic of the Indian politics whereby barring a few traditional allies of the BJP almost all the parties from left or right had made up their mind to oust the BJP from power. Further when the question arose about formation of the alternative government, the different parties agreed upon facilitating the formation of a Congress-led coalition government that would work on the basis of common minimum programme. Thus, the UPA emerged as a plausible alternative to the NDA led by the BJP and was invited to form the government depending on the support of several parties either by becoming part of the government or supporting that from outside. The formation of the new government did succeed in driving BJP out of power, yet the moot question before the coalition, in general, and the Congress, in particular, was to evolve such plans and policies that would ensure short-term acceptability of the government as well as long-term electoral benefits for the party. Thus, clientelism became the governing mantra of the new government in accordance with which numerous programmes were designed to provide direct benefits to the people.

CHAPTER 9

Centrality of the Right in Indian Politics

Although all the general elections in India have been important landmarks in the political history of the country, some of them have proved to be turning points in the sense that their outcomes have altered the political texture in fundamental ways. The criticality of such elections lay both in reversing some of the long-standing trends or conventions of the electoral dynamics of the country or heralding newer tendencies having potential to reshape the Indian political landscape in a refreshing manner. Such elections are usually in contrast to the general elections that have tended to perpetuate or facilitate continuation of the long-standing phenomena of the Indian politics. That way, the 16th general elections held in 2014 may be considered as defining moment for a number of reasons. Although the hegemony of the Congress in the Indian electoral politics has already been ruptured through the electoral victories of the non-Congress-led political formations in several general elections in the past, the decisive victory of the BJP-led NDA in 2014 has tended to marginalize the Congress to such an extent that it appeared unbelievable that the party that stood routed now had been the epicentre of the Indian politics so much so that the entire spectrum of the Indian party system had famously been described as nothing but the 'Congress system'.

However, more than the unprecedented routing of the Congress party, the 16th general elections are recognized more as the momentous event that catapulted the political right on centre stage of the Indian politics.[1] Until these elections, while no one denied the gradual ascendance of the right on the political firmament of the country, very few, if any, could foresee such a formidable rise of the rightist forces to become the fait accompli of India. In comparison to the Congress party that has remained the ruling party of the country for a large number of years with handsome majorities in both houses of the parliament, the previous role of the right in formation of the government at centre appeared to be shaky and untenable given the large number of coalition partners that joined hands together to form the government. Although the government led by former Prime Minister Atal Bihari Vajpayee was indeed able to complete its full term, the internal fissures of the coalition remained visible throughout the four plus years during which the government lasted. But the 2014 general elections have tended to make such unimpressive performances of the BJP in the Lok Sabha elections a matter of the past. With Narendra Modi presented as the prime ministerial candidate of the party in these elections, the support for the party on the part of the common electors of the country had been so convincing that the results of these polls appeared most surprising in the electoral history of the country. The present chapter seeks to critically examine the significance of the 16th general elections in reshaping the democratic contours of the country.

Context

The circumstances preceding the 16th general elections presented a complex scenario in which all the political parties operating at different levels geared themselves up for reaping rich dividends out of the ensuing elections.[2] In such a scenario, the stakes of different political

[1] Suhas Palshikar and K. C. Suri, 'India's 2014 Elections: Critical Shifts in the Long Term, Caution in the Short Term', *Economic & Political Weekly* 49, no. 39 (2014): 43.

[2] For contemporary nature of party system in the country, see Pradeep Chhibber, Francesca Jensenius, and Pavithra Suryanarayan, 'Party Organisation and Party Proliferation in India', *Party Politics* 20, no. 4 (2014): 489–505.

parties, both ruling and opposition have become quite high. These stakes appeared embedded in the social, economic and political milieus in which different claimants to power sought to position their perspectives during these elections. The social churning in the country that had begun with the implementation of the reservation for the OBCs has still been tried to be made relevant by the proponents of social justice particularly in the Hindi heartland. The rise of the hitherto marginalized sections of Indian society has indeed imparted a new texture to the body politic of the country.[3] But amidst the resurgence of these classes that has immensely facilitated the realignment of the political forces in the numerically preponderant states of Uttar Pradesh and Bihar, the parties like the Congress remained in the forefront of the electoral dynamics banking upon the mosaic of political forces in different parts of the country. At the same time, the regional parties particularly in the southern and eastern parts of India also appeared ferocious in keeping their social support bases intact to put up a robust show in the ensuing elections. But the party that has been gearing itself to spoil the electoral march of the incumbent forces has undoubtedly been the BJP.

Apart from the caste, ideology has also been a very significant normative goalpost of the parties like the BJP and left parties in the country. While left parties tried to combine their ideological predilections with class perspective of the Indian politics, the BJP has tried to conjoin the ideology of Hindutva with the caste dynamics. Interestingly, while the social support base of most, if not all, of the major political parties has been expanding or contracting depending upon the electoral promises or leadership patterns of different parties, in case of the BJP, such an observation could not be held with much conviction. For, the social support base of the party has traditionally been confined to the relatively less numerical social groups of Brahmans and banias. Even among the two, only banias have been argued to be steadfast in extending their unflinching support to the BJP ever since its inception. Brahmans have not been the original supporters of the BJP given their earlier support to the Congress

---

[3] Satish Deshpande, 'Caste in and as Indian Democracy', *Seminar* 677 (January, 2016): 29.

even from the days of the national movement. In such circumstances, the constrictive social support base of the BJP has proved to be its nemesis in getting a majority on its own in the Lok Sabha. The party has, therefore, sought to trigger the realignment of the social forces by putting forth the ideology of Hindutva in the face of the forces of social justice and economic empowerment represented by caste-based parties and the Congress party, respectively. The ideology of Hindutva has in fact been presented as the cementing element that could bind all the social groups within the fold of the party just by virtue of them being Hindu first and harbouring other social markers of identity later. This has been a calculated gamble that the party played amidst its two previous consecutive defeats.

The political configuration of the country at the time of the 16th general elections has admittedly been on the conventional lines in which no major stakeholder appeared to be yielding any ground for any other party. While the two formidable coalitions, the NDA and the UPA, have their coalition partners holding on to their traditional strongholds, peculiar situations existed for the dominant partners of both the coalitions in expanding their areas of influence in different states. For instance, given that the crucial states of Uttar Pradesh and Bihar have been out of the comfort zones of the Congress for a number of years, the party did have the intention of entering into electoral alliances with the major players in these states. But barring the RJD in Bihar, no major political party in both the states has positively responded to the overtures of the Congress for entering into a pre-poll alliance. Almost similar, if not identical, fate has also beckoned for the BJP whose efforts at expanding its support base in the states of southern and eastern India did not appear to be very successful as important regional parties in these regions refused to accede to demands of the BJP for electoral alliances. Insofar as the regional and other national parties were concerned, they sensed a chance of making big electoral gains in these elections on the back of the public resentment against the incumbent UPA government.

Clearly, the 2014 general elections were seen by the regional and left parties as the golden opportunity for them to maximize their gains in the Lok Sabha for obvious reasons. For, they could clearly see an anti-UPA, more particularly anti-Congress wave sweeping differ-ent parts of the country on account of a number of policy failures of the government, on the one hand, and the series of scandals getting unearthed one after another in quick succession on the other. At the same time, they were also quite confident that the NDA, particularly the BJP, would not be able to go beyond its traditional strongholds of the Hindi heartland. They appeared convinced that the Hindutva politics of the BJP would not have much takers in the southern and eastern states as a result of which the party would not be in a position to secure a majority in the lower house of parliament. That way, the 16th Lok Sabha polls appeared for many as the stepping stone for the regional and left parties to bounce back on the political centre stage of national politics by holding keys for the formation of any majority in the Lok Sabha. So much so that a few of the coalition partners in both the NDA and the UPA exhibited signs of restlessness to break ranks with the coalitions so as to make more gains in these elections. Thus, the general elections in 2014 happened to be fairly poised for all the stakeholders to make best of their previous electoral performances.[4]

Vital Stakes

In the 16th general elections, all the major contestants had very high stakes. But the most vital stake was that of the BJP for both ideological and tactical reasons. Ideologically, the BJP has been championing the cause of right enmeshed in the framework of Hindutva ever since its formation in 1980. In the face of the Congress's left of the centre ideology, the BJP has been seeking to present an alternative to the ideology of the Congress by offering the right of the centre approach to almost all the issues and challenges facing the country right since the Independence.[5] With the arrival of the forces of social justice on the political scene in big way in the aftermath of the implementa-tion of the Mandal recommendations, the ideological landscape in

[4] Rajdeep Sardesai, *2014: The Election that Changed India* (New Delhi: Penguin, 2014), 16.
[5] Pradeep Chhibber and Rahul Verma, 'Why the Congress Needs the BJP', *Indian Express*, 19 March 2014.

the country got muddied with these forces eschewing the ideology of either left or right for the sake of social justice. Yet the Congress's overt or covert collaborative political engagements with the left from time to time has surely strengthened the leftist genre of the party, and imparted a distinct ideological space to it. What the BJP has been trying to offset is the dominance of this leftist leaning policies of the Congress by pushing that to political marginalization through electoral politics. The BJP had already made significant inroads in the Hindi heartland and replaced the Congress as the dominant political player in these states. But the dominance at the central level was yet to come.

Alongside the ideological pursuits, the BJP also wanted to present an alternative vision for the country in terms of its radical views on the important issues and challenges facing the country. Given that the previous experiences of the NDA government under the leadership of Atal Bihari Vajpayee did not allow the party to materialize its vision of India owing to the coalitional nature of the government in which securing support for its agenda would not have been possible, the party was surely eying these elections as the stepping stone for it to arrive at the seat of power in New Delhi with comfortable majority of its own.[6] Moreover, with Narendra Modi declared as the prime ministerial candidate, the leadership position of the party had already experienced a generational change in which the old guards no longer remained the shepherd of the party. As a result, these elections were both a challenge and an opportunity for the second-generation leadership of the party to prove their mettle in running the party and making it acceptable to the people on the basis of the long-drawn avowed goals and objectives for which it had stood steadfastly over the years. So, for the BJP, the stakes in the 2014 general elections were as high as a matter of life or death. For, the third consecutive defeat at the national polls would have foretold the doomsday for the party from the political scene of the country.

As the dominant party of the ruling coalition, stakes for the Congress in these elections could not have been less, if not more, than

[6] Pradeep Chhibber, Harsh Shah, and Rahul Verma, 'The Art of Building Majorities', *The Hindu*, 14 March 2017.

that of the principal opposition party. As a matter of fact, the sliding down of the Congress party on the electoral scale in the country in the absence of a member of the Gandhi–Nehru family at the helm of affairs of the party had presumably convinced Sonia Gandhi to step in and take charge of the party at an opportune time. The veracity of her decision to become president of the party was proved somewhat right when she was able to cobble up the coalition in the name of the UPA to offer a plausible alternative to the NDA. Further, the decision of the coalition partners to choose her as the prime ministerial candidate of the coalition and her subsequent decision to decline the offer and name her trusted aide Manmohan Singh had amply proved the political acumen of the 'foreigner' in protest against whom a number of senior leaders of the party had left the Congress. The political morale of the party, in general, and Sonia Gandhi, in particular, was enormously boosted when she was able to steer the coalition for a back-to-back victory in the 2009 general elections. In such a situation, the third straight win for the party could surely have turned Sonia Gandhi into the persona of her mother-in-law who played defining role in the Indian politics.

For the other parties, these elections presented a win-win situation for two reasons. One, the regional and left parties were sure that the straight fight between the two dominant national parties, the Congress and the BJP, would surely be an advantageous position for them. They appeared quite sure that the performance of the ruling party in these elections would not be as thumping as it was in the two previous general elections. The series of corruption charges against senior ministers of the government and the anti-incumbency wave after 10 long years of rule by the Congress appeared as the plausible reasons for them to be hopeful of Congress's dismal performance in these elections. Alongside, they were also expecting that the BJP, as the epitome of the right ideological perspective, would not be able to cut much ice with the teeming millions of the country, given the social and economic orientations of such people to unhesitatingly go for the left leaning parties. Two, the regional and left parties, after improving their tallies in the wake of the dismal performance of the two national parties, also looked to vie for their greater role in the national politics, as part of the ruling coalition that was likely to be constructed after the indecisive results of the polls. Thus, the stakes of the regional and left parties also seemed to be very high as handsome results in these elections could have secured them the passport for becoming the kingmaker at the national level.

Electoral Outcomes

Given the high stakes of all the contestants of the 16th general elections, their efforts for maximization of their gains also appeared commendable. However, as far as the electoral preparedness of different parties was concerned, three interrelated trends could be discerned. First, the vital stakes of both the UPA and the NDA in these elections also ingrained in them the fear of not being able to secure a majority in the Lok Sabha after these elections. As a result, the dominant partners of both the coalitions were found to be in search for newer alliance partners that could help them improve their final seat tally in these elections. In other words, both the Congress and the BJP did not appear to be confident of securing even a working majority in the lower house of parliament so as to form the government on their own. So the most plausible course of action seemed to them was to go for more and more alliance partners at the pre-poll stage to augment their seat tally. Second, the search for more alliance partners by the two major coalitions did not yield much result as the battle lines had already been drawn in different parts of the country with major players in various regions having already opened their political cards for the electoral fray. Moreover, the changing fortunes of the two coalitions have also acted as the significant marker for the regional parties to become a part of one or the other political alliance.

Third, and the most important, weakening of the UPA even in its conventional strongholds and the perceived inability of the NDA, particularly the BJP, to replace the Congress as the formidable political force in those areas apparently emboldened the spirits of the regional parties to an unprecedented level. So much so that, barring the traditional allies of the two coalitions such as the RJD for the UPA in Bihar and the SAD for the NDA in Punjab, other regional parties refused tersely to respond positively to the alliance overtures of either of the two national political alliances. These parties appeared convinced of their invincibility in their respective states in view of the slippery presence of the two dominant national parties in those states. Given the persisting trend of political bargains amidst the situation of a hung house in the aftermath of the election, the regional parties very well sensed the possibility of playing kingmaker in the case of none of the two national coalitions securing a majority in the lower house of parliament. In such a scenario of uncertainty and unpredictability of mood of the common voters, the electioneering during the 16th general elections reached a crescendo with the major stakeholders holding no bar in putting the best of their performances. Although the electoral management of the NDA, in general, and the BJP, in particular, seemed to be better than its rivals, the other parties including the Congress did not seem to leave any stone unturned to reap rich electoral dividends from these elections.

An important feature of the 16th general elections has been the highest ever voter turnout in any of the Lok Sabha polls till that date. Despite the spectacular regularity of the parliamentary elections in the country, the voter turnout in the successive elections for the lower house has hovered around 50–60 per cent over the years. Such somewhat stable percentage of voting in the Indian general elections has been tried to be explained with the argument that the electors remain indifferent to the elections in the absence of any radical issue over which people might wish to express their protest or approval by casting their vote. Before the 2014 general elections, the best voting percentage for Lok Sabha elections was registered for the 1984 general elections which stood at 64 per cent. As a matter of fact, the 1984 general elections were held in the aftermath of the assassination of Prime Minister Indira Gandhi. After her death, Rajiv Gandhi had taken over as the prime minister and went for the polls. Thus, during these elections people got an opportunity to express their anguish over the assassination of Indira Gandhi and put their stamp of approval on Rajiv Gandhi stepping into the footsteps of his mother. Pollsters tried to discern similar indicators in the wake of 66.4 per cent of polling in the 16th general elections that must be considered as reflection of the public opinion on the political scenarios prevailing in the country.

When the results of these elections started pouring in, the shape of things in the political landscape of the country had begun to be clear. The anti-incumbency wave against the Congress and its allies was sweeping all around the country. The party was up for its worst electoral performance in its history. Out of the 464 seats it had contested in these elections, the party could manage to win only 44 seats. Even its allies contested a sizeable number of 75 seats but were able to win just 14 seats. In all, the Congress and its allies had contested 539 Lok Sabha seats but were able to secure winning mandate in 58 seats only. As against that, the juggernaut of the BJP seemed to have arrived in full measure as, for the first time, the party could manage to win comfortable majority of 282 seats out of the 428 the party had contested. Riding on the wave of the BJP, its NDA allies also won 54 seats out of 114 they had contested in different states. Overall, of the 542 seats the NDA had contested, it won 336 seats (Table 9.1) which was a sort of record for the coalition. Interestingly, in the states where neither the NDA nor the UPA could put up a formidable fight, the regional parties could make maximum gains. As a result, as many as 132 seats in Lok Sabha were won by the regional parties and independents. Thus, the results of the 16th general elections spelled doom for the Congress and made the lotus bloom as the ruling icon of the country.[7]

The record number of seats won by the BJP in these elections was due to a major jump in its share of votes polled primarily cutting

Table 9.1 *Performance of Various Parties/Coalitions*

Parties/Coalitions	Seats Contested	Seats Won
NDA	542	336
UPA	539	58
Others	6,806	132

Source: Computed from the *Statistical Report on 2014 General Elections* (New Delhi: Election Commission of India, 2014), accessed 12 August 2019, https://eci.gov.in/statistical-report/statistical-reports/

[7] Prashant Jha, *How the BJP Wins: Inside India's Greatest Election Machine* (New Delhi: Juggernaut, 2017), 82.

Table 9.2 *Changes in Vote Share of Different Parties/Coalitions*

Parties/Coalitions	Vote Share (in %)	Change from 2009 General Elections (in %)
NDA	38.3	+12.25 (-0.3)
UPA	23	-19.6
Others	26.2	+2.46

Source: Computed from the *Statistical Report on 2014 General Elections* (New Delhi: Election Commission of India, 2014), accessed 17 August 2019, https://eci.gov.in/statistical-report/statistical-reports/

deeper into the vote share of the Congress and its allies. On the whole, though 31.1 per cent of votes polled by the party in these elections cannot be considered a big percentage, what made the party secure a majority of seats were the multi-cornered contests in most, if not all, of the seats contested by the party. Thus, the first-past-the-post electoral system helped the party win the majority of seats by polling the highest number of votes among all the contestants. Nevertheless, the vote share of the party registered a magnificent jump of over 12.25 per cent compared to its share of votes in the 2009 general elections (Table 9.2). Interestingly, the vote share of BJP's other NDA allies registered a negative shift making them lose a marginal 0.3 per cent votes as compared to their performance in the previous Lok Sabha polls. As against the rise in the polling percentage of the BJP, the Congress suffered in a big way by polling just 23 per cent of the total votes cast in these elections. In comparison to its performance in the 2009 Lok Sabha polls, the party lost as much as 19.6 per cent of votes polled. Even the regional parties including the left parties polled more votes at 26.2 per cent as compared to the Congress that helped them replace the Congress as the formidable challenge to the BJP in a number of states. Thus, the shifting pattern of the voting percentage of different parties showed the changing fortunes in their performances in the 16th general elections.

The 2014 general elections saw the spectacular rise of the BJP on the strength of its thumping performance in two distinct regions of the country that have traditionally been its stronghold over the years. As Table 9.3 shows, an overwhelming majority of seats for the BJP and

Table 9.3 *Expansion of the NDA in Different Regions of India*

Regions	Total Seats	BJP		BJP Allies	
		Vote %	Seats	Votes %	Seats
Hindi speaking states	225	43.7	190	2.2	11
Western India	78	38.5	53	15.4	19
Rest of India	240	17.3	39	9.7	25
Overall	543	31.0	282	7.4	54

Source: Computed from the *Statistical Report on 2014 General Elections* (New Delhi: Election Commission of India, 2014), accessed 17 August 2019, https://eci.gov.in/statistical-report/statistical-reports/

its allies came from the Hindi heartland where the coalition won as many as 190 seats out of 225 Lok Sabha seats. While the Congress was the worst performer in these states, the rest of the seats were grabbed by the regional parties. The other region from where the NDA kitty of seats got replenished was the western states such as Gujarat and Maharashtra that helped the coalition bounce back to power at the centre after a gap of 10 years. In these regions, the vote share of the BJP and its NDA partners was well above its national average at 38.3. In these states, the performance of the Congress and its allies was quite dismal and their vote share dipped markedly resulting in substantial loss of seats for them. Further, in these elections, the social support base of the BJP has been significantly supplemented by the vote of all the classes.[8] At the same time, even the rural–urban divide also got shattered as the party could secure the majority of votes in both the rural and urban constituencies in a number of states.[9] BJP's stellar performance in the northern and western parts of the country could however not be carried over to the eastern and southern parts where the regional satraps held on to their bastions disallowing the national parties, particularly the BJP, to creep in. Thus, what these elections proved was the further consolidation of the reach of the BJP and its

[8] E. Sridharan, 'Class Voting in the 2014 Lok Sabha Elections', *Economic & Political Weekly* 49, no. 39 (2014), 75.

[9] Neelanjan Sircar and Milan Vaishnav, 'The Rural-Urban Divide Dies Out', *Financial Express*, 2 April 2014.

allies in their conventional strongholds of the northern and western states rather than their expansion into the hitherto unreached territories of the eastern and southern regions. But the Congress's rout in these elections appeared complete as the party could not put up an impressive show in any major state. The states where BJP juggernaut could not roll out, the gainers were the regional parties and the Congress was pushed to the third position in most, if not all, of the states.[10] Thus, though the winning spree of the NDA might be said to be lopsided, it was indeed able to replace the Congress as the ruling coalition at the centre.

Centrality of the Right

The most significant outcome of the 16th general elections has been that it catapulted the right to the political centre stage of the country.[11] This cannot be considered as an aberration in the conventional framework of the Indian politics as the outcome of the 17th Lok Sabha polls also proved the well-entrenched character of the right in the Indian political landscape in the contemporary times. This is actually a complete turnaround in the texture of Indian politics. As a matter of fact, right from the days of the national movement, dominance of the left of the centre ideology has been a proven fact owing to the infatuation of a number of prominent national leaders with the socialist ideology. After Independence, with the ascendance of Nehru as the towering personality of the Indian political system in his capacity as the prime minister, the leftist orientation of the Indian electorate remained intact with people voting for Nehru and his Congress party unhesitatingly for a number of years. The parties that espoused the cause of the right ideology such as the Jana Sangh and the Swatantra Party could not cut much ice with the voters who continued with their love for the socialist ideology that was carried forward by Indira Gandhi after the death of her father. Although the Congress in the early 1990s tried to

[10] K. K. Kailash, 'Regional Parties in the 16th Lok Sabha Elections: Who Survived and Why', *Economic & Political Weekly* 49, no. 39 (2014): 65.

[11] Pradeep Chhibber and Rahul Verma, 'The BJP's 2014 "Modi Wave": An Ideological Consolidation of the Right', *Economic & Political Weekly* 49, no. 39 (2014): 50.

embrace the neoliberal economic agenda and implement the structural adjustment programmes, the party remained the pall-bearer of left of the centre politics in the country.

Clientele-based welfare policies have been the hallmark of almost all the left of the centre political parties having powerful presence at centre as well as the different states.[12] In these elections, however, the support for the left of the centre politics dwindled decisively. The Congress's clientele politics of weaning away the voters through a number of welfare measures could not persist in the face of the nationalist onslaught of the BJP-led rightist forces. As a result, the Congress got comprehensively decimated at the hands of the BJP in the political heartland of the country. But the loss of Congress need not be understood as the rejection of the socialist ideology in the politics because many of the regional parties that were able to hold on to their bastions despite the ascendance of the BJP in different parts of the country are subscribers to the socialism as the mainstay of their political belief. They have also been in the forefront of accepting clientelism as the crucial policy of government once they come to power in the state.[13] At times, such clientelism becomes as good as buying the votes of the electors on the promise of paying a price for their votes, though in certain cases practical buying of votes also takes place.[14] What therefore these elections have proved is the fact that the rise of the generation next in the country would tend to underplay, if not forget, the value of the socialist ideology that remained the core of the plan for social and economic reconstruction of the country in the aftermath of the Independence. For the new voters, the nationalist legacies of the Congress no longer remained the cementing factor to bind them with the party. As a result, the days of dominance of the

[12] See Louise Tillin, Rajeshwari Deshpande, and K. K. Kailash, eds. *Politics of Welfare: Comparison across Indian States* (New Delhi: Oxford University Press, 2015).

[13] For a lucid discussion on the role and relevance of clientelism as the major policy perspective of regional parties in the country, see Adam Ziegfeld, *Why Regional Parties? Clientelism, Elites and the Indian Party System* (New York, NY: Cambridge University Press, 2016).

[14] Avantika Chilkoti, 'Indian Elections: A Festival of Vote Buying', *Financial Times*, 6 May 2014.

Congress in Indian political system seemed to have run out its course leaving space for other parties or coalitions to take charge.

Although in these elections the pollsters did anticipate that things were not going to be easy for the Congress, nobody in fact anticipated that the party that had been heading the government for the last 10 years would be reduced to such a miserable condition. But a number of factors seemed to have gone against the party in tandem with each other that it was made to bite the dust in the electoral arena like never before.[15] For instance, there was widespread belief that the 10 long years of governance of the party would surely have driven in the psyche of the people the element of anti-incumbency. Moreover, the public welfare measures that the party had initiated during its first stint had started losing their sheen on account of poor implementation and related issues. They have arguably been seen as the replacement for the relatively poor performance of the institutions and buying the votes of the people.[16] But the most important factor that almost discredited the government and helped the BJP capitalize upon was the series of scandals and cases of corruption. The last few years of the government were so much marred by the cases of corruption that it seemed as if nothing moved in that government without speed money. Amidst these circumstances, the BJP, particularly its prime ministerial candidate Narendra Modi was able to effectively drive the impression in the minds of the electorate that the Congress was a party of corrupt and unscrupulous politicians getting rid of which would probably be in the best interests of the country.[17]

Relative marginalization of the left in the Indian politics has correspondingly been matched with the centrality of the right.[18] BJP's

---

[15] Suhas Palshikar, 'The Defeat of the Congress', *Economic & Political Weekly*, 49, no. 39 (2014): 57.

[16] Oliver Heath and Louise Tillin, 'Institutional Performance and Vote Buying in India', *Studies in Comparative International Development* 53, no. 1 (2018): 99.

[17] Pradeep Chhibber and Susan Ostermann, 'The BJP's Fragile Mandate: Modi and Vote Mobilizers in the 2014 Lok Sabha Elections', *Studies in Indian Politics* 2, no. 2 (2014): 143.

[18] Subrata K. Mitra and Jivanta Schottli, 'India's 2014 General Elections: A Critical Realignment in Indian Politics?' *Asian Survey* 56, no. 4 (2016): 89.

avowed detest for the left ideology has been reflected in the host of policies and programmes that have been placed and reiterated in the manifestos of the party from time to time. Further, the party has tried to embed its overt subscription to the rightist ideology with the indigenous construct of Hindutva that is considered as the raison d'être for the party. It has always been the public stance of the BJP that the government is not meant to provide the basic livelihood needs of the people. Rather, what the government should do is to empower and enable the people to make their own efforts for fulfilling the basic needs of their life. That way, the party has consistently been against the freebies and other tangible promises made by the Congress to provide to people in case it is voted to power. Thus, the 16th general elections acted as the watershed from where the economic means to the political ends would not remain the cardinal principle of the electioneering in the country. In other words, the promises of economic well-being of the people on the part of the government got trumped on the hands of those who espoused the cause of self-dependence of the people with the government only acting as the facilitator rather than the provider of public goods and services as in the past.

The convincing victory of the BJP-led coalition in these elections also proved the growing acceptability of Hindutva as the defining feature of Indian polity in place of what the BJP calls the pseudo secularism. The public discourse in the country has always got mired in the intense debate as regards the veracity of secularism to be underlining feature of Indian polity. On this issue, while a section of intelligentsia claims that India has always been a secular country where all the people irrespective of faiths they believed in have enjoyed equal rights and privileges, the left group has tried to ingrain the idea of secularism more as a ritual through constitutional stipulation than a norm of public life. On this count, although the BJP subscribes to the RSS's belief that Hindutva is the core building block of the Indian society, it had not found so much support for its ideology among the majority of the electors in the past. But the 16th general elections helped the party break the glass ceiling through which the electors were made to disprove Hindutva as the fundamental ideological belief of the party. In turn, the party's election campaigns did revolve around convincing the electorate about Hindutva being the foundation value for the idea of India. The most valuable support in this vigorous thrust of the party has been provided by the formidable use of social media and other digital resources available to ensure that the party's policies and programmes reach the common people effectively.[19] Although the recourse to social media has been taken by almost all the parties, the clear march of the BJP over its rivals was apparent right from the beginning which seemingly helped the party reach to the vast majority of the people and secure a decisive victory.[20] Thus, the convincing victory of the party in these elections surely brought about a radical shift in the discourse of democratic politics in the country whereby Hindutva got public acceptance to be the core belief around which the BJP would seek to reshape the polity of the country.[21]

Leadership styles and characteristics of the personality of the leaders have also been important factors in determining the outcome of these elections.[22] The phenomenon of personality cult through the persona of Narendra Modi seemed to have made a comeback with the results of the 16th general elections. Needless to mention that personality cult in the Indian democracy has got deep-rooted with the long stint of Nehru as the prime minister of the country. Drawing upon his nationalist legacy, Nehru had indeed been able to keep Indian masses mesmerized with his personality and make personality cult an infallible feature of the Indian democracy. The same tendency was carried forward by his daughter as well as his grandson. But the departure of the Nehru–Gandhi stalwarts from the scene during the closing years of the 1980s, the era of personality cult seemed to have lost

[19] Rahul Verma and Shreyas Sardesai, 'Does Exposure to Media Affect Voting Behaviour and Political Preferences in Indian Elections', *Economic & Political Weekly* 49, no. 39 (2014): 85.

[20] Neena Talwar Kanungo, 'India's Digital Poll Battle: Political Parties and Social Media in the 16th Lok Sabha Elections', *Studies in Indian Politics* 3, no. 2 (2015): 217.

[21] Suhas Palshikar, 'The BJP and Hindu Nationalism: Centrist Politics and Majoritarian Impulses', *South Asia: Journal of South Asian Studies* 38, no. 4 (2016): 726.

[22] Sandeep Shastri and Reetika Syal, 'Impact of Leadership in the 2014 Lok Sabha Elections: Leadership in Context', *Economic & Political Weekly* 49, no. 39 (2014): 79.

its relevance in Indian democracy with the electorates casting their votes on the poll promises as well as qualitative assessment of the candidates in their constituencies. But with the arrival of Narendra Modi on the national level, Indian democracy appeared poised for the return of the era of personality cult. The entire electioneering of the BJP during these elections revolved around the personality of its prime ministerial candidate who was portrayed as the person who brought a turnaround in the fortunes of Gujarat as its chief minister for many years. In fact, to magnify his personality, Gujarat model of development was presented as the ideal model of development that would be replicated at the national level once Narendra Modi becomes the prime minister. Thus, personality cult made a dramatic comeback in Indian democracy through the 2014 Lok Sabha polls that may have debilitating effect on the democratic credentials of the party organizationally.[23]

Concluding Observations

The BJP's stunning victory in the 16th Lok Sabha polls, held in 2014, is not simply an event but one that has created new vocabularies of politics, a new narrative that appears to have caught the national political imagination or devised a new *zeitgeist* in the Indian politics. The fact that the BJP had a consistent share of roughly 40 per cent of total votes across Uttar Pradesh's various regions is perhaps indicative of its success in creating 'sincere' and not 'strategic' voters,[24] and also, the spread of its support base cutting across social segments and regions supports the contention that it is clearly broken out of its 'Brahman–Bania' and urban-centric party image. While the BJP has, by reinventing its approach, reaped the benefit, the opposition seems to have lost its viability by failing to address the newer developmental

---

[23] K. C. Suri and Rahul Verma, 'Democratising the BJP', *Seminar* (November, 2017): 26.

[24] In Political Science parlance, a sincere voter is one who casts votes consistently for a party with the belief that its ideological priorities correspond with him/her; a strategic voter is one who does not want to waste his/her vote on candidates who have no chance of winning, so he/she votes for the preferred candidates among the candidates in the fray.

concerns of the people. The decline of the regional parties and the steady drubbing of the Congress in Uttar Pradesh is indicative of their failure to gauge the changing popular mood which is no longer inspired by identity considerations but by the implementation of the developmental promises that are made to them by the political masters. The BJP and its mascot, Modi, seem to have established an image of being true to their promises. Even his hard-core critic, P. Chidambaram of the Congress admitted this by saying 'the man at the moment is Narendra Modi [who] has convincingly demonstrated that his appeal is pan-Indian'.[25] He represented the idea of India that majority wanted. In his endeavour, the RSS functionaries contributed by building a solid booth-level network during elections with its creative model of social engineering leading to the consolidation of an inclusive social group among the Hindus and also by couching of an appeal (in a very subtle way) in Hindutva terms. As a result, the BJP stands out not only as a party that instils 'a sense of destiny' among the rank and file but also an outfit conveying the message 'the party is doing *deshseva* (service to the motherland) while others have been doing politics'.[26] This is a new brand of aggressive politics representing newer concerns which cannot be understood in the available politico-ideological vocabulary. In the past, especially during the Nehruvian era, the Congress remained invincible because of its success in building 'an umbrella social-political coalition'; this appears to have exhausted its potential. With BJP's convincing victory, there has emerged a powerful ideological force built around a creative mix of hope, Hindutva and personal magnetism of Narendra Modi.

These elections acted to shift the goalposts of Indian democracy in probably as fundamental ways as was done during the time of its foundation. The results of these elections heralded the onset of a number of such processes and forces that have had the potential of transforming the nature of Indian polity and democracy in subtle ways. Interestingly, the approval for such sweeping transformations in the

[25] P. Chidambaram, 'Across the Aisle: The People Have Voted: Now, We Hope', *The Indian Express*, New Delhi, 12 March 2017.
[26] Suhas Palshikar, 'Party with a Difference', *Economic & Political Weekly* 52, no. 15 (April 15, 2017): 11.

Indian democratic landscape was obtained from none other than the people of India. As a matter of fact, the BJP as the cornerstone of the new political order has unhesitatingly been presenting such an alternative vision to the politics, society, democracy and economy of the country that would inevitably be radically different from the visions implemented by the Congress through its long years of rule.[27] While the alternative vision of the BJP could not get approval of the majority of the Indians for a long period of time, the 16th general elections categorically placed the vision of the BJP ahead of the other perspectives claiming to be the dominance discourse of Indian democracy. But what seems startling about these elections is the fact that its denouncement of the Congress appeared more comprehensive than its approval of the BJP.[28] In other words, the Indian democracy allowed ample space for its reinvention in the years to come through the victory of an alternative vision that vied for its acceptance by the Indian masses for the last many decades.[29]

[27] Rekha Diwakar, *Party System in India* (New Delhi: Oxford University Press, 2018, 75.

[28] Suhas Palshikar, 'Congress in the Times of the Post-Congress Era: Surviving sans Politics', *Economic & Political Weekly* 50, no. 19 (2015): 44.

[29] Pratap Bhanu Mehta, 'A BJP-Dominant System', *The Indian Express*, 20 May 2016.

CHAPTER 10

Predominance of the Right

Despite being routine affairs in the established democracies, elections sometimes prove to be turning points in the history of a nation. The outcome of certain particular elections not only demolishes the long-held political beliefs, systems, patterns and processes but also set the stage for their replacement with novel alternatives. In this regard, the 17th general elections, held in 2019, may really be termed as momentous in India's recent political history. The outcomes of these elections have not only unsettled many of the well-established tendencies and practices of Indian democracy but have also acted to provide decisive perspectives on a number of competing issues and challenges facing the Indian political system for long. In fact, during more than 70 years of successful working of the Indian democracy, numerous issues both constitutional and political have remained contentious with varying perspectives being put forward to settle them accordingly. However, the long period of the Congress rule has tended to provide the foundational shape in terms of both ideology and institutions to the practical working of the Indian democracy which has not been taken easily by certain sections of political class. Moreover, the conventional wisdom in fighting elections in India has also come under severe constraints during the last few years. On all such issues and many more, the 2019 general elections have tended to set the futuristic perspective for the shape of things to come in the country. Apart from the processes through which these elections were fought, the outcomes of this battle of ballots have gone to bring about serious transformations in the Indian political system whose long-term implications are likely to be novel and uncharacteristic of the traditional view of Indian politics.

To grasp the results of these elections in terms of just victory for the BJP as a party and Narendra Modi as the prime minister would probably be an underestimation of their long-term implications for the country. In other words, these elections may be taken as the watershed that would mark a divide between India before 2019 and after. Such divisions have both short- and long-term implications. For example, the results of these elections have signalled the end of electoral formidability for a number of parties and individuals. They have also established seemingly irreversible dominance of *kamandal* over *Mandal*. Primordial affinities such as caste, region, language and ethnicity have also been reduced to a large extent to somewhat irrelevance with the relegation of their proponents in the political oblivion. Left as a formidable force in the democratic processes of the country has ceased to exist. But these short-term transformations in the wake of these elections would look pale if one ponders over the likely changes that might be going to take place in the long run. For the party that has emerged as the unchallenged master of India's destiny is the one that has been born with a vision and ideology stand which is in stark contrast to what has been professed and practised hitherto in the country. Although these results might not be able to convert India into a *Hindu Rashtra* as of now, they would certainly put the prospective trajectory of political processes in India on a hitherto unchartered path. The chapter has thus two aims: on the one hand, it is directed to conceptually understand the 2019 national poll which is not an ordinary election since it has contributed to the creation of a new template for reconceptualizing the idea of India. Given the thumping majority that the BJP-led NDA secured, the chapter, on the other hand, seeks to address the veracity of the claim that is articulated with the suggestion that the Nehruvian nationalist project does not seem to be tenable in the changed socio-economic and political environment.

In other words, by raising pertinent questions, the main objective of the chapter is to help us understand whether the 2019 electoral responses are merely ripples or they represent a clear beginning of a new India in which some of the highly publicized politico-ideological preferences that India has, so far, nurtured seem to have lost their appeal to the masses.

Contextualizing the 2019 National Poll

The high stakes of the important players in the 2019 general elections apparently made them both nervous and anxious to leave no stone unturned in securing their best electoral performances. At the same time, none of the parties appeared confident enough from within so as to roll out their solitary juggernaut in the elections despite the public posturing of exhibiting confidence of winning majority of seats in their respective strongholds. Such a visible lack of confidence inevitably compelled almost all the parties to look out for electoral understanding, if not outright alliances, with the probable allies apart from their conventional coalition partners. The most interesting part of the coalition building exercises during these elections has been the dilemmatic situations of a number of parties in weighing their short-term and long-term interests in going for a coalition with different political parties in various parts of the country. In this context, the most precarious position has been that of the Congress whose short-term interest could surely have been entering into alliances with probably every non-BJP party in order to prevent the division of votes so that decisive defeat of the ruling party could have been secured. But amidst the allurements of such alliances, the party also had to look at its long-term interests as the prospective formidable player in certain states where conceding ground to the competing parties could have proved suicidal for the party. The party, therefore, decided to go alone, defying alliance offers from dominant players in the states like Uttar Pradesh, Haryana and Union Territory of Delhi because in these states the party's future stakes are very high and it could not have afforded to play second fiddle or even transfer its traditional votes to the parties that could have emerged as its rivals in future.

As far as coalition building exercises during these elections are concerned, three patterns could be seen at both national and state levels in different parts of the country. One, the major parties such as the BJP and the Congress, apart from carrying forward with their traditional coalition partners, went for strategic alliances with only a few smaller parties who could have provided them with the winning edges on different seats. In this context, BJP's strategic move of aligning with the smaller regional parties in north-east really helped the party not only enhance its tally in the Lok Sabha but also increase its penetration deeper in the hitherto dicey region for the party.[1] Otherwise, these parties, more or less, desisted from entering into political alliances in the major states with the other rival dominant parties so that their political ground would not be lost in both short and long runs. Two, as the march of BJP's victory juggernaut in the major states like Uttar Pradesh during the previous general elections had reduced the caste-based regional parties to almost a naught even in their respective strongholds, the fear of repeat of the same story presumably drove the sworn enemies such as the SP and the BSP to enter into electoral partnership.[2] But such pattern has been rare and could not see its emulation in other parts of the country given the long-term rivalry of the prospective alliance partners.

However, in majority of the states, the dominant political parties shied away from forging formidable alliances for two distinct reasons. First, they appeared to be well placed in their citadels to sail through on majority, if not all, of seats on their own without support of or understanding with any other party. Second, entering into electoral alliances means conceding certain number of seats to the alliance partners which eventually eats into the total seat tally of the dominant party. For these reasons, in many of the states, the electoral contest remained multi-polar due to the presence of more than two political formations. Interesting part of these electoral alliances has been that while the national parties, especially the BJP appeared confident to go

[1] Wasbir Hussain, 'BJP & Allies Make Saffron Sparkle in Northeast', *The Asian Age*, New Delhi, 31 May 2019, 7.

[2] Rajeev Dikshit, 'SP-BSP Picks Ravidas Temple for Grand Rally to Bolster Core Vote Bank', *The Times of India*, New Delhi, 7 May 2019, 7.

alone in many of the states, the regional parties were not far behind the national parties to assert their autonomous spheres of influence. It was presumably for this reason that in most of the states the regional parties contested against the national parties banking upon their strategy of arousing regional aspirations of the people to garner their support and vote. The electoral scenario during the 17th Lok Sabha polls, therefore, witnessed multi-cornered contest in the states excepting the ones that have traditionally remained bipolar throughout all these years, and as has been the case, multi-polar contests have always been in favour of the BJP.[3]

Electoral Pledges

The 2019 general elections saw the clear continuation of the long-drawn beliefs and priorities of major political parties in terms of their avowed electoral promises presented in their manifestos. The BJP has unfailingly been a champion of a nationalist vision for a country in which in place of social and economic issues of the people, priority has been accorded to the issues concerning national defence and overall security scenario of the country. In its election manifesto, named 'Sankalp Patra' (Dossier of Commitments), the party offered 75 promises that it would attempt to fulfil by the time India turns 75.[4] Indicating its intent of according top priorities to unity and integrity of the country over the issues of social welfare and economic development, the first set of promises were related to the core issues facing the internal security and external defences of India. Curiously enough, party's long-standing promise of getting Ram temple constructed at Ayodhya got only passing reference in face of the muscular nationalistic promises getting focused over all other issues.[5] Although the party indeed offered a number of welfare measures for the farmers, such

[3] Barkha Dutt, 'The 2019 Election: Lack of a National Alternative Means Advantage Modi', *The Hindustan Times*, New Delhi, 18 May 2019, 16.

[4] Bharatiya Janata Party, *Sankalp Patra: Lok Sabha 2019*, accessed 12 June 2019, https://www.documentcloud.org/documents/5798075-Bjp-Election-2019-Manifesto-English.html

[5] Kumar Uttam, 'Nation First' Approach Won the Day', *The Hindustan Times*, New Delhi, 24 May 2019, 2.

promises were surely not in the mould of socialistic freebies offered during the heyday of the Congress. Rather, the manifesto aimed at inching towards the 'New India' in which nothing would probably come without a price.

In comparison to the BJP's security-centred nationalist fervour, the Congress continued with greater reliance on the social and economic welfare of the people with the promise of depositing ₹72,000 per year in the bank account of a female member of each poor family through its ambitious 'NYAY' scheme. Politically, this scheme was visualized to be a master stroke to wean away the billions of poor households and regain its lost ground particularly in the less developed but populous states. The party also sought to attract the attention of the youth who are basically floating votes in comparison to the more mature and experienced voters by promising to go big way towards generation of greater employment opportunities in the government sector. The major promises of the party revolved around the catchy phrases like '*kaam*, *daam* and *shaan*' pointing towards its intent for employment and growth, an economy that works for all, and pride in the soft and hard powers of the country, respectively. In fact, most of the entries in the Congress manifesto read like routine references to the conventional issues and challenges which no longer bother the mindset of the electorate. Moreover, inclusion of the subjects such as electoral reforms, non-discriminatory anti-corruption measures, taxation reforms, rights of gay and lesbians, and planning appeared totally incongruent with the contemporary realities of India. The Congress manifesto, therefore, failed to either offer newer perspectives for the aspiring India or a better and concrete plan of action to rid the country of its current challenges.

Apart from the national parties, electoral promises of other parties presented a mosaic of affirmations aimed at impressing the electorate in the concerned areas to vote for them. In this regard, the ideology-based parties like the CPI (M) carried forward their ideological commitments by promising comprehensive social and economic reforms and initiation of public welfare policies. Moreover, these parties also cautioned electorate on the dangers emanating from the ruling of the BJP over the last five years with the promise of reverting back to the previous thrust on socialistic pattern of society if voted to power. On the other hand, regional parties such as the SP, the Aam Aadmi Party (AAP) and the YSR Congress (YSRC) presented quite long list of promises which appeared either routine or a reiteration of certain long-drawn promises made by the party over the years. Interestingly, many of the parties standing on a diametrically opposed viewpoint in comparison to ruling party presented somewhat reactionary points in their manifestos in relation to the works and policies of the government. For instance, the SP made it an important promise to debar public use of the Armed Forces in any kind of electoral or political processes in clear reaction to BJP's claim over Balakot air strikes in Pakistan.[6] Other parties issued region- or state-centred manifestos in order to present their specific concerns for their citadels. Thus, the AAP came out with a special manifesto for Delhi to lure away voters in the national capital. Carrying forward its long-standing demand of statehood for Delhi, the AAP promised to do the needful to elevate Delhi from the position of a union territory to state apart from reserving seats for local residents in jobs and educational institutions.[7] Similarly, YSRC focused its manifesto to specific issues and concerns of its stronghold Andhra Pradesh. In all these manifestos, national issues and concerns were either brushed aside or addressed in a very cursory manner without offering any particular perspective on those issues.

Looking at the electoral promises made by different parties, both national and regional, it is clear that there did not exist any consensus among various parties on any of the vital issues that could have been called as national consensus. Even the priorities accorded to different issues and problems faced by country as well as people also varied drastically in such a way that each of the manifestos reflected varying priorities as per the perspectives of the parties. The only common ground covered by almost all the opposition parties appeared to be their scathing critique of the policies and programmes of the ruling party. In fact, these parties, while coming down heavily on the ruling

---

[6] Samajwadi Party, *Manifesto for Lok Sabha Elections, 2019*, accessed 1 June 2019, https://www.firstpost.com/lok-sabha-elections-2019/sp-manifesto

[7] Alok K. Mishra, 'AAP Promises 85% Quota in Edu, Jobs for Delhi-NCR Locals', *The Times of India*, New Delhi, 26 April 2019, 12.

party for destroying the constitutional bodies and national institutions, also promised to undo the harms done to them if voted to power. The electoral promises of the parties eventually became the major plank upon which they based their campaigns.

Campaign Strategy

The long-drawn period of polling spanning over seven phases provided the parties and their star campaigners sufficient time to hop different parts of the country to put forward their perspective before voters. In elections, campaigning happens to be the most important mechanism to reach out to the common voters and establish a personal rapport with them by highlighting their issues and concerns from public platform. At the same time, it also provides the parties and candidates an opportunity to enter into a public debate with their opponents on the contentious issues over which wider disagreements prevail among them. The campaign strategy for the 17th general elections, thus, presents a bird's-eye view of the issues raised by different parties and their leaders which reflected their vision and action plan. While the campaign strategy of different parties more or less hovered around the conventional wisdom of fielding their star campaigners at strategic areas to reap maximum benefits, a remarkable feature of these parliamentary elections was their special focus on certain key areas where they expected to make rich dividends. Such a strategy was most visible in the campaigns of the major national parties.

BJP's campaign strategy was overwhelmingly centred on the personality of its charismatic leader and Prime Minister Modi. But apart from Modi, party also banked upon the massive electoral tours of its President Amit Shah as well as other party heavyweights.[8] A remarkable aspect of the campaign strategy of the party was to focus on those areas where it could sense bright prospects of bettering its previous records of seats in addition to paying sufficient attention to its traditional strongholds lying mainly in the Hindi heartland and western

[8] Rajdeep Sardesai, 'The BJP Juggernaut Is in High Gear', *The Hindustan Times*, New Delhi, 10 May 2019, 16.

part of the country. For instance, the party could very well visualize fair prospects for it to have a strong foothold in the hitherto unexplored territories in eastern part of India with special stress on West Bengal.[9] It began with weaning away dissenter leaders of the TMC like Mukul Roy who acted to mobilize a number of TMC supporters in support of the BJP.[10] Moreover, the party stationed one of its very seasoned strategist to be in charge of the state on a long-term basis so as to have the feel of ground realities of the state, issues and challenges faced by the people, governmental responses to their problems and how the party could convert the public disenchantment with the ruling party into its favour. Such a master stroke of the party really worked well in the state and the party was indeed able to emerge as a formidable force in the state in terms of both Lok Sabha seats and percentage of votes polled in its favour.[11] The issues that became the punch line for the party to put forward its vision and action plan consisted mainly of such problems and rhetoric that would help in arousing people's nationalistic passion. Beginning with the drafting of its manifesto till the last day of election campaign, the party stuck to the core issues facing national defence and internal security of the country.

Comparative analysis of campaign strategies of the BJP and the Congress shows stark contrast in both planning and execution. While the former was marching ahead with a well-planned strategy of raising only those issues and concerns that would have emotive appeal to voters, latter began with a misplaced focus on demonizing the mascot of the BJP as a corrupt man on the basis of the Rafale deal. The fallacy of the most important plank of the Congress was proved disastrous when midway through the election campaign, the Supreme Court on a petition debunked the Congress chief's claim that Modi has been proved corrupt in the Rafale deal. The engine of Congress' campaign machinery was, thus, punctured midway and the party had to look for some other plank to base its electoral strategy on. On the contrary,

---

[9] Romita Datta, 'Battle for Bengal', *India Today*, 20 May 2019, 52.

[10] Pratick Mallick, 'Poll Perceptions and Strategies in West Bengal', *Economic & Political Weekly* 54, no. 23 (8 June 2019), 10.

[11] Kumar Uttam, 'Behind BJP's Bengal Inroads, Month of Planning, Silent Toil', *The Hindustan Times*, New Delhi, 24 May 2019, 5.

the BJP continued with its focus on security and related concerns throughout with only minor additions or deletions in speeches of its star campaigners as per needs of the local circumstances. The glaring mismatch between the campaign strategies of the two major contenders for power, in fact, set the stage for penultimate day when the voters had to make up their mind to cast their vote. Eventually, the poll outcomes proved the relative effectiveness of campaign strategies of the two parties.

Outcomes

The long-drawn voting schedule had resulted in torturous election campaigns in different parts of the country with varying stakeholders and differing mood of the voters. It had always, therefore, been anybody's guess to visualize what could have been the outcome of these polls. The BJP being the only pan-India formidable stakeholder with the probable exceptions of the southern most states of Kerala and Tamil Nadu (though party has played its cards well by entering into an electoral alliance with AIADMK in Tamil Nadu), throughout all the seven phases of polls, the party never lowered its guard and kept its tempo of campaign in full throttle. Hence, it was quite obvious that the party is likely to emerge as the single largest party even if it fails to secure a clear majority in the Lok Sabha. Conjectures were also put forward by certain analysts and activists that these polls would result in the non-BJP, non-Congress parties nearing majority in the house in which case there would be clear probability of the BJP getting unseated from the power in Delhi. The most reluctant participant in these elections appeared to be the Congress whose aging top leadership had almost bestowed the responsibility of steering the party's electoral engine on the shoulders of its president Rahul Gandhi.

The declaration of results came as a shock for the political pundits who were foreseeing the prospects of either a hung Lok Sabha or a working majority for the Third Front parties drawn from various states. A cursory look at the poll outcome confirms that there is hardly a fool-proof mechanism to fathom how Indian voters make the choice

Table 10.1 *Seats and Vote Share of Select Parties/Groups*

BJP	BJP Allies	Congress	Congress Allies	BSP	Left
303 (37.4)	48 (7.4)	52 (19.4)	39 (7.1)	15 (6.4)	01 (2.2)

Source: Lokniti Election Survey (courtesy Dr Sanjay Kumar of CSDS, New Delhi).
Note: Figures in the parentheses indicate the share of the votes in percentages.

before casting their votes. The results were stunning and neither the pollsters nor the party activists had any clue to what had happened in an election in which the voters' turnout was reasonably high. That the voters wanted the incumbent government to come back was crystal clear as Table 10.1, showing the number of seats won by the parties and their share of votes, underlines.

The poll outcomes indicated a clear wave sweeping across the country in the name of Prime Minister Narendra Modi catapulting his party at the top of all.[12] As Modi himself has said in his post-victory speech, his chemistry with the common people of the country has decisively trumped the mathematics of poll pundits.[13] What appeared unique in case of BJP's electoral fortunes has been that Modi's charisma has adequately been matched by the moves of master strategist Amit Shah as party president. As a matter of fact, on the issues of entering into electoral alliances as well as identifying the states and seats where his party stood in an advantageous position in comparison with other parties, Shah's calculations hit almost cent per cent mark.[14] On the contrary, in gauging the public mood, the seasoned politicians like N. Chandrababu Naidu also failed to arrive at right conclusion even if one ignores the calculations of political novices such as Akhilesh Yadav in Uttar Pradesh and Tejashwi Yadav in Bihar.

[12] Venkitesh Ramakrishnan, 'Right on Top', *Frontline*, 7 June 2019, 6.

[13] Sanjay Singh, 'Its Victory of Chemistry over Arithmetic: Modi', *The Economic Times*, New Delhi, 28 May 2019, 2.

[14] Shishir Gupta, 'Shah of Strategy Has Emerged as Leader of Masses', *The Hindustan Times*, New Delhi, 24 May 2019, 4.

Table 10.2 *Position of Different Groups in the 17th Lok Sabha*

Alliances	No. of Seats Won
NDA	354 (44.9%)
UPA	91 (26.8%)
Others	97 (29.2%)

Source: Election Commission of India, 'General Election 2019' (New Delhi: Election Commission of India, 2019), accessed 29 January 2020, https://eci.gov.in/general-election/general-elections-2019/
Note: Figures in the parenthesis indicate the share of popular votes.

A look at the figures in Table 10.2 shows a clear landslide for the BJP and its NDA allies sweeping across the country. By winning 354 seats out of 542, the NDA has proved to be the most formidable political alliance ever made at the national level. In fact, right from the days of Janata Party, the electoral alliances in India have never been able to secure such a landslide victory. In the previous elections, electoral alliances had just been able to secure a workable, or on occasions, only comfortable majorities that allowed them to complete the full terms of the government. Moreover, in the past, partners in an alliance were powerful players in their respective states or areas of influence and did not owe their good electoral performances to the dominant partner or the charisma of its leader. But in the case of the position of the NDA in the 17th Lok Sabha, the things would not have been same had the alliance partners would have to contest the polls on their own.

In the run-up to the elections, as usual, there came a time when some sort of alliance swapping appeared on the scene. Given the five years of iron-handed rule of Modi, certain degree of apprehensions was natural in the minds of some of the NDA partners who either thought of striking hard bargain with the BJP in the seat sharing parleys or decided to leave the alliance altogether. In such a scenario while the long-term allies such as the Shiv Sena and the Janata Dal (United) bargained hard with their dominant partners to extract as many seats in their respective states as possible, a suspicious ally like the Rashtriya Lok Samta Party led by Upendra Kushwaha, a minister of state in the

Modi government, decided to leave the alliance in the hope of reaping rich dividends out of anti-incumbency against the central government. Naturally, he joined the *Mahagathbandhan* (grand alliance) in Bihar to contest the polls. But to his great surprise, the result of his move proved counterproductive and his party lost all the seats it contested including his own.

What is, therefore, being argued here is that the Modi wave that clearly swept these elections proved very advantageous for the allies as well apart from the BJP. Indeed, barring a few states where the Modi wave was stymied by regional factors or leaders, the NDA allies in different states were able to defy any kind of anti-incumbency presumably on account of the Modi wave only. As a result, while most, if not all, of the seats contested by alliance partners in different states were won by them, in certain cases a few alliance partners dramatically improved their kitty of seats riding on the Modi wave. A clear example in this regard is that of the Lok Janshakti Party led by a seasoned politician and cabinet minister in Modi government, Ram Vilas Paswan. His party which had just two members in the 16th Lok Sabha trebled its tally by winning all the six seats it had been allotted under the seat sharing formula in Bihar. Thus, the outcome of these elections proved to be landslide not only for the BJP but also for most of its allies that made the NDA win historic mandate in these elections. Comparatively, when one looks at the performance of alliance partners of UPA, the story is just opposite to that of the NDA.

BJP's Landslide

The most spectacular outcome of the 17th general elections may be considered to be the historic landslide for the BJP that has moved it to the centre of the Indian politics.[15] Such a landslide was probably not expected even by the leaders of the party themselves, though in their public addresses as well as media interviews they claimed that the party would be able to return to power again with absolute majority.

[15] Sanjay Baru, 'Right Moves Closer to Centre', *The Economic Times*, New Delhi, 27 May 2019, 16.

Given the enormous hue and cry raised by the elements opposed to the BJP government over the policies and programmes of the government including certain untoward incidents such as cow vigilantism and lynching of certain individuals, path-breaking economic measures like demonetisation, it appeared even in the general perception that the party was going to face a very tough challenge in the ensuing polls. The situation was further made challenging for the party with coming together of even sworn enemies in the critical states like Uttar Pradesh just for the purpose of checking BJP's return to power again at the centre. In such scenarios, though the party leadership could definitely visualize the enormity of the situation and made earnest efforts to initiate appropriate public posturing including concerted publicity and propaganda to browbeat opposition's moves, the situation, nevertheless, did not permit any space for complacency in the party cadres as well as top leadership.[16]

The BJP secured 37.3 per cent of the popular votes in the 2019 election. The NDA received nearly 45 per cent of the votes which is the highest vote share by any of the pan-Indian conglomeration of parties in any of the earlier national polls since the BJP was formed in 1980. The Congress-led UPA failed to regain its popularity and had won only in 91 constituencies. The 2019 Lok Sabha poll outcome provides inputs to suggest that Hindu nationalism was not just a slogan but an effective mobilizing device. When the results of the polls started pouring in on 23 May 2019, the deep penetration of the Modi wave even into the unchartered territories of the country began to get exhibited. In the place of mandatory 272 seats required to secure a working majority in the Lok Sabha, the party's individual seat tally swelled to cross the magical 300 marks and landed at as much as 303 (Table 10.3).

As Table 10.3 demonstrates, the BJP-led NDA coalition (along with Shiv Sena, the Janata Dal (United), the Shiromani Akali Dal, Dravida Munnetra Kazhagam, among others) had won a comfortable majority with nearly 45 per cent of the popular votes, which is higher

---

[16] Sunita Aron, 'How the Saffron Party Overcame the Opposition in UP', *The Hindustan Times*, New Delhi, 26 May 2019, 10.

Table 10.3 Seats Contested and Won by Different Parties/
Coalitions with Select Allies

Name of the Parties	Contested	Won	Change from 2014	Vote (%)	Change from 2014
NDA	540	352	00	44.9	5.6
BJP	436	303	21	37.4	6.4
Janata Dal (United)	17	16	14	1.5	0.4
Shiv Sena	23	18	00	2.1	0.2
Akali Dal	10	02	-2	0.6	-0.04
UPA	525	91	27	26.8	0.9
Congress	421	52	08	19.5	0.2
Rashtriya Janata Dal	21	00	-04	1.9	-0.3
National Congress Party	19	04	00	1.4	-0.04
Dravida Munnetra Kazhagam	23	23	23	2.3	0.5
Communist Party of India	03	02	02	0.2	0.1
Communist Party of India (Marxist)	03	02	02	0.2	0.1

Source: Lokniti National Election Survey (We are grateful to Dr Sanjay Kumar for sharing the data on the 2019 election).
Note: NDA (National Democratic Alliance); UPA (United Progressive Alliance).

than what it had secured in the last national poll, held in 2014. In contrast, the Congress-led UPA failed to improve its vote share of 19.5 per cent which it captured in the 16th Lok Sabha poll in 2014. When one looks at the contributions of different states and union territories in such a landslide for the party, three categories of states and union territories could be discerned in accordance with the performance of the party in these regions. At the top of all, comes the traditional strongholds of the party where it could land up monopolizing the seats leaving no scope for any other contender to even open their account. Interestingly, the sweep of such states did not remain confined to any particular region and spanned to different parts of the country as shown in Table 10.4. For instance, if the landslide was most visible in the Hindi heartland of Rajasthan, Haryana, Himachal Pradesh, Uttarakhand, it was also witnessed in the western part of the country

Table 10.4 *States/Union Territories Where the BJP Had a Clean Sweep*

States/Union Territory	Total Seats	Won by BJP
Arunachal Pradesh	02	02
Delhi	07	07
Daman and Diu	01	01
Chandigarh	01	01
Gujarat	26	26
Haryana	10	10
Himachal Pradesh	04	04
Tripura	02	02

Source: Election Commission of India, 'General Election 2019' (New Delhi: Election Commission of India), accessed 29 January 2020, https://eci.gov.in/general-election/general-elections-2019/

like Gujarat.[17] Similarly, apart from the capital city of Delhi, BJP's juggernaut also rolled out fantastically in the north-eastern states of Tripura and Arunachal Pradesh.[18]

In many other states, presented in Table 10.4, though other parties could also manage to secure a few seats, the overwhelming majority of seats in these states also went in favour of the BJP in alliance with its coalition partners. Such a situation prevailed not only in the most critical states such as Uttar Pradesh and Bihar but also in many of the states where even the party did not expect such a landslide. The caste-ridden politics of Hindi heartland, especially Uttar Pradesh and Bihar, was trumped by Modi's lucrative economic and emotive security measures.[19] For instance, while the party was able to defy all sorts of doomsayers to establish its dominance of the political scenarios

[17] Nilanjan Mukhopadhyay, 'Clean Sweep', *The Economic Times Magazine*, New Delhi, 26 May 2019, 10.

[18] Vivek Chhetri, 'Triumphant BJP Takes All in Hills', *Telegraph*, Kolkata, 24 May 2019, 8.

[19] Kunal Singh, 'How Modi Conquered Caste in 2019', *The Hindustan Times*, New Delhi, 30 May 2019, 16.

in Uttar Pradesh, Bihar, Jharkhand and Maharashtra, it apparently bounced back in the states such as Madhya Pradesh and Chhattisgarh where it had just lost the state assembly elections a few months back. Most importantly, the Modi wave really helped out the party to reach even to hitherto unchartered territories of eastern, north-eastern and southern parts of the country and secured handsome, if not over-whelming, number of seats in the states such as West Bengal, Odisha, Assam and Karnataka. Of these, the party's stunning performance in West Bengal has probably signalled the ouster of the regional parties from the state.[20]

Decimation of Congress

If the BJP emerged as the most significant gainer from the 2019 Lok Sabha polls, the concomitant losers have surely been the Congress along with some regional satraps such as Lalu Prasad Yadav clan in Bihar and N. Chandrababu Naidu in Andhra Pradesh. In the case of the Congress, the losses arising out of these elections are not only of seats in the lower house of parliament but much more than that. In fact, the party's debacle in these elections might result in existential crisis for the party in the sense that it might not be able to find even capable people in the states to lead the party in future. At the same time, apart from losing the great number of seats, the party may argu-ably have lost its face along with a number of prospective trump cards that would have been used to rebuild the party in future. The losses of certain seemingly unbreachable bastions of the party like Amethi for party president Rahul Gandhi and Guna for party veteran Jyotiraditya Scindia must be recognized as inflicting immeasurable damages to the physical as well as psychological health of the party, recovering from which might take very long time.[21]

What could be seen as the most shocking part for the Congress has been the consistency with which newly appointed party president

---

[20] Kanchan Gupta, 'Bengal's Green Fort Falls', *Business Standard*, New Delhi, 24 May 2019, 4.

[21] Neerja Chowdhury, 'Reaching for the Empty Hand', *The Economic Times*, New Delhi, 27 May 2019, 16.

Rahul Gandhi has performed to lead party from one failure to another in different assembly and parliamentary elections. He could neither infuse new vigour in the party nor streamline its working methodology. Even the party leadership could not improve its as small working style as that of selection of the candidates.[22] As a matter of fact, given that the Congress seems to be destined to be led by a Gandhi despite all the failures and disasters that Gandhi could bring for the party, Rahul Gandhi's coronation as the party president was construed by many to infuse new energy and vigour in the rank and file of the party. It was also expected that with the waning of popularity of Modi and anti-incumbency factor likely to be working against the BJP, Gandhi would stand on a solid pedestal to bounce back as the epicentre of the Indian politics. But the way Modi wave built up progressively and the BJP was able to reap rich electoral dividends out of that wave, the naive expectations of the Congress leadership were dashed and the party was thrown into the vortex of serious uncertainty. These elections, thus, instead of acting as the salvagers of the diminishing fortunes of the Congress led to deterioration in its physical and psychological health.

The party's performance in these elections has been presented in Table 10.5. The most worrying scenario emerging out of these elections for the Congress consists of mainly three ominous portents. At the outset, all kinds of programmes and strategies for the party's revival in the key states of Uttar Pradesh and Bihar have failed to show any sort of positive indicators based upon which the party could have been assured of bouncing back in these states sooner or later. Second, party's long-awaited gains in the states of Hindi heartland such as Rajasthan, Madhya Pradesh and Chhattisgarh could not be retained, if not to talk about consolidation, for any longer duration of time as the results for the parliamentary elections produced diametrically opposite position in comparison to the elections for state assemblies. Rather, these gains tended to make the party complacent.[23] Third, arrival of Rahul Gandhi

[22] Gilles Verniers, 'What Candidates Selection Tells Us about BJP, Cong Strategies', *The Hindustan Times*, New Delhi, 18 May 2019, 15.

[23] Partha Mukhopadhyay, 'Winner's Curse', *The Indian Express*, New Delhi, 30 May 2019, 15.

Table 10.5 *Seats Won by the Congress in Different States/ Union Territories*

States/Union Territories	Total Seats	Seats Won by Congress
Andaman and Nicobar Islands	01	01
Assam	14	03
Bihar	40	01
Chhattisgarh	11	02
Goa	02	01
Jharkhand	14	01
Karnataka	28	01
Kerala	20	15
Madhya Pradesh	29	01
Maharashtra	48	01
Meghalaya	02	01
Odisha	21	01
Puducherry	01	01
Punjab	13	08
Tamil Nadu	39	08
Telangana	17	03
Uttar Pradesh	80	01
West Bengal	42	02

Source: Election Commission of India, 'General Election 2019' (New Delhi: Election Commission of India), accessed 29 January 2020, https://eci.gov.in/general-election/general-elections-2019/

as the party president was a long-cherished dream for most, if not all, of Congressmen who wished to see the Gandhi scion lead the party to recovery and secure majority in the Lok Sabha to take up the reins of the country.[24] Amidst such high hopes, the scenario in which the party president could not save his own seat that has been the family bastion for long naturally caused consternations in the party circles.

[24] Ravi Shankar Kapoor, 'The Free Congressman's Burden', *The Times of India*, New Delhi, 30 May 2019, 22.

State of Regional Parties

The post-1990s era in the Indian politics has not only been marked by dominance of coalition politics in place of the one-party dominant system but also growing clout of the regional parties. Strengthening of the regional parties while providing them a formidable foothold in their respective states has also afforded them a quite respectable and, at times, decisive role in the making or unmaking of the central government. As such, the 17th general elections produced a mixed bag of results for the regional parties as shown in Table 10.6. In this regard, three distinct trends may be noticeable. One, in certain states, particularly in the southern and north-eastern parts of the country,

Table 10.6 *Seats Won by Major Regional Parties*

Name of Party	State	Total Seats	Seats Won
Apna Dal	Uttar Pradesh	80	02
Bahujan Samaj Party	Uttar Pradesh	80	10
Biju Janata Dal	Odisha	21	12
Dravida Munnetra Kazhagam	Tamil Nadu	39	23
Indian Union Muslim League	Kerala	20	02
Janata Dal (United)	Bihar	40	16
J&K National Conference	Jammu and Kashmir	06	03
Lok Janshakti Party	Bihar	40	06
Nationalist Congress Party	Maharashtra	48	04
Samajwadi Party	Uttar Pradesh	80	05
Shiv Sena	Maharashtra	48	18
Shiromani Akali Dal	Punjab	13	02
Telangana Rashtra Samithi	Telangana	17	09
Telugu Desam Party	Andhra Pradesh	25	03
Trinamool Congress	West Bengal	42	22

Source: Election Commission of India, 'General Election 2019' (New Delhi: Election Commission of India), accessed 29 January 2020, https://eci.gov.in/general-election/general-elections-2019/

regional parties have reasserted their primacy in the political scenario of these states. Two, many of the regional parties have indeed been able to show their continued grip over the electoral dynamics of their respective states in a kind of all-weather electoral performances. Three, some parties that had been formidable at certain points of time have, however, been reduced to naught in these elections and now stare at crisis of identity for them.[25]

The southern comfort of the regional parties has, by and large, remained intact even during these elections. Barring Karnataka and Kerala where national parties, that is the BJP and the Congress, respectively, have been able to hold their grounds, rest three states witnessed assertion of supremacy of the regional parties. The most significant aspect of these elections has been the emergence of the YSRC from a sort of political wilderness to become a force to reckon within Andhra Pradesh to give a new shape to the nature of party politics in the state along with the TDP. Rise of the YSRC may indeed be taken as a great loss for the Congress which has remained the countervailing force to the TDP in the state to provide a political alternative for the people. The nature of party politics in the state may, probably, follow the pattern of Tamil Nadu in future in which the two Dravidian parties alternatively share the honours with each other leaving not much scope for the national parties to dabble in the politics of the state. At the same time, the DMK in Tamil Nadu and the Telangana Rashtra Samithi in Telangana continued to dominate the political scenes in their respective states.[26]

In other parts of the country, political fortunes of regional parties have varied from state to state. In Odisha, though Navin Patnaik led BJD has been able to return to power, the rapid pace with which the BJP has increased its areas of influence in the state should ring warning bells for the regional party sooner or later. In the north-eastern states, majority of the regional parties have been able to hold on to

[25] Hemant Karnik, 'Regional Parties: Hardly an Existential Problem!' *The Asian Age*, New Delhi, 26 May 2019, 5.

[26] Sugata Srinivasaraju, 'Seesaw in the South', *The Economic Times Magazine*, New Delhi, 26 May 2019, 14.

their citadels despite earnest efforts on the part of the BJP to make inroads in as many north-eastern states as possible with the strategy of alliances and coalition governments in different states.

Of all the provinces, the poll outcomes in West Bengal seem to have baffled many pollsters presumably because they failed to read how public wrath could become a source of political mobilization; they, in other words, completely misread the public anguish against the incumbent government that, despite having adopted many welfare schemes, did not appear to be as tough as was expected to contain the miscreants who, by resorting to muscle power and other extra-constitutional means, utilized the government machineries for realizing their personal goals. The TMC supremo, Mamata Banerjee, notwithstanding her declared objective of weeding out corruption and other means for misusing the institutionalized authorities for gratifying personal agenda, was hardly effective to halt the electoral slide in West Bengal. She suffered the most serious defeat which is indicative of a clear erosion of her support base across various social strata and districts. Being disillusioned with the TMC, a large number of her supporters shifted their loyalty to the BJP, which explains, to a significant extent, the astounding victory of its candidates. In fact, the rise of the BJP to take pole position in the politics of the state may be considered to be one of the most unexpected outcomes whose implications would not be felt only in the state but in the whole country in the times to come. Table 10.7 substantiates the claim that in a democracy, the voters are the final determinant.

Table 10.7 Poll Results in West Bengal, 2019

Name of the Party	Vote Share (%)	Change (%)	Seats Won	Change
TMC	43.3	+3.5	22	-12
BJP	40.3	+22.3	18	+16
Congress	5.6	-4.1	02	-2
CPI (M)	6.3	-16.7	00	-2

Source: Election Commission of India, 'General Election 2019' (New Delhi: Election Commission of India), accessed 29 January 2020, https://eci.gov.in/general-election/general-elections-2019/

It is evident that the BJP's electoral gain is directly linked with the drubbing of the TMC which lost many of its parliamentary seats that it had won in 2014. That it had lost in 12 parliamentary constituencies shows its failure to retain its support base in areas which were considered to be its strongholds. What is most striking is the near decimation of the left, especially the CPI (M) in the 2019 elections; not only did the CPI (M) candidates fail to win even a single parliamentary seat, there was also a massive reduction of its vote share which also shows that a mere ideological appeal is not enough to garner votes. So is true of the Congress that has ceased to be a critical player in West Bengal as its vote share shows. The 2019 national poll is about a new political map in which the BJP has emerged as a chief contender for power in the 2021 assembly elections. This was unthinkable in a province in the past since the BJP was hardly a force to talk about presumably because of its association with overtly religious appeal. The gradual but steady decline of the parties that held the citadel of power in West Bengal, namely the Congress, the Left Front and the TMC, reinforces the point that in democracy no political party is invincible.

The decline of the TMC is generally attributed to the lack of governance, especially in rural areas, where its members, by being blatantly partisan in distributing government funds for welfare, alienated even its erstwhile supporters who stood by the party in the past in opposition to the Left Front. In other words, the misuse of government machineries for partisan gains and for protecting those involved in anti-people activities are reasons which created a chasm between the party and the voters. This was the context which need to be taken into account to explain the phenomenal growth of the BJP voters in West Bengal. It is fair to argue that in West Bengal, the increasing importance of the BJP as a decisive player has followed a different trajectory in comparison with what is usually the case elsewhere in India. As history has shown, the growth of the BJP is attributed to the sustained organizational activities of the RSS; wherever the BJP has emerged as a stronger contender for power, it is the RSS that had a significant role creating conditions in which the BJP rose in importance. That was surely not the case in Bengal because, due to historical reasons, the RSS, or for that matter any other right-wing organization had never succeeded in winning mass support ever.

Besides the border districts, the presence of the RSS was negligible. In view of the well-entrenched radical traditions in the province, the RSS, being identified with Hindutva, had hardly had social influence which also explains why it failed to create a strong support base in the province. This was evident in the pre-2019 national elections: the BJP failed to win more than two parliamentary seats. What is little puzzling is the fact that despite being the birthplace of one of the top right-wing leaders, Shyama Prasad Mukherjee, West Bengal did not seem to have created a conducive environment for Hindutva to strike roots. It is also surprising that most of the Hindu nationalist ideologues came from Bengal, and yet, the Hindu Mahasabha, the RSS and the BJS remained confined to few pockets in West Bengal. Mukherjee's campaign against the United Bengal scheme[27] which the Congress and the Muslim League leadership had espoused just on the eve of India's freedom in 1947 helped build a constituency for the right-wing ideological preferences; the plans that he forced the independent government to adopt to ameliorate the conditions of the refugees who came from East Pakistan also established him as a popular leader among the displaced and dispossessed Hindus. There was thus a possibility for the right-wing politics to prosper. His untimely death in 1953 however nipped that hope in the bud. In the absence of Mukherjee, it was the left activists who fought for the refugee resettlement in West Bengal which helped them build and also consolidate a strong support base in the state. Being opposed to the Congress and the Left those championing the right-wing ideological preferences always remained peripheral. It was the decimation of the Left at the hands of the TMC during the period when the BJP was steadily growing in importance as a pan-Indian party which created a definite space for the party in West Bengal.

[27] Chakrabarty elaborated the United Bengal scheme that the Bengal Congress and the Muslim League floated to carve out a third dominion following the partition; the campaign fizzled out since Mukherjee convinced the Congress high command and the Bengali Hindus that it was essentially a ploy to create a Greater Pakistan of which both the Bengals were to be constituents. Bidyut Chakrabarty, 'An Alternative to Partition', in *The Partition of Bengal and Assam, 1932–47: Contour of Freedom* (London: Routledge, 2004), 85–131.

The story of the rise of the BJP reveals that its growth in West Bengal needs to be understood contextually because neither the RSS nor typical Hindu nationalist appeal seem to have aided the BJP candidates to win in the 2019 elections. Instead, it was primarily the misgovernance and the obvious adverse consequences which catapulted the BJP to the centre stage indicating how mass disenchantment resulted in the defeat of the TMC candidates. There is a wider point here: the Left Front that ruled West Bengal uninterruptedly for 34 years was voted out of power in 2011 largely due to its failure to control the cadre-raj which flourished at the behest of some of the top leaders for fulfilling personal aims and objectives. The story does not seem to be very different with the TMC. With its inability to contain the power brokers and those activists resorting to means for attaining their personal goals, the TMC appears to have significantly lost its public credibility which explains its drubbing in the Lok Sabha poll and the consequent rise of the BJP as a formidable contender for power in the forthcoming assembly elections in 2021.

Demise of the Left

An important ideological goalpost in the Indian politics has always been provided by the left parties despite their own ideological differences and political bickering. The pivotal significance of left parties in the Indian politics, therefore, might not lie in their forming government in a state or joining in a government at the centre. Rather, as part of the ideological plurality, left parties provide a refreshing perspective on all the major issues and concerns facing the country at different points of time. Absolute wiping out of the left parties from the vortex of the Indian politics should not, therefore, be considered as a good pointer for the agility and longevity of the Indian democracy. Despite that, due to their misplaced priorities, disconnection with the genuine common issues and concerns of the people, and their rowdy run of being in power in West Bengal over a long period of time has somehow made them an unattractive alternative to the mainstream political ideologies and actors of Indian politics. As a result, in the 17th general elections, the left parties acted as a sort of irrelevant

Table 10.8 *Seats Won by Left Parties*

Party	States	Seats Won
Communist Party of India (Marxist)	Kerala	01
	Tamil Nadu	02
Communist Party of India	Tamil Nadu	02
Revolutionary Socialist Party	Kerala	01

Source: Election Commission of India, 'General Election 2019' (New Delhi: Election Commission of India), accessed 29 January 2020, https://eci.gov.in/general-election/general-elections-2019/

participant in the festival of votes whom people have also refused to take seriously and vote for them.

General electors' apathy towards the left parties was omnipresent and quite comprehensive in these elections as proved by the number of seats won by them as presented in Table 10.8. When one looks at the plight of once mighty CPI (M) whose writ used to run in number of states including West Bengal and Tripura, the party has now been reduced to such a position where it could not open its account in these states. The most surprising results have however come from West Bengal where the penetration of the BJP into the erstwhile left bastions has almost obliterated the presence of left in these areas.[28] Although it continues to be the ruling party in Kerala, party's performance even in that state deep down in south did not help it do better. In all, the party could win just three seats in these elections which have been contributed by the two southern states of Tamil Nadu and Kerala. Of the three, interestingly, two seats came to the kitty of the party arguably not on its perseverance but riding on the wave of the DMK that not only stymied the Modi wave in the state but also helped even DMK's allies to improve their overall seat tally. The only seat which could be considered as coming out of hard work of the party was the one it won from Kerala amidst the Congress dominance in the state.

Along with the CPI (M), the other important left party, the CPI also met almost similar fate as that of its dominant partner. When

[28] Sai Manish, 'BJP Bengal Breach Obliterates Left', *Business Standard*, New Delhi, 24 May 2019, 2.

elections for the Lok Sabha were declared, the party sought to ride piggyback on a number of pseudo celebrities who had hogged the limelight in the previous months for all wrong reasons. The party, therefore, decided to take the calculated risk of throwing its full weight behind such candidates instead of giving ticket to its seasoned leaders who had been toiling for the party for years. A classic case in this regard happened to be that of Kanhaiya Kumar, the former Jawaharlal Nehru University Students' Union (JNUSU) president who was sought to be accorded a larger than life status by fielding him as the party candidate from Begusarai in Bihar. In fact, Kumar has become the poster boy of not only the CPI but the entire left intellectuals who took the position that even by winning just Begusarai seat, left may attain salvation in Indian politics. But he lost miserably. Like the CPI (M), the two face-saving seats for the CPI also came from Tamil Nadu where its alliance with the DMK helped it win the two seats contested as alliance partner.

There was a time when the left politics in India was represented by a number of leftist parties led by their dominant partner the CPI (M). There used to be at least three more important parties apart from the CPI (M) that constituted what was known as the Left Front in different parts of the country. The other three partners of the Left Front, namely the CPI, the Revolutionary Socialist Party (RSP) and the Forward Block used to be important stakeholders in both ideological maturity and electoral broad base of the left politics in India. But after the loss of power of these parties in West Bengal, the Left Front, per se, ceases to exist and the other left partners have virtually been driven into oblivion. In these elections, therefore, apart from the CPI (M) and the CPI, the only other left party that could win a seat was the RSP which was able to sail through its solitary gain in Kerala. But for Forward Block, even such a consolatory win in any part of the country could not materialize. Thus, even collectively, the Left Front which used to be a formidable bloc in Lok Sabha has been reduced to just six seats in the 17th Lok Sabha.

Now, the moot question that arises in the face of the present status of left in the Indian politics is: Does this parliamentary election indicate the demise of the left in Indian politics? Such a question gains validity in view of the fact that in as vast a country as India where 543

Lok Sabha seats were at stake, the left parties could not win the support of the voters even in dozens of constituencies. Their miserable performance in the states like West Bengal where they used to be in power for almost four decades tells a ton about the voters' alienation with these parties. In fact, the left parties have now been reduced to such a position that their probability of emerging as all India parties would have been reduced to almost zero. It was indeed their fortune that the major left parties decided to become part of the DMK-led coalition in Tamil Nadu and got opportunity to contest a few seats that they won riding on the anti-Modi wave in the state. Otherwise, they would have faced the spectre of remaining thoroughly unrepresented in the 17th Lok Sabha which in itself would have signalled the demise of the left in the country.

BJP as the Epicentre of Indian Politics

Ever since its formation in 1980 to replace its previous incarnation in the form of the BJS, the BJP has gradually but consistently been inching towards the pole position in Indian politics.[29] The remarkable growth of the BJP over the years as the dominant party in the Indian political system tells an amazing journey of a party that began its forays in Indian politics by winning just single digit seats in Lok Sabha over a number of general elections. But the party's parentage to the formidable RSS did not let it brood over its dismal performances in its early phases and it was always assured of a grand future in Indian politics in the years to come. So, in the 17th Lok Sabha elections when the party has been able to secure a landslide of 303 seats in the lower house of Indian parliament, it should really be considered as a result of not just hard work and perseverance of its leaders and cadres but the veracity of its ideological commitment which has now gained wider acceptability among the cross sections of Indian political spectrum. In fact, all through these elections, the parent organization of the BJP was at the forefront to boost its electoral prospects.[30]

[29] Abhinav Prakash, 'BJP Cement Its Position as Central Pole of Indian Polity', *The Hindustan Times*, New Delhi, 25 May 2019, 11.
[30] Smriti Kak Ramachandran, 'RSS Tweaks Outreach Plan to Boost Polling on May 19', *The Hindustan Times*, New Delhi, 15 May 2019, 1.

Given the mind-boggling social, economic and cultural diversities prevailing in the vast countries like India, winning electoral battles decisively must be considered as the product of a multitude of factors working in tandem with each other to produce an intended result. As all sorts of cleavages, divisions and fault lines are visible in different parts of the country, electoral management becomes one of the most complex managerial exercises for the people tasked with the responsibility of ensuring wins for their parties. In India, such a unique competence was shown by the Congress leaders until the time of Rajiv Gandhi when various leaders singlehandedly steered the Congress to its numerous electoral victories since the independence of the country. But then, the Congress did have the background of the national movement which helped it reap rich emotional crop which the sacrifices of the people made during the national movement had ingrained in the minds of people for the years to come. Hence, what becomes more startling for the BJP is the fact that the party has been able to reach the highest possible marks in the Indian parliamentary elections by dint of sheer hard work and appropriate strategy in place of emotive historical legacies of the Congress.

BJP's unprecedented mandate in these elections has also been attributed to its well-planned massive expansion into the rural and semi-urban areas. Traditionally, given the dominance of the RSS in urban and semi-urban centres ever since its inception, the initial presence of the BJP remained confined to urban and semi-urban areas only. However, with the installation of the BJP governments in various states, the process of party's entrenchment even into the countryside also began. As a result, during the last Lok Sabha elections, the BJP had indeed been able to make its presence felt in its non-traditional constituencies. However, what has happened in the current general elections has really been phenomenal. The sweep of the party in many states proved its deep presence in all kinds of human habitats whether rural, urban or semi-urban. Such a pan-Indian all-habitat presence was previously commanded only by the Congress under the leadership of Gandhi–Nehru scions. Other mass-based parties had their dominance confined to certain state or states only. But in these elections, the BJP has shown its prowess of occupying the universal space vacated by the Congress as the mass party without any kind of geographical or class-based restrictions.

In charting out the grand success of the BJP, the pivotal contribution of two of its top leaders—Modi and Shah—is unparalleled. Long association of the two right from their days in Gujarat has helped them develop the highest degree of understanding and mutual respect for each other which could be reckoned as the rarest in the contemporary Indian politics.[31] In this context, the role of Prime Minister Modi is truly historical.[32] It was his personal appeal to the voters in different parts of the country that a sort of massive wave of support started building up in his favour which was called the Modi wave. In states where the state units appeared jittery, they invariably fell upon the charisma of Modi.[33] His capacity to effortlessly connect with the common voter has truly turned into rare brand of politicians who are able to draw maximum mileage even out of minuscule welfare of the people.[34] In caste-ridden states like Bihar, it was Modi who breached that seemingly impregnable shield of the caste-based parties.[35]

The two significant factors that presumably went in favour of Modi to get personal rapport with the people have been his personal character and concern for all. Given that political power has been the den of corruption in India out of which very few politicians have come out unscathed, Modi's famous slogan that he would neither indulge in corruption nor allow anybody else to do so has probably captured the attention of the people like never before. His corruption-free governance has presumably proved his credible leadership in doing, he says.[36] This precisely was the reason that the Congress president Rahul Gandhi's affront to Modi as 'chor' could not move common people even an inch in giving credence to his charges. At the same time, Modi's repeated commitment in public that despite a party

---

[31] Bhavna Vij-Aurora, 'Applied Chemistry', *Outlook*, 10 June 2019, 28–31.

[32] Suhas Palshikar, Sandeep Shastri and Sanjay Kumar, 'Modi All the Way', *The Hindu*, New Delhi, 30 May 2019, 11.

[33] A. S. R. P. Mukesh, 'Jittery in J'khand, BJP Banks on Modi Rally Wave to Swing Votes', *The Times of India*, New Delhi, 1 May 2019, 18.

[34] Patralekha Chatterjee, 'Modi's Welfarism: Some Action, a Lot of Emotion', *The Asian Age*, New Delhi, 31 May 2019, 6.

[35] Prashant Jha, 'In Bihar, It's Modi Factor versus Caste, Candidate', *The Hindustan Times*, New Delhi, 6 May 2019, 9.

[36] Pradeep Bhandari, 'Credible Leadership Crucial', *Organiser*, 7 April 2019, 18.

member, as Prime Minister, his endeavours would be for the welfare and development of all including the ones who would not have voted for him probably made him loved by all cutting across their primordial affinities such as caste, religion, region, language and gender.[37] Modi's pan-India appeal has indeed made doomsayers who called him the great divider of India change their stance to call him the great unifier of the country.[38]

The positive atmosphere in favour of his party created by Modi through his credible promises and convincing arguments has been taken full advantage of by party president Amit Shah who has over the years emerged as the top political strategist in the country.[39] Keeping in mind both the short-term and long-term visions for the growth and development of his party, Shah has really propelled the growth of the BJP even in such areas which would have seemed improbable just a few years back. The classic examples in this context are that of West Bengal and Uttar Pradesh. West Bengal under the long period of rule by communists and Mamata Banerjee is considered to have become the citadel of anti-BJP sentiments. But the way Shah planned the BJP inroads into different parts of the state has really been appreciated. Similarly, in Uttar Pradesh, once considered to be the bastion of casteist parties, the phenomenal rise of the BJP has demolished the dominance of the well-entrenched parties in such a way that they would probably not be able to overcome the shocks of defeat in the near future.

Dominance of the BJP candidates in majority of the constituencies is also proved by the fact that they have won their seats with overwhelming majorities.[40] In the states where the party could manage to have clean sweep, the wining margins of its candidates generally crossed over lakhs, though ironically the narrowest winning margin for

[37] Abhishek Lodha, 'An Election of Trust', *The Indian Express*, New Delhi, 30 May 2019, 15.

[38] IANS, 'Modi Has United India! Time Does Somersault', *The Pioneer*, New Delhi, 30 May 2019, 1.

[39] Archis Mohan, 'Chanakya Niti', *Business Standard*, New Delhi, 24 May 2019, 6.

[40] Times News Network, 'Margins Tell Story of BJP Dominance', *The Times of India*, New Delhi, 25 May 2019, 1.

a candidate also went to B. P. Saroj of the BJP who won by just 181 votes from Machhlishahr constituency of Uttar Pradesh. Clearly, the victory margins of different candidates indicated two distinct patterns for standing of the BJP in different constituencies. One, where the party was in a predominant position, the opposition could simply not put up a formidable fight as a result of which the victory margins of the BJP candidates soared to greater heights. But even where the opposition candidates won, the BJP has surely been able to put up a strong fight making sure that the victory margins of opposition candidates could go up extraordinarily.[41] The only exception to these generalizations could be seen in Tamil Nadu where the BJP could not come into the reckoning at all. Resultantly, the DMK candidates in the state won with huge margins. But for other opposition parties, none of their candidates could come anywhere near to the BJP trendsetters.

A creditable feat for the BJP in these elections has been the demolition of stereotypical behaviour of the voters based on their primordial affinities like caste.[42] Given that caste has acted as the most significant determinant of voting behaviour, particularly in the Hindi heartland, it was a point of great interest for the analysts to see how the parties fare in terms of obtaining the votes of the castes that traditionally have been their vote bank. Another marker of the universal social acceptability of the parties, particularly parties like the BJP that has been accused of being dominated by upper-caste people, is how their candidates fare in the reserved constituencies over which the caste-based parties pay special attention. Even on this count also, the BJP virtually outnumbered all other parties by bagging majority of seats reserved for Scheduled Castes and Scheduled Tribes.[43] That way, it was not only able to trounce the caste-based electoral alliances called *Mahagathbandhan* in Uttar Pradesh and Bihar by winning majority of seats reserved for Scheduled Castes but also cut to size the parties

[41] Neelanjan Sircar, 'BJP's Win Margins Rose in 2019', *The Hindustan Times*, New Delhi, 25 May 2019, 11.

[42] Sudha Pai, 'Other Aspirational Class', *The Economic Times Magazine*, New Delhi, 26 May 2019, 16.

[43] Vishwa Mohan, 'Half of BJP's Additional MPs from SC/ST Constituencies', *The Times of India*, New Delhi, 26 May 2019, 14.

like the JMM that has taken the seats reserved for Scheduled Tribes as their traditional citadels. The Modi wave, thus, acted to defeat the calculated social machinations of a number of parties looking forward to improve their tallies counting on reserved seats and establish Hindutva as more cementing force than caste.[44]

Undoubtedly, the landslide victory for the BJP in these elections could not have been possible without portraying Hindutva as the major ideological plank for the party. In fact, given the parentage of the party to the RSS, Hindutva has been the raison d'être for the BJP and it has never shied away from presenting it as the saviour of Hindus in the country. Such a categorical stand of the party has obviously tended to widen the religious divide in the country which has further widened with the astounding victory of the BJP in these elections.[45] Although BJP's stand on the Muslims as a community has been categorical, even the parties that have been claiming to be the facilitator of the community would also not take them more than vote bank.[46] The stereotyping of the Muslims, therefore, has tended to do more harm to the community than serving their cause.

BJP's failure to make inroad among the Muslims is comprehensible; its inability to sway the women voters in its favour is also intriguing despite the fact that the Modi government had undertaken many welfare schemes specifically for women, including the Ujjwala Yojana which distributed cooking gas connection, almost free of cost. Nonetheless, it hardly gave the BJP dividends in the 2019 national poll. A careful look at the proportion of women voters who voted for the BJP in the 17th Lok Sabha elections demonstrates that despite having increased its share of popular votes, BJP's women voters have dwindled. So, the BJP continues to suffer on this count which means that there can hardly be a pattern in voting behaviour. This is an interesting facet of the 2019 elections because notwithstanding its

[44] Avinash M. Tripathi, 'BJP's Performance a Result of Deep Social Churn', *The Hindustan Times*, New Delhi, 25 May 2019, 10.

[45] Shreyas Sardesai and Vibha Attri, 'The Verdict Is a Manifestation of the Deepening Religious Divide in India', *The Hindu*, New Delhi, 30 May 2019, 11.

[46] Sagarika Ghosh, 'The Othered Muslim', *The Times of India*, New Delhi, 24 April 2019, 14.

growing political dominance lesser number of Indian women than men support the BJP which is indicative of 'the arrival [and consolidation] of a distinctive women's constituency in Indian politics'.[47] This is also an interesting development which also reinforces the point that while casting their votes, women voters are guided by considerations which may not have been critical for men's electoral choice. Implicit here is a fundamental point exposing the in-built limitations of the claim for the 'one-size-fits-in-all' approach.

The results of the 17th Lok Sabha polls have also gone to demolish a number of ominous tendencies prevalent in Indian politics for fairly long period of time. Among such tendencies, the phenomenon of dynastic politics has been quite conspicuous by its presence in almost all parts of the country despite being despised by political analysts. Traditionally, while the Congress has been charged with perpetuating the trend of dynastic politics, there undoubtedly are more vigorous champions of dynastic politics than the Nehru–Gandhi family. For instance, in Uttar Pradesh, the political expansion of the Mulayam Singh Yadav family has outnumbered any other by fielding six members of the family in different parts of the state.[48] However, in the wake of the Modi wave, only two members have been able to get elected: father Mulayam Singh Yadav along with the son Akhilesh Yadav. Other members of the family including wife of Akhilesh have met with drubbings in their erstwhile strongholds. As far as the BJP is concerned, the dynastic traditions at the national level have been perpetuated again by the BJP brand of Gandhi scions: mother Maneka Gandhi and son Varun Gandhi.[49] While both the mother and the son got elected, the same fate did not augur for other dynasts mainly from the Congress and other regional parties.[50]

---

[47] Rajeshwari Deshpande, 'Gender-wise Politics: To What Extent Did Women's Vote Contribute to the BJP's Spectacular Victory?' *The Times of India*, New Delhi, 17 July 2019.

[48] Subhash Mishra, 'With 6 Members, MSY's Is the Largest Family Contesting Polls', *The Times of India*, New Delhi, 25 April 2019, 2.

[49] Kanchan Chandra, 'This May Not Be a Verdict against Dynastic Politics', *The Times of India*, New Delhi, 25 May 2019, 19.

[50] Ramesh K. Singh, 'Dynasts Get Mixed Results', *The Pioneer*, New Delhi, 24 May 2019, 5.

Clearly, the BJP has jumped to take the credit for ridding the Indian polity of the dominance of dynastic politics by ensuring the defeat of well-entrenched dynasts while keeping the party away from this malaise to a large extent.[51]

Concluding Observations

Elections are a litmus test for the political parties to gauge their popularity among the voters. In the first-past-the-poll system, the idea of majority is little deceptive since by securing the majority of the votes polled a candidate wins. Nonetheless, this design of electoral democracy has been accepted and the political authority is being reconstituted regularly since 1952 when the first general elections were held in India. India is unique in that respect because despite having the same colonial legacies, the former British colonies in the subcontinent failed to sustain the Westminster democracy for reasons connected with the socio-economic and political milieu in which they rose as independent polities following decolonization. Except the period of Emergency between 1975 and 1977, India has an enviable track record of democratic governance that does not seem to be a mere outward show, but one that has evolved organically.

The results of the 2019 Lok Sabha elections have arguably ushered in a new era in the Indian politics upsetting a number of well-entrenched tendencies, perceptions, parties and processes that have underpinned the political system for a fairly long period of time. Although the notion of 'Congress system' was shattered long ago, these elections have gone to bury the idea even deeper to make that irreversible. Moreover, the 2019 mandate has also driven home the point that the grand old party of India needs to reinvent itself in more substantive manner than just passing resolution in the Congress Working Committee to repose its faith in the eternal leadership of the Gandhi–Nehru scion despite all the losses. At the same time, it also signalled that mass of clichéd slogans emphasizing the basic

---

[51] Times News Network, 'Mandate Rid Nation of Dynasty Politics: Shah', *The Times of India*, New Delhi, 26 May 2019, 14.

demands of '*roti, kapda, makaan*' (food, cloth and roof) as well as '*bijli, sadak* and *pani*' (electricity, road and water) seemed to have lost their appeal to the voters. Caste, the most formidable determinant of voting behaviour until recently, has now been reduced to irrelevance, if not discredited. In view of the BJP's astounding electoral success, the argument defending the contention that coalition is inevitable in India may no longer be valid. What attracts the voters now is a more muscular posturing of India as the regional, if not global, hegemon, who not only could hit anti-India elements across the border deep inside Pakistan but also could stand with global powers on equal footing. These results have indeed gone into radically transforming the term of political discourse in the country.

The 2019 Lok Sabha poll is a watershed in the annals of elections in India. The first national poll, held in 1952, was a departure with the past since it was held immediately after the 1947 transfer of power following the withdrawal of colonialism. There was a pattern which continued until the 1967 state assembly elections in which the ruling party, the Congress, lost miserably. By forming the government in 1996, the BJP ushered in an era in which the Congress no longer remained the focal point in the Indian politics. The journey continued until 2004; having failed to win a majority in 2004 and 2009 national elections, the BJP seemed to have lost its sheen to the rest of the world which was however temporary since the Modi-led BJP got a majority in 2014 which was repeated in 2019. The purpose of this short briefing is two-fold. On the one hand, what it confirms is the point that democracy is not merely a format of governance, it is also a spirit governing the prevalent politico-ideological priorities. This is also to argue that democracy offers a level-playing field in which these preferences jostle for space. On the basis of an analysis of the poll results, one is now well-equipped to argue that Hindu nationalist ideas prevail over other competing ideological choices. The 2019 poll outcome also underlines, on the other, the point that Indian voters are perhaps the most judicious when they are asked to choose the future rulers with reference to what they deem most appropriate for the country. Here too, that the BJP-led NDA had won a majority in the 2019 elections firmly establishes the point that the Hindu nationalist voice helped build a strong constituency for the conglomeration in opposition to those drawing upon the age-old Enlightenment values. So, the 2019 poll was a battle of ideas in which those seeking to rework on the idea of India by reference to her rich socio-cultural and academic traditions seem to have edged out their counterparts espousing the Nehruvian idea of India.

Conclusion

I

Recognized as the largest democracy in the world, free and fair elections have been the foundational characteristic of the Indian democracy. India has been able to successfully hold 17 general elections so far, the latest being held in 2019. Although the Constitution stipulates that the lower house of the Parliament would have a term of not more than five years, quite a number of times premature general elections have also been organized in case of the fall of a government and the house unable to provide a stable government. There have been occasions when the term of the Lok Sabha has been sought to be extended beyond the constitutional stipulations. There have also been times when the scheduled elections to the Lok Sabha could not be held on account of the executive arbitrariness as has been experienced during the period of Emergency in 1977. Thus, the regularity with which the general elections in India take place cannot be taken as a mean achievement given the multiple challenges arising out of different individuals and contingencies. But after all, the democratic process of the country has remained on the track braving all kinds of challenges.

When the democratic system of government was envisaged for the country by the Constitution makers, apprehensions were raised in a number of quarters regarding the capability of the institutions and individuals to keep the process of democratic government intact if not to talk of its deep rooting. The situation further seemed complicated for the alarmists on account of the introduction of universal adult franchise as the guiding principle of the Indian democracy. Such apprehensions of some people were presumably based on their perception of taking democracy and democratic processes as the monopoly of the Western countries. Moreover, they appeared convinced that the mass of people having all sorts of social and economic backwardness—poor, illiterate, caste ridden, having predominant primordial affinities and prone to all kinds of threats and allurements—could never succeed in making democracy a successful experimentation in their societies. Above all, the failure of democratic experiments in many other parts of the world has been the empirical case for them to foretell the failure of the democratic experiment in the country. But having experienced the democratic government for over 70 years, Indians are now well placed to show the world how democracy is designed and implemented in the traditional societies.

The democratic experience of the people of India has not remained confined only to the elections for the apex bodies like the Parliament. On the contrary, the democratization of the Indian polity has been sought to be taken to the lower possible levels. Thus, elections are held regularly to elect the representatives of the people at the state, district, block, village, municipality, urban centres, cooperative societies and everywhere else if that body or institution has been engaged in the management of the public affairs. For successful conduct of all these elections, appropriate bodies and administrative units have also been created at suitable levels. In fact, the administrative and logistical paraphernalia of the election machinery have been so efficiently organized and managed in the country that a number of other countries look up to India to assist them in organization of free and fair polls in those countries as well. Thus, the vision of the Constitution makers to make the Indian democracy successful and vibrant has been facilitated by the creation of competent machinery, provision of men and materials and design of standard operating procedures for conducting free and fair polls.

Elections may be considered as both the cause and effect of democratic process in the country. At the heart of democracy lies the election of the people's representatives to take charge of the government on behalf of the people electing them. Thus, election has indeed been the cause of democracy. In other words, the idea of democracy could simply not be visualized without thinking of the appropriate system through which the people would be able to articulate their opinions or views to the people likely to be their representatives. But the ingenuity of the people still has not allowed them to imagine any other institution or process through which the true representatives of the people could be identified and placed in the position of government. As a result, elections remain the basic system through which democracies attain functional vibrancy. However, the democratic processes also result in the refinement of the processes and methods of elections in such a way that constant innovations and creativities are experienced in the conduct of elections in different parts of the world. Elections, therefore, affect and get affected by the democratic processes in a number of subtle ways all across the globe. Insofar as India is concerned, elections have been important factors in reinvention of the democratic institutions and processes in the country.

II

Conceptualization of the Indian democracy through the prism of elections being held in the country at regular intervals is a refreshing exercise. As a matter of fact, democratic experimentation in India since Independence has been underpinned by different kinds of institutional, functional, procedural and behavioural innovations each of which has gone to add creative dimensions in understanding and conceptualizing democracy in the country. Although adoption of a democratic system of government based on universal adult franchise has been considered as a gamble on the part of fathers of Indian Constitution, the gamble has undoubtedly paid rich dividends in terms of establishing India as one of the most vibrant and respected democracies in the world. However, the moot question that arises in analysing the institutional vibrancy and functional dynamism of democratic experiences in India is the way it is looked at and conceptualized to bring out the creative inputs it has provided to the body of literature on democracy and democratic experiences across the world.

Among the different factors that have gone to make democracy a way of life for the people of India, elections stand out prominently. Initially, under constitutional stipulations, regular periodicity of elections has been ensured only for the higher legislative bodies such as Lok Sabha and state legislative assemblies. But after the Seventy-third and Seventy-fourth Amendments to the Constitution, regularity of elections for the bodies of local-level democracy, in both rural and urban areas, has also been guaranteed with creation of suitable structures and procedures for the same. Contemporaneously, India may be reckoned as one of the most election-oriented democracies in the world. Various other substantive features of democracy such as social cohesion and egalitarian nature of society may not be underlining characteristics of the Indian democracy, but what has definitely gone to make the Indian democracy make its mark is the elections taking place without fail, and each election adding a novel theoretical dimension to the understanding of democracy.

Although elections are held in the country for electing the people's representatives at different levels of government, the elections that have motivated a number of fundamental transformations in the democratic system of the country are the ones held for electing the members of Lok Sabha. Even of such elections, the elections held up to the fourth general elections could be taken as routine given the nationalistic fervour in which they were held. As a result, successive re-election of the Congress party had become a sort of certainty, thereby making those elections monotonous and uneventful. The real churning in the political psyche of the common people of India came in the elections for the fifth Lok Sabha when the major personalities in the fray were the ones seeking public support not on the basis of their role in the national movement but on issues very relevant for the life of the people during that time. In other words, the elections for the fifth Lok Sabha held in March 1971 may be seen as a reinvention of democratic ethos in the country in view of the fact that the main contestants in the election joined the electoral fray with a vision of life for the people in contrast to the previous elections when nationalistic fervour continued to sway the voters to cast their franchise in support of the party steering India to Independence.

Indira Gandhi's penchant for establishing a strong chord with the psyche of the common people of India appeared to be at its best with her sui generis call for *garibi hatao*. With this exemplary call, she had indeed been able to transform the imagery of democracy in the minds of masses of people from a routine *jalsa* (gathering) to that of an emancipatory tool which might bring about a turnaround in the conditions of their life. This arguably seems to be a path-breaking moment in the march of democracy in the country given its impact on repositioning of democracy from a ritualistic to an instrumental value. Marking an outright break from the past, the fifth general elections apparently stirred the Indian masses from their slumber to make them perceive the democratic processes in a more egalitarian and ameliorative sense than before. Democracy in India, thus, transcended the formalistic and procedural overtones through which it had been carried forward by important stakeholders to attain a substantive place whereby it tended to percolate down to the masses. It no more remained a bastion of the social, economic and political elites of the country. Raising the hopes of the plebeian classes, democracy in India now appeared poised to run into the blood of the people instead of remaining confined to the provisions of the Constitution.

III

Real churning in the democratic polity of India started taking place in the aftermath of lifting of the Emergency and holding the sixth general elections. As a matter of fact, declaration of the Emergency by Indira Gandhi and the atrocities committed on the hapless people had produced the scenario in which the Indian democracy seemed to have lapsed into non-existence forever. The dreams of leaders like JP to make India a true democracy appeared like improbable. But the sudden declaration of the general elections put the democracy back on the track in the country. Now, the prospects of regaining the democratic space appeared brighter. That way, translation of JP's dream of creating a truly democratic India into reality through the sixth Lok Sabha elections in 1977 has been a revolutionary aspect of the Indian democracy. Indira Gandhi's magical moves getting converted into bumper support for her in the previous general elections had somehow drove an impression in her to become a democratic despot whom people would adore and accept forever. Apparent result of this was the declaration of the Emergency and the dark phase of democratic experience in India. This, however, offered an opportunity to the people of India to relook at the empty rhetoric and false promises made during elections and turn towards the creative alternatives to such hoaxes.

As a result, the 1977 general elections proved to be historical in three senses. One, the common people of India showed their prowess in voting out a government whom they voted just a few years back to power with thumping majority precisely on account of the fact that the same government tried to curtain their constitutionally ordained basic rights and sabotage the democratic processes in the country. Two, for the first time, the country was to witness the inauguration of a non-Congress government consisting of a diverse range of ideological and identity standpoints in sharp contrast to what had been professed and practised by the Congress till date. Thus, the demarcation of Indian party system as 'Congress system' was decisively shattered through this election. Three, a refreshing theoretical perspective was provided to the idea of democracy through the ideas of JP who also acted as the conscience keeper of participatory democracy in the country. For JP, democracy has to be participatory enough to include all the sections, particularly the marginalized ones so as not to remain the bastions of the elite sections or a few individuals.

The restoration of democratic processes and the democratic institutions in the country offered new theoretical perspectives on the understanding of the finer points of Indian democracy. For instance, analytical forays in understanding the democratic process in the country need to engage with two interrelated processes critical to the Indian democracy. One, apart from the centrist ideological space occupied predominantly by the Congress, there also exist two parallel ideological streams of left and right whose theoretical premises vary so much from each other that there does not appear to be a fair possibility of any congruence between them. Such a conceptual premise was at its full play during the working of the Janata Party government which presented a picture of disparate incongruent groups coming together for certain pressing cause rather than providing a plausible political alternative to the Congress. Two, the sentimental nature of Indian electorate which had been exhibited right since the Independence through mass voting by the people for leaders of the national movement got reinforced in wake of the assassination of Indira Gandhi in October 1984.

Amid these underlying considerations, the elections for the seventh Lok Sabha happened to be unprecedented in the democratic history of India because the Congress was able to secure a historical majority in the lower house of the Parliament which even Jawaharlal Nehru could not secure in the first general elections fought amid the nationalistic fervour. Thus, theoretically, this general election was underpinned by virtual elimination of non-Congress forces in almost all parts of the country barring Andhra Pradesh where the TDP under the leadership of N. T. Rama Rao was indeed able to stem the sympathy wave in support of the Congress. It also corroborated the argument of erosion of the Congress base in the southern India. Rajiv Gandhi's ascendance to the position of Indian prime minister from being a commercial pilot in the Indian Airlines further strengthened dynastic tendencies in Indian politics with massive support of the people.

The real churning and game of one-upmanship by scrupulous or unscrupulous means began in the democratic process of India with the ninth general elections. Fought in the shadow of Bofors scandal, this election saw the greater fragmentation of Indian electorate on the basis of corruption, religion, ideology and regional factors in such a way that the idea of a consensual politics got virtually buried in the electoral hustle. Thus, this election provided an open space for all the stakeholders in the democratic process to increase their areas of influence vacated by the Congress. However, the dilemmatic situation in front of the opposition parties was not less formidable. While most, if not all, of them based their electoral forays on anti-Congress stand, their ideological orientations also dissuaded them from forging a powerful alliance so as to take on the Congress in a united manner. The electorate now had the widest possible choice to cast their franchise which was really used in the most disparate manner in this election. During this election, different political parties saw an expansion in their support base in proportion to the decline in support base of the Congress. So, while left parties were able to consolidate their position in their traditional strongholds of West Bengal, Kerala and Tripura, the BJP was able to make great strides in the northern and western parts of India. For the rest of India, regional parties did assert their primacy in certain states, whereas the Congress was able to put up an impressive show in a number of states. Thus, these elections helped in eroding the hegemonic position of the Congress in almost all the states, thereby creating opportune scenario for the opposition parties to deep root their presence in different parts of the country.

IV

Elections to form the 10th Lok Sabha witnessed the reconfiguration of social groups on the lines of caste and religion. The announcement of the implementation of Mandal Commission recommendation by the government started a new stir in the political dynamics of the country given the potential of these recommendations to put OBCs in the political and administrative mainstream of India. Although the proponents of the Mandal recommendations sought to reap rich electoral dividends in the ensuing elections, their plans fell flat midway with the assassination of Rajiv Gandhi at Sriperumbudur in Tamil Nadu on a campaign trail. To counter the move of Mandal, the rightist political forces raised the bogey of the Ram temple in Ayodhya. Thus, the elections to the 10th Lok Sabha witnessed the toying of novel ideas on the electoral firmament of the country so as to influence the voting behaviour of the people in their favour. Although the death of Rajiv Gandhi helped in turning the electoral tide in support of the Congress in the later phases of elections, the electoral bars were definitely raised during these elections by the proponents of social justice and Hindu right elements. The terms of political discourse in the country appeared set for a new conceptualization based on the primordial parameters as opposed to the secular and progressive elements of government and politics practised during the preceding elections. The political landscape of India appeared fertile for germination of seeds of caste and religion having potential of turning into formidable factors of political mobilization in the country. It also set the stage for reinvention in the political dynamism of the Congress which appeared settled to the fact that the days of it commanding clear majority in the Lok Sabha are over and it needed to be mentally prepared for coalition governments.

Results of the seeds sown in the 10th general elections started showing up in the subsequent elections for the 11th and 12th Lok Sabha in 1996 and 1998, respectively, whose theoretical implications in conceptualization of the Indian democracy have been quite striking. Democratic processes in India had now become more and more polarized with caste and religion taking centre stage, especially in north Indian Hindi heartland. The parties based on secular credentials without apparently espousing the cause of any particular dominant caste groups started facing greater marginalization in the electoral battles. As a result, the Congress, at one time the epitome of party system in the country, appeared to be pushed to insignificance in the Hindi heartland states such as Uttar Pradesh and Bihar. The caste-based parties started reaping rich electoral dividends which were rivalled only by the BJP. Thus, the period of one-party majority or dominance of a single party in the electoral arena had almost been over. Politicization of primordial affinities of the people tended to introduce the element of identity politics that acted to provide a new sense of political vitality and eminence to different caste groups in the democratic processes of the country. Hitherto marginalized sections of society started asserting their new-found political power and a novel era of coalition politics began in India. It became clear that the electoral arena would now be dominated only by those parties who are able to forge grand coalitions with the regional and caste-based parties. But given the inhibitions of different parties to join hand together on long-term basis, the country was faced with two general elections in a short span of just three years. The Indian democracy had now come full circle with politicization of the masses to an unprecedented scale.

Held in 1999, elections for the 13th Lok Sabha may be termed as historical given the fact that it produced a coalition of political forces that were able to form the first non-Congress government which was able to complete its full term. Coalitional nature of the Indian democracy had by now become well entrenched whose practical manifestation came in the form of two important coalitions in the name of NDA led by the BJP and the UPA led by the Congress. Forming nucleus of the democratic processes in India, these two alliances presented themselves as national alternatives before the electorates. At the regional levels, most, if not all, of the states became witness to the rise of one or more than two regional parties that preferred to keep them aloof from the national alliances presumably owing to the regional dynamics of their core vote bank. During the elections for the 13th Lok Sabha, democratic process in the country was marked by sharp polarization of the voters around a number of issues ranging from social justice to the Ram temple. Given the internal divisions among the parties standing for social justice, the votaries of ideologically right-wing forces led by the BJP were indeed able to make deep impressions on the psyche of the masses, thereby securing a majority in the Lok Sabha. The Indian democracy, thus, apparently completed its ideological shift full circle beginning with socialistic pattern of society of the Congress to the Hindu revivalism of the BJP. Amid these sharp ideological goalposts, the caste-based parties remained firmly rooted in their pockets of influence playing only marginal role in the national politics. At the same time, the left parties were increasingly reduced to insignificance in view of their clamour to become the nucleus of a viable non-BJP, non-Congress force.

V

Theoretical underpinnings of the 14th and 15th general elections could be discerned with particular reference to their impact on the democratic process in the country. These elections were fought between the national coalitions with certain parties shifting their allegiance from one to another. But the nucleus of these coalitions remained intact with the two major national parties—the BJP and the Congress—leading them. The increasing formidability of the BJP in democratic process apparently acted as deterrent for the smaller regional parties to keep their independent status intact. As a result, most, if not all, of them preferred to join the Congress-led UPA to keep them relevant in the national politics. Even the parties that desisted from joining the UPA tried to hammer out some sort of electoral understanding with the friendly parties in the UPA so as to offer a strong challenge to the BJP. Thus, the democratic landscape in the country was marked by deeper politicization of different sections of society with caste and religion vying with the developmental clientele agenda of the Congress. Amid the claims and counterclaims by the caste-based and religion-based parties, the masses tended to be swayed by the public-oriented policies of the UPA that helped it sail through the electoral battle. In the absence of any viable alternative presented by the NDA or any major bickering appearing in the UPA conglomerate, the same electoral behaviour got repeated in the 15th Lok Sabha elections as well. At the state level, different regional parties continued to hold sway over their core vote bank that helped them not only remain ruling dispensation in the state but also an important player in the national politics.

The 16th Lok Sabha elections have been the most creative intervention in the theoretical understanding of the Indian democracy. It has apparently changed the goalposts of democratic processes in the country in such a way that what appeared to be the fringe at the time of inception of democratic politics in India has come to attain the central place in the Indian democracy. Such an unprecedented turnaround has probably been made possible by the spadework done by the parent organization of the BJP, the RSS, through its enormous efforts towards integration of hitherto marginalized sections of society such as Scheduled Castes and Scheduled Tribes. The obvious result of such a social churning in the democratic process of India has been quite clear. In other words, the BJP has not only been able to keep its traditional support base intact in these elections but has also been able to garner massive support from marginalised sections of society including women. Thus, the nature of Indian democracy has largely become pluralized with existence of not only two powerful coalitions in the form of the NDA and the UPA but also an equally, if not more, powerful bloc of non-BJP, non-Congress forces operating at regional levels.

VI

The Indian democracy is a puzzle for all since the established conceptual categories that had clear Western roots failed to persuasively explain its growth and gradual consolidation. Elections are held regularly, and the authority is transferred to the winning political parties. The Indian political experiment is thus unique since there is hardly a parallel in history. Despite being routine affairs in the established democracies, elections sometimes prove to be turning point in the history of a nation. The outcome of certain particular elections not only demolishes the long-held political beliefs, systems, patterns and processes but also set the stage for their replacement with novel alternatives. In this regard, the 17th general elections, held in 2019, may really be termed as momentous in India's recent political history. The outcome of these elections have not only unsettled many of the well-established tendencies and practices of the Indian democracy but have also acted to provide decisive perspectives on a number of competing issues and challenges facing the Indian political system for long. In fact, during more than 70 years of successful working of the Indian democracy, numerous issues both constitutional and political have remained contentious with varying perspectives being put forward to settle them accordingly. However, the long period of the Congress rule has tended to provide the foundational shape in terms of both ideology and institutions to the practical working of Indian democracy which have not been taken easily by certain sections of political class. Moreover, the conventional wisdom in fighting elections in India has also come under severe constraints during the last few years. On all such issues and many more, the 2019 general elections have tended to set the futuristic perspective for the shape of things to come in the country. Apart from the processes through which these elections were fought, the outcomes of this battle of ballots have gone to bring about serious transformations in the Indian political system whose long-term implications are likely to be novel and uncharacteristic of the traditional view of the Indian politics.

VII

The 2019 national poll stands out in the history of Indian elections for one principal reason, namely the fulfilment of one of the major election pledges. The BJP included the scrapping of controversial Articles 370 and 35A of the 1950 Constitution in its election manifesto. On assumption of power, the newly elected BJP government abandoned these provisions as they were contrary to the principles of equality, fraternity and unity; Articles 370 and 35A remained integral to India's Constitution even seven decades after its inauguration in 1950. It was both a puzzle and a paradox: paradox because despite India being federally united, Kashmir with her special constitutional status sustained a semi-independent identity; puzzle since Article 370 was allowed to continue despite being contrary to the claim of India being a nation. With the recognition of the 1954 Constitution of Jammu and Kashmir as the supreme guiding design for the province, the argument that it was not exactly a part of India gained ground. In his address in Srinagar in 1953, Shyama Prasad Mukherjee, the founder of Jana Sangh, held Articles 370 and 35A to be unwarranted special favour to Jammu and Kashmir and argued for 'one country, one emblem and one constitution' because, as he believed, 'separateness creates separatism'.[1] In other words, Article 370 which provides special constitutional status to Jammu and Kashmir is a source of contestation, if not irritation, since a guarantee of special status to a constituent state in federal India is constitutionally untenable within the framework of a federal nation. The scrapping of Articles 370 and 35A does not seem to be an aberration because by endorsing special constitutional status to Jammu and Kashmir, the provision was an impediment to India's identity as a nation state. In the present context, the argument has substance although the founding fathers were persuaded to extend special privileges to the province perhaps due to contingent circumstances in which it was perhaps the best option available to them.

The banning of Article 370 is thus, constitutionally, legitimate since the presidential abrogation order is derivative of the core values of democratic governance justifying diversity within the framework of India being a republic. The annulment is also justified because the insistence of Jammu and Kashmir being separate from India is contrary to the inherent syncretism of Kashmiriyat which hardly corresponds with the sectarian appeal in which Jinnah's two-nation theory was couched. A syncretic philosophical discourse, Kashmiriyat

---

[1] Rudrangshu Mukherjee, ed., *Leaves from a Diary: Syama Prasad Mukherjee* (Calcutta: Oxford University Press, 1993), 8.

is an articulation of processes leading to secularization of Islam also by being drawn to Buddhism, Sikhism and by giving equal space and even patronage to the localized philosophical traditions. So long as Articles 370 and 35A, being legitimately dubbed as 'the architecture of otherness',[2] were allowed to continue, it not only militated against Kashmiriyat, it also consolidated a constitutional design 'to discriminate against man and woman, insider and outsider [and] Indian and Kashmiris' which is constitutionally ultra vires and also indefensible.[3] In other words, in the guise of autonomy, discrimination along the axes of caste, religion and gender was allowed to be justified. In these circumstances, notwithstanding the self-defeating hue and cry by those privileging sectarian appeals over the nation, the redundancy of Article 370 can thus be said to have brought back the core concerns of the founding fathers for building a unified India which is culturally diverse but constitutionally one.

The converting of 'the iconic Article 370 of the Constitution from reality to history'[4] is undoubtedly a concrete step to defend the point that 'the old Nehruvian left-liberal consensus has given way to an alternative understanding of India in her own civilizational lens [which] ... may have annoyed some, but generated a zeal to critically evaluate the derivative wisdom', drawn on Western intellectual antecedents which was, so far, considered axiomatic.[5] There is a conceptual point here: contrary to the view that Article 370 was universally accepted in view of its historical roots, the mute repercussion following its revocation in 2019 also reveals that the Nehruvian model of Indian identity did not seem to have been as persuasive as was believed in a context when contrary views and ideas were not encouraged, if not brutally suppressed. Basic to the design was an endeavour to build a hegemonic discourse around

[2] Rahul Shivshankar, 'What Binds J&K to India? It Is Kashmiriyat, Article 370 Merely Set Up an Architecture of Otherness, Thankfully Annulled', *The Times of India*, Kolkata, 8 August 2019.

[3] Ibid.

[4] Swapan Dasgupta, 'The Miniscule Support for Article 370 Indicates a Big Mood Shift in India: Smooth Road Ahead', *The Telegraph*, Kolkata, 8 August 2019.

[5] Ibid.

the Nehruvian politico-ideological priorities that had, for historical reasons, flourished in India presumably because of the success of the capable nationalist leadership in effectively containing alternative conceptual yardstick and views. The 2019 Presidential Order rescinding Articles 370 and 35A is therefore not only a break with the past but also a significant constitutional intervention in creating a discursive space for alternative discourses to strike roots. It will thus not be exaggeration to argue that India's journey to nationhood was complete with the abrogation of Articles 370 and 35A of the 1950 Constitution of India following the Constitution (Application to Jammu & Kashmir) Amendment Order, 2019.

VIII

A careful analysis of national elections held so far in India reveals that there is a discernible pattern which will help us understand the contention that voters usually make up their mind, not on the basis of the merits of the party's electoral pledges, but by being persuaded by issues which are generally couched in emotional terms. In other words, there is substance in the argument that elections in India are generally decided by the voters' responses to those issues which might not have been drawn on policy preferences that the contestants endorse in their election manifestos. The idea is clear: polls in India do not seem to reflect the choice of the voters based on their comprehension of the issues that might have been critical before the elections. The argument is testified very sharply in the 2019 Lok Sabha poll.

The spectacular victory of the BJP-led NDA in the 17th general elections in 2019 is a testimony to the claim that Hindu nationalism is also a vote-catching device. An analysis of the poll results confirms the argument that the Indian voters' preference for the ruling party was reflective of their conscious choice for an ideological priority in which the concern for the nation figured prominently. At one level, the election results represented an opinion which drew on an idea of India that hardly received critical attention in the past. It was a verdict which was thus politically contrived and ideologically governed; it was, in other words, a voice, a neglected one, which gradually gained momentum, especially since the 16th Lok Sabha poll. The 2019 poll was also, at another level, a referendum on the leadership of Prime Minister Narendra Modi, who was hailed in the contemporary media reports as 'a game-changer' in the midst of adverse campaigns by his political opponents. A careful view of the nature of the campaign suggests that the opposition that endeavoured hard to cobble up a *Mahagathbandhan* (grand alliance) was almost decimated in a milieu in which the NDA juggernaut appeared to have been unstoppable. Two factors seem to have worked in tandem: on the one hand, the BJP's organizational networks, complemented by the support of the RSS cadres, explain, to a large extent, how the party succeeded in spreading its tentacles across the length and breadth of the country. It is therefore fair to claim that it was BJP's organizational back up which resulted in this astounding triumph of the incumbent government. This is also attributed, on the other, to the immense popularity of BJP's star campaigner, Narendra Modi, who, by his electrifying presence in innumerable pre-poll meetings, consolidated an opinion which was translated into votes in BJP's favour. There was another factor that also need attention, namely the 2019 surgical strike in Balakot (in Pakistan) by the Indian Air Force demolishing the terrorist camps that acted favourably in creating a nationalist fervour that the BJP activists utilized to generate support for their candidates. For the BJP and the RSS ideologues, the Balakot episode helped them create an environment in which the idea of the nation being prior to everything was privileged. The strike had established India's military capability vis-à-vis terrorism that instantaneously generated pro-BJP sentiments, especially among the new voters who saw in this a perfect design for the nation to emerge as a formidable global player. For a large number of voters, the Balakot attack by the Indian Air Force consolidated the nationalists who remained marginalized in view of growing disenchantment, especially among the youth, with the past governments largely because of their prejudiced policy designs opposing endeavours towards developing 'a strong India'. As argued, the election results are an outcome of complex socio-ideological processes which are reflected in voters' choice. What had begun with the capture of power by the BJP-led NDA in 2014 continued in the 2019 elections. It can now be persuasively argued that being a national party, the BJP is no longer confined to the Hindi heartland, although its staggering electoral performance in the 17th general elections has been possible due to having won large number of seats in Hindi-speaking areas. Furthermore, besides its geographic expanse, the party has also, as the evidence suggests, succeeded in creating constituencies of support across social strata. No longer an upper-caste party, the BJP has supporters among the OBCs, besides the Dalits. The book therefore pitches its argument at two levels: at an empirical level, it argues that Hindu nationalism, as it is interpreted by the BJP and the Sangh Parivar, is effective enough to garner votes for the NDA coalition which substantiates the claim that the idea of India cannot be so simplistically conceptualized as is usually done in the so-called secularist discourse. At a conceptual level, the argument is also an endeavour, perhaps most well-designed one, to suggest that Hindu nationalism has its viability as a powerful mobilizing mechanism in an India that hardly had the capacity to sway the voters in the immediate past.

Within the frame of plebiscitary democracy, individual leadership has become more important than both the party structure and the ideology it professes. At the dawn of India's rise as an independent nation, it was Jawaharlal Nehru who rose as an uncontested leader of the newly emerged polity. With Gandhi throwing his weight behind Nehru, the leadership issue was decided amicably in his favour. As long as he was on the political scene, Nehru appeared formidable probably because of his ability to carry the masses with him. His rise as the only able and effective Congress leader was relatively easy due to the demise of his equally competent and charismatic colleague, Vallabhbhai Patel. Congress's victory in elections both at the national and provincial levels under Nehru's stewardship made the party dependent on a single individual for his remarkable vote catching ability. The party therefore looked redundant in the absence of a charismatic leader—this is the beginning of a process which assumed massive proportions with the passage of time. Although Nehru did not groom his daughter Indira Gandhi consciously as his successor, the mantel of the Congress leadership had fallen on her owing to Lal Bahadur Shastri's prema-ture death. The Congress syndicate comprising senior Congressmen, such as Atulya Ghosh, K. Kamaraj and S. Nijalingappa, accepted her as she would, they thought, serve their interests better than other contenders. Through a direct communication with the people, Indira Gandhi reduced the Congress party to a mere name. Her emergence as a charismatic leader who swayed the masses and brought victory to her party countered other possible majority for her party in the 1971 Lok Sabha elections. It was essentially a verdict of the people on her performance as a leader amid crisis.

The 1971 electoral victory made Indira Gandhi's position invincible.[6] This election was also the beginning of plebiscitary politics that 'opened direct relation between Indira Gandhi's personalized leadership and individual voters rather than of an issue-oriented politics that mobilized classes and interests in support of Congress programmes and candidates'.[7] Indira Gandhi became Congress's most vital resource, the key to political power and personal advancement; the party and the person ended to become one. As a result, not only was the party reduced to 'an individual fiefdom', an attempt was also made to retain its leadership within the family by grooming her son, Sanjay Gandhi, as her probable successor. The young Gandhi was projected as the future prime minister by the party which depended largely on Indira Gandhi for its survival. Within a brief period, Sanjay Gandhi appeared acceptable to the Congressmen irrespective of factions showing probably the extent to which Nehru–Gandhi lineage prevailed over other considerations in so far as the leadership was concerned. A sizeable section of contemporary politicians, both inside and outside the Congress (I) owed their rise in politics to Sanjay Gandhi. Since Indira Gandhi's capacity to sway the masses in her favour was enviable, there was not a single protest against her deliberate attempt of establishing a dynastic rule by projecting her youngest son. Her defeat in 1977 was more due to the excesses of the Emergency than personalization of politics. Her victory in 1980 corroborates the plebiscitary democracy model. The slogan for stability acted favourably in view of the chaos experienced during the 1977–1979 Janata rule.

The accidental death of Sanjay Gandhi, anointed as Indira Gandhi's successor, in 1980, created a break in the line of succession

---

[6] For details see: Paul Brass, *The Politics of India since Independence* (Delhi: Orient Longman, 1990); Rudolph and Rudolph, *In Pursuit of Lakshmi*.

[7] Rudolph and Rudolph, *In Pursuit of Lakshmi*, 137.

which appeared temporary following the induction of Rajiv Gandhi into national politics; so, Nehru–Gandhi lineage continued. The unanimous choice of Rajiv Gandhi as Indira Gandhi's successor following her tragic end in 1984 seems to have been drawn on the consideration that 'if the Congress remains the central fact of India, [the Nehru family] has become the central fact within it'.[8] Indira Gandhi's brutal killing and the rising tide of divisive tendencies made 'desh bachhao' the most effective vote catching slogan in the 1984 elections. Rajiv was projected as a natural heir to the victory with an unprecedented 49 per cent popular votes to his credit ensuring the importance of the individual leadership rather than the party in obtaining votes.

The sudden and tragic death of Rajiv Gandhi created an obvious vacuum in the Congress leadership. There were attempts to make his widow, Sonia Gandhi, the Congress president which she declined. The move was probably prompted by one of two reasons or perhaps a combination of both: it may have been a strategic move to avoid internal power struggle that was inevitable given the internecine feud within the party, and second, it might have been a well-calculated endeavour to exploit a brutal killing for electoral gain on the promise that the slain leader's sorrowing wife would be an asset in the election campaign. Resolutions adopted by various provincial Congress committees supporting the suggestion seem to explain the deplorable state of affairs within the party which gave the impression that without the stewardship of Nehru–Gandhi family it looked completely disarrayed. The apparent bankruptcy of the party is probably obvious because with organizational elections long overdue, it had become an organization of subservient camp followers. As a result, it became a fact of political life that the only people 'who shone at court were either those who had no home base to draw strength from, or flunkeys who were able to assist the leader in a secretarial capacity'.[9] Although the

[8] M. J. Akbar, 'Wolves at the Dynasty's Door', *The Telegraph*, Calcutta, 2 June 1991.

[9] Khushwant Singh described the people surrounding the Congress (I) leader in a more pejorative way: 'Whatever political importance they got in the past was a *chamchas* (parasites) hanging round our recently assassinated former Prime Minister and his family;' see, Khushwant Singh's column in *The Telegraph*, Calcutta, 3 June 1991.

Congress cobbled up a majority by forming a coalition, it remained a minority coalition. A Congress-led minority government assumed power under the leadership of Narasimha Rao who was tipped by the Sonia-supported Congress High Command simply because he lacked political base and hence would never become a threat to the party authority. Despite being the prime minister of a Congress-led minority government, the Rao regime will be remembered in history for its failure to prevent the destruction of the Babri Masjid in 1992 by the Hindu right wing. Perhaps to regain the Hindu vote bank for the Congress, Rao seemed to have gone slow even after he had had clear indications of vandalism that was to follow on 6 December 1992. The uncertainty that followed in the aftermath of the Babri Masjid episode catapulted the BJP to the centre stage of the Indian politics. Along with the increasing importance of L. K. Advani who led the Rath Yatra, Atal Bihari Vajpayee rose as an invincible leader who articulated a new voice supportive of the Hindu right wing. The 11th, 12th and 13th Lok Sabha polls, held in 1996, 1998 and 1999, respectively, are illustrative here since BJP's rise to power was largely due to the acceptance by the majority of the voters of the leadership of Advani and Vajpayee. The trend did not appear to have continued in 2004 and 2009 Lok Sabha poll when it was the Congress Party which was effective in garnering votes for the coalition of parties with diverse socio-political interests though the importance of the Gandhi family, especially the widow of late Prime Minister Rajiv Gandhi, Sonia Gandhi, cannot be ignored. Following the landslide victory of the BJP-led NDA in the 16th poll, held in 2014, in which the role of Narendra Modi was decisive, it was again proved how individual leadership was critical in India's polls. The convincing victory of the same coalition in 2019 is a further confirmation of the argument emphasizing the immense importance of an individual leader. In fact, it will not be an exaggeration to suggest that the 2019 Lok Sabha poll was referendum on the leadership of incumbent premier. Being the star campaigner in the 2019 elections, it was Modi who helped the candidates belonging to the NDA coalition win the electoral battle. One must add a caveat by stating that Modi succeeded because (a) the prevalent environment was conducive for BJP's electoral pledges to gain an easy acceptance by the voters, (b) he was ably supported by the regional leaders who also had a strong support base in the respective regions which they had represented and also (c) the consolidation of a popular mindset being opposed to the Congress leadership and also those parties which formed a grand coalition to defeat the NDA. Except Kerala, partly in Telangana, Punjab, Tamil Nadu and West Bengal, the opposition parties failed to retain the number of seats which they had won in the earlier election. The most striking results were visible in West Bengal where the BJP, which was almost non-existent as an organization, managed to enhance the number of seats from just 2 in the 2009 elections to 18 in the last Lok Sabha poll out of a total number of 42 seats. What it leads us to conclude that in Indian elections the importance of an individual leader cannot be overlooked, as the history bears testimony to this contention.

There is another flip side also because the rise of plebiscitary politics creates an environment in which the parties no longer remain as decisive as they are expected to be in Westminster-type parliamentary democracy. In order to obtain votes, individual leadership appeal became far more critical than the party which appeared insignificant in elections. Between 1947 and the death of Jawaharlal Nehru in 1964, however, the Congress party remained a crucial political institution sustaining India's democracy. Nehru who described the Congress party as the central fact of India guarded the party which won freedom against tendencies undermining its democratic structure. So strong and widespread was its organization throughout India that the Congress party appeared to be the only viable alternative to run the state. The commentators such as W. H. Morris-Jones and Rajni Kothari,[10] impressed by the continuity of the party as a ruler despite serious challenges, attributed the durability of the 'one party dominance' or 'the Congress system' to its historic role in the freedom struggle and its ability to mediate between different conflicting interest which were dominant on the contemporary political scene. The party held India's

---

[10] Rajni Kothari, 'The Congress System in India', *Asian Survey* 4, no. 12 (March, 1964), 1170 and also, 'Integration and Exclusion in Indian Politics', *Economic & Political Weekly* 23, no. 43 (1988), 2224; W. H. Morris-Jones, 'Stability and Change in Indian Politics', in *Politics in Southern Asia*, ed. Saul Rose (London: Macmillan, 1963), 9–32.

democracy in safe custody because, as James Manor explains, it was 'a huge, hierarchically structured party, broadly rooted throughout the country side, apparently provided the mechanism whereby a plurality of elites, sub elites and groups could both voice their claims and attempt to realize them'.[11] At the same time, the Congress could adequately mediate and settle these multiple and often conflicting claims. If necessary, the extreme faith in the constitutional and legal system and second, the fact that the ruling party which fought for independence was held in high esteem and therefore what was decided by the Congress party and its leadership was accepted by the masses at large. Moreover, the party also mirrored grievances of other groups too. It reveals thus that 'the principle of consensus' helped the Congress system work so smoothly for the first two decades after Independence. Following the landslide victory of the BJP-led NDA in 2014 and 2019 national poll, the argument that the individual leadership matters does not seem to be overstretched. As the campaign and the scintillating victory of the ruling coalition in 2019 demonstrates, one is thus persuaded to believe in the effectiveness of the electoral appeal of the incumbent prime minister in garnering votes for the coalition that he represented.

[11] James Manor, 'Party Decay and Political Crisis in India', *The Washington Quarterly*, Summer, 1981, 26.

Bibliography

Note: A book usually ends with a bibliography. The reason is simple. It helps the beginners because the list of texts that are included in the bibliography introduce them to a specific area of knowledge; it also provides inputs to the researchers seeking to pursue the enquiry further. In other words, a bibliography is always useful. There is however a cautionary note since no bibliography is exhaustive for obvious reasons. The author picks up those texts which he/she deems appropriate for the kind of issue that he/she is interested to explore. Hence, a bibliography is also a list of selective texts and written tracts which are chosen by the author according to his/her preferences. Despite this apparent conceptual limitation, there are however many advantages of a bibliography which is an unavoidable part of any published book. A bibliography is also a pertinent methodological exercise because while including specific books and texts, the author applies certain criteria which, according to him/her, are justified to make an argument that he/she builds and expands in the narrative. The bibliography has thus to be a reason-based document.

Reconceptualizing Indian Democracy is an endeavour to comprehend the changing texture of Indian polity with reference to the electoral behaviour of the voters. In simple terms, it is a study of how Indian democracy has undergone a metamorphosis over the years. Implicit here are two important points: on the one hand, the book provides an argument to suggest that no study of Indian polity is likely to be persuasive independent of the context. In other words, the context is too important to be ignored. One of the indices of change is visible in electoral behaviour which the book argues, on the other, to substantiate the claim. This is not an unusual point as the available literature shows. What is unique here is the argument that Indian democracy is the outcome of a very complex interplay of processes which are largely context-driven. There are many studies in this genre. Similarly, Indian elections have also attracted many scholars. In reconceptualizing Indian democracy, these studies have provided very useful inputs in grasping how voters cast their votes in elections; as evidence shows, there is hardly a pattern since the voting behaviour is seldom static, but changes in response to the social, economic and political circumstances.

Books on Indian democracy are in abundance. It is therefore difficult to include all of them in this bibliography. Hence, they are selectively chosen as per the principal theme that runs through the book. A scan of the available literature suggests that there are three broad categories in so far as the studies on Indian democracy are concerned: first, there are books and well-researched monographs which focus on Indian democracy per se by delving on both its constitutional character and political texture; the second category contains those texts which are region-specific studies. These are useful because it is difficult to conceptually capture the studies in a uniform format given the variation in electoral behaviour in India from one region to another. In the third category, one can safely place those studies which are attempts at building conceptual models on the basis of thorough studies of selective national elections, being held in India since 1952. The purpose here is to narrativize the evolution of Indian democracy by reference to the elections at regular intervals.

There is another cautionary remark here which merits attention. A bibliography is prepared by the author on the basis of his/her conceptual/theoretical priorities. Hence it is reflective, for obvious reasons, of the ideational inclinations of the author which further confirms the claim that no bibliography is perfect. Despite the easily understandable limitations, no author can afford not to include a bibliography since it constitutes a significant part of the text. Two important ideas are relevant here: on the one hand, bibliography is critical to the text, which means it cannot be done away with; the fact that the bibliography is always author-specific also confirms, on the other hand, the claim that it is unidirectional and cannot be universal. Fundamental here is the idea that in view of the claim of the bibliography being drawn on authors' choice, it is impossible to draw a comprehensive bibliography which will be acceptable to all. In other words, it is neither conceptually viable nor logical to even endeavour to prepare a list of books or texts which are equally provocative and also intellectually persuasive to all since 'the one-size-fits-in-all formula' is inherently debilitating, for obvious reasons.

The above brief note has two purposes: on the one hand, by putting forward those ideas which are usually critical to the preparation of a bibliography, it helps readers understand the nature of the argument that the book seeks to make; there is also the point, on the other hand, that the bibliography is also a powerful academic tool which one cannot ignore since it is an entry point for the future researchers to an area of enquiry in which he/she is interested.

Books and Published Articles

Adeney, Katharine, and Lawrence Saez. *Coalition Politics and Hindu Nationalism*. Oxford and New York, NY: Routledge, 2005.

Austin, Granville. *The Indian Constitution: The Cornerstone of a Nation*. New Delhi: Oxford University Press, 1966.

———. *Working a Democratic Constitution: A History of the Indian Experience*. New Delhi: Oxford University Press, 1999.

Bajpai, Rochana. 'Constituent Assembly Debates and Minority Rights'. *Economic & Political Weekly* 35, no. 21–22 (May 27, 2000): 1837–1845.

———. *Debating Difference: Group Rights and Liberal Democracy in India.* New Delhi: Oxford University Press, 2011.

Basrur, Rajesh M., ed. *Challenges to Democracy in India.* New Delhi: Oxford University Press, 2009.

Basu, D. D. *Introduction to the Constitution of India.* Gurgaon: LexisNexis, 2015.

Berlin, Isaiah. *Four Essays on Liberty.* New York: Oxford University Press, 1969.

Bernstein, James. *Dawning of the Raj: The Life and Trials of Warren Hastings.* Chicago, IL: Ivan R Dee, 2000.

Bhagwati, Jagdish, and Arvind Panagariya. *India's Tryst with Destiny: Debunking Myths That Undermine Progress and Addressing New Challenges.* Noida: Collins Business, 2012.

Bhargava, Rajeev, ed. *Politics and Ethics of the Indian Constitution.* New Delhi: Oxford University Press, 2008.

Bhatia, Gautam. *Offend, Shock or Disturb: Free Speech under the Indian Constitution.* New Delhi: Oxford University Press, 2016.

Bombwall, K. R. *Indian Constitution and Administration.* Ambala Cantt: Modern Publication, 1978.

Bose, Sumantra. *Transforming India: Challenges to the World's Largest Democracy.* New Delhi: Picador India, 2013.

Brass, Paul. *Language, Religion and Politics in North India.* Cambridge: Cambridge University Press, 1974.

———. *The Politics of India since Independence.* Cambridge: Cambridge University Press, 1994.

Bussell, Jennifer. *Clients and Constituents: Political Responsiveness in Patronage Democracies.* New Delhi: Oxford University Press, 2019.

Chakrabarty, Bidyut. 'BR Ambedkar and the History of Constitutionalizing India'. *Contemporary South Asia* 24, no. 2 (2016): 133–148.

———. 'BR Ambedkar: A "Rebel" Liberal in the Gandhian Universe'. *Indian Historical Review* 23, no. 2 (2016): 289–315.

———. *India's Constitutional Identity: Ideological Beliefs and Preferences.* Oxford: Routledge, 2019.

Chakrabarty, Dipesh. *Provincializing Europe: Postcolonial Thought and Historical Difference.* New Delhi: Oxford University Press, 2000.

Chandhoke, Neera. *Rethinking, Pluralism, Secularism and Tolerance.* New Delhi: SAGE Publications, 2019.

Chatterjee, Angana P., Thomas Blom Hansen, and Christophe Jaffrelot, eds. *Majoritarian State: How Hindu Nationalism Is Changing India.* London: C Hurst & Co, 2019.

Chaube, Shibanikinkar. *Constituent Assembly of India: Springboard of Revolution.* New Delhi: Manohar, 2000.

———. *The Making and Working of the Indian Constitution.* New Delhi: National Book Trust, 2009.

Chiriyankandath, James. 'Creating a Secular State in a Religious Country: The Debate in the Indian Constituent Assembly'. *Commonwealth and Comparative Politics* 38, no. 2 (2000): 1–24.

Chopra, Pran, ed. *The Supreme Court versus the Constitution: A Challenge to Federalism*. New Delhi: SAGE Publications, 2006.

Chowdhury, Sujit, Madhav Khosla, and Pratap Bhanu Mehta, eds. *The Oxford Handbook of the Indian Constitution*. New Delhi: Oxford University Press, 2016.

Conniff, James. 'Burke and India: The Failure of the Theory of Trusteeship'. *Political Research Quarterly* 46, no. 2 (1993): 291–309.

Dalmia, V. *Nationalism of Hindu Traditions: Bharatendu Harishchandra and Nineteenth Century Benaras*. New Delhi: Oxford University Press, 1997.

Dasgupta, Jyotirindra. *Language, Conflict and National Development*. Berkeley, CA: University of California Press, 1970.

Dasgupta, Sandipto. 'A Language Which Is Foreign to Us: Continuities and Anxieties in the Making of the Indian Constitution'. *Comparative Studies of South Asia, Africa and the Middle East* 34, no. 2 (2014): 228–242.

Dasgupta, Swapan. *Awakening Bharat Mata: The Political Beliefs of the Indian Right*. Gurgaon: Penguin, 2019.

De, Rohit. *A People's Constitution: The Everyday Life of Law in the Indian Republic*. Princeton, NJ and Oxford: Princeton University Press, 2018.

Devare, Aparna. *History and the Making of a Modern Hindu Self*. New Delhi: Routledge, 2011.

Dirks, Nicholas. *Castes of Mind: Colonialism and the Making of Modern India*. Princeton, NJ: Princeton University Press, 2001.

Doniger, Wendy, and Martha C. Nusbaum, eds. *Pluralism and Democracy in India: Debating the Hindu Right*. New York, NY: Oxford University Press, 2015.

Dworkin, R. *A Matter of Principle*. Massachusetts, MA: Harvard University Press, 1986.

———. *Freedom's Law*. Massachusetts, MA: Harvard University Press, 1986.

———. *Law's Empire*. Massachusetts, MA: Harvard University Press, 1986.

———. *Taking Rights Seriously*. Delhi: Universal Law Publishing House, 1999.

Elangovan, Arvind. 'Constitutionalism, Political Exclusion, and Implications for Indian Constitutional History: The Case of Montague-Chelmsford Reforms (1919)'. *South Asian History and Culture* 7, no. 3 (2016): 271–288.

———. 'Provincial Autonomy, Sir Benegal Narsing Rau, and an Improbable Imagination of Constitutionalism in India, 1935–38'. *Comparative Studies of South Asia, Africa and the Middle East* 36, no. 1 (2016): 66–82.

———. 'The Making of the Indian Constitution: A Case for a Non-nationalist Approach'. *History Compass* 12, no. 1 (2014): 1–10.

———. 'The Road Not Taken: Sir Benegal Narsing Rau and the Indian Constitution'. In *Decolonization and the Politics of Transition in South Asia*, edited by Sekhar Bandyopadhyay. New Delhi: Orient BlackSwan, 2016.

Gajendragadkar, P. B. *Law, Liberty and Social Justice*. Bombay: New Age Printing Press, 1965.

Galanter, Marc. 'Who Are the Backward Classes?' *Economic & Political Weekly* 13, no. 43–44 (October 28, 1978): 1812–1828.

———. *Competing Equalities: Law and the Backward Classes in India*. New Delhi: Oxford University Press, 1984.

———. *Law and Society in Modern India*. New Delhi: Oxford University Press, 1997.

Gudavarthy, Ajay. *Maoism, Democracy and Globalization: Cross-currents in Indian Politics*. New Delhi: SAGE Publications, 2014.

Guha, Ranajit. *Dominance without Hegemony: History and Power in Colonial India*. New Delhi: Oxford University Press, 1998.

Hansen, Thomas Blom. *The Saffron Wave: Democracy and Hindu Nationalism in Modern India*. New Delhi: Oxford University Press, 1999.

Hansen, Thomas Blom, and Christophe Jaffrelot, eds. *The BJP and the Compulsions of Politics in India*. New Delhi: Oxford University Press, 1998.

Hasan, Zoya. Politics of Inclusion: Castes, Minorities and Affirmative Action. New Delhi: Oxford University Press, 2009.

Hasan, Zoya, E. Sridharan, and R. Sudarshan, eds. *India's Living Constitution: Ideas, Practices, Controversies*. Ranikhet: Permanent Black, 2002.

Hayek, F. A. *The Constitution of Liberty*. Chicago, IL: University of Chicago Press, 1978.

HM Stationery Office, *Proceedings of Indian Round Table Conference 12 November, 1930–19 January, 1931*. London: HM Stationary Office, 1931.

Jacobsohn, Garry. *The Wheel of Law: India's Secularism in Comparative and Constitutional Context*. New Delhi: Oxford University Press, 2003.

Jacobsohn, Gary Jeffrey. 'Constitutional Identity'. *The Review of Politics* 68, no. 3 (2006): 361–397.

Jaffrelot, Christophe. *The Hindu Nationalist Movement in India*. New Delhi: Viking, 1993.

———. *India's Silent Revolution: The Rise of the Low Castes in North Indian Politics*. Ranikhet: Permanent Black, 2003.

———. *Dr. Ambedkar and Untouchability: Analysing and Fighting Caste*. Ranikhet: Permanent Black, 2005.

Jayal, Niraja Gopal, ed. *Democracy in India*. New Delhi: Oxford University Press, 2001.

———. *Citizenship and Its Discontents: An Indian History*. Ranikhet: Permanent Black, 2013.

———, ed. *Reforming India: The Nation Today*. Gurgaon: Penguin, 2019.

Kalekar Commission (1956). *Report of the Backward Classes Commission*. New Delhi: Government of India, 1956.

Kashyap, Subhash C. *Our Constitution: An Introduction to India's Constitution and Constitutional Law*. Reprint, New Delhi: National Book Trust, 2015.

Kashyap, Subhash C. *The Indian Constitution: Conflicts and Controversies.* New Delhi: Vitasta Publications, 2010.

Khilnani, Sunil. *The Idea of India.* London: Hamish Hamilton, 1997.

Khosla, Madhav. *The Indian Constitution.* New Delhi: Oxford University Press, 2012.

King, Robert D. *Nehru and the Language Politics of India.* New Delhi: Oxford University Press, 1997.

Komireddi, K. S. *Malevolent Republic: A Short History of India.* London: C Hurst & Co, 2019.

Krishnaswami, Sudhir. *Democracy and Constitutionalism in India: A Study of the Basic Structure Doctrine.* New Delhi: Oxford University Press, 2009.

Kumar, Aishwary. *Radical Equality: Ambedkar, Gandhi and the Risk of Democracy.* Stanford, CA: Stanford University Press, 2015.

Kumar, Ravinder. 'Gandhi, Ambedkar and Poona Pact, 1932'. *South Asia: Journal of South Asian Studies* 8, no. 1 (1985): 87–101.

Kymlicka, Will. *Multicultural Citizenship: A Liberal Theory of Minority Rights.* Oxford: Clarendon Press, 1995.

———. *Politics in the Vernacular.* Oxford: Oxford University Press, 2001.

Larson, Gerald. 'Mandal, Mandir, Masjid: The Citizen as an Endangered Species in Independent India'. In *Religion and Law in Independent India*, edited by Robert D. Baird. New Delhi: Manohar, 1993.

———. *Religion and Personal Law in Secular India: A Call to Judgment.* Bloomington, IN: Indiana University Press, 2001.

Legg, Stephen. 'Dyarchy: Democracy, Autocracy and the Scalar Sovereignty of Interwar India'. *Comparative Studies of South Asia, Africa and the Middle East* 36, no. 1 (2016).

Ludden, David, ed. *Contesting the Nation: Religion, Community and the Politics of Democracy in India.* Philadelphia, PA: University of Pennsylvania Press, 1996.

Mahajan, Gurpreet. *Identities and Rights: Aspects of Liberal Politics in India.* New Delhi: Oxford University Press, 1998.

Maharaj, Ayon. *Infinite Paths to Infinite Reality: Sri Ramakrishna & Cross-cultural Philosophy of Religion.* New Delhi: Oxford University Press, 2018.

Mehrotra, S. R., and Dinyar Patel, ed. *Dadabhai Naoroji: Selected Private Papers.* New Delhi: Oxford University Press, 2016.

Mehta, Uday Singh. *Liberalism and Empire: India in British Liberal Thought.* New Delhi: Oxford University Press, 1999.

Metcalf, Thomas R. *Ideologies of the Raj.* Cambridge: Cambridge University Press, 1998.

Michelutti, Lucia. *The Vernacularization of Democracy: Politics, Caste and Religion in India.* New Delhi: Routledge, 2008.

Mukherjee, Mithi. 'Justice, War and Imperium: India and Britain in Edmund Burke's Prosecutorial Speeches in the Impeachment Trial of Warren Hastings'. *Law and History Review* 23, no. 3, (Fall 2005): 589–630.

Mukherjee, Ramkrishna. *The Rise and Fall of the East India Company.* New York, NY: Monthly Review Press, 1974.

Naoroji, Dadabhai. *Poverty and Un-British Rule in India.* London: S. Sonnenschein, 1901.

Nehru, Jawaharlal. *An Autobiography.* London: John Lane the Bodley Head, 1941.

———. *The Discovery of India.* Reprint, New Delhi: Oxford University Press, 1989.

Noorani, A. G. *Constitutional Questions in India: The President, Parliament and the States.* New Delhi: Oxford University Press, 2000.

Nussbaum, Martha C. *Political Emotions: Why Love Matters for Justice.* The Belknap Press of Harvard University Press, Cambridge, MA and London, 2013.

O'Hanlon, Rosalind. *Caste, Conflict and Ideology: Mahatma Jotirao Phule and Low Caste Protest in Nineteenth-Century Western India.* Cambridge: Cambridge University Press, 1985.

Omvedt, Gail. *Cultural Revolt in a Colonial Society: The Non-Brahmin Movement in Western India, 1873–1930.* Bombay: Scientific Socialist Educational Trust, 1976.

———. *Dalits and the Democratic Revolution: Dr Ambedkar and Dalit Movement in Colonial India.* New Delhi: SAGE Publications, 1994.

Oommen, T. K. 'Religious Nationalism and Democratic Polity: The Indian Case'. *Sociology of Religion* 55, no. 4 (1994): 455–472.

Parekh, Bhikhu. *Debating India: Essays on Indian Political Discourse.* New Delhi: Oxford University Press, 2015.

———. *Debating India: Essays on Political Discourse.* New Delhi: Oxford University Press, 2015.

Petit, Philip. *Republicanism: A Theory of Freedom and Government.* Oxford: Oxford University Press, 1999.

Philips, Anne. Oxford: *The Politics of Presence.* Oxford: Clarendon Press, 1995.

Philips, C. H. *The East India Company, 1784–1834.* Manchester: Manchester University Press, 1961.

Prakash, Gyan. *Emergency Chronicles: Indira Gandhi and Democracy's Turning Point.* Gurgaon: Penguin, 2018.

Prasad, Ganesh. 'Whiggism in India'. *Political Science Quarterly* 86 (1966): 11–19.

Pylee, M. V. *Constitutional Government in India.* London: Asia Publishing House, 1965.

Rajagopal, Arvind. *Politics after Television: Hindu Nationalism and the Reshaping of the Public in India.* Cambridge: Cambridge University Press, 2001.

Ramnath, Kalyani. 'We the People: Seamless Webs and Social Revolution in India's Constituent Assembly Debates'. *South Asia Research* 32, no. 1 (2012): 57–70.

Ram-Prasad, C. 'Hindutva Ideology: Extracting the Fundamentals'. *Contemporary South Asia* 2, no. 3 (1993): 285–309.

Rao, Shiva. *The Framing of India's Constitution*, 5 vols. New Delhi: Universal Law Publishing Company, 1968.

Rathore, Akash Singh. *Indian Political Theory: Laying the Groundwork for Svaraj*. Oxford and New York, NY: Routledge, 2017.

Rau, Benegal Narsing. *Outlines of a New Constitution, 1946*. Reproduced in B. Shiva Rao, ed. *The Framing of India's Constitution*, vol. 1. Delhi: Universal Law Publishing House, 1967.

Rege, Sharmila (selected and introduced). *Against the Madness of Manu: BR Ambedkar's Writings on Brahmanical Patriarchy*. New Delhi: Navayana Publishing Pvt Ltd, 2013.

Roover, Jakob De. Europe, India and the Limits of Secularism. New Delhi: Oxford University Press, 2015.

Rosenfeld, Michel. *Affirmative Action and Justice: A Philosophical and Constitutional Enquiry*. New Haven, CT: Yale University Press, 1991.

Roy, Anupama. *Mapping Citizenship in India*. New Delhi: Oxford University Press, 2010.

———. *Citizenship in India*. New Delhi: Oxford University Press, 2016.

Roy, Srirupa. *Beyond Belief: India and the Politics of Postcolonial Nationalism*. Durham, NC: Duke University Press, 2007.

Rudolph, Lloyd, and S. H. Rudolph. *The Realm of the Public Sphere: Identity and Policy*. New Delhi: Oxford University Press, 2008.

Saez, Lawrennce. *Federalism with a Centre*. New Delhi: SAGE Publications, 2002.

Sampath, Vikram. *Savarkar: Echoes from a Forgotten Past, 1883–1924*. Gurgaon: Penguin, 2019.

Saxena, Rekha. *Situating Federalism: Mechanisms of Intergovernmental Relations in Canada and India*. New Delhi: Manohar, 2006.

Sen, Amartya. *Development as Freedom*. New Delhi: Oxford University Press, 1999.

———. *The Argumentative Indian: Writings on Indian History, Culture and Identity*. New York, NY: Picador, 2005.

———. *Identity and Violence: The Illusion of Destiny*. London: Allen Lane, 2006.

———. *The Idea of Justice*. New York, NY: Allen Lane, 2009.

———. *Collective Choice and Social Welfare*. Reprint, New Delhi: Penguin, 2017.

Sen, Sarbani. *The Constitution of India: Popular Sovereignty and Democratic Transformations*. New Delhi: Oxford University Press, 2007.

Seth, Sanjay. 'Rewriting Histories of Nationalism: The Politics of "Moderate Nationalism" in India, 1870–1905'. *American Historical Review* 104, no. 1 (February, 1999): 95–116.

Sharma, Brij Kishore. *Introduction to the Constitution of India*. New Delhi: Prentice Hall of India, 2005.

Sharma, Jyotirmaya. *Hindutva: Exploring the Idea of Hindu Nationalism*. New Delhi: Penguin, 2003.

———. *Terrifying Vision: MS Golwalkar, the RSS and India*. New Delhi: Penguin, 2007.

Smith, D. E. *Nehru and Democracy: The Political Thought of an Asian Democrat.* Calcutta: Orient Longman, 1958.

Somanathan, Rohini. 'Assumptions and Arithmetic of Caste-Based Reservations'. *Economic & Political Weekly* 41, no. 24 (June 17, 2006): 2436–2438.

Sowell, Thomas. *Affirmative Action around the World: An Empirical Study.* New Haven, CT: Yale University Press, 2004.

Stokes, Eric. *The English Utilitarians and India.* Cambridge: Cambridge University Press, 1959.

Sutherland, Lucy. *The East India Company in Eighteenth-Century Politics.* Oxford: Clarendon Press, 1962.

Tilly, Charles. *Durable Inequality.* Berkeley, CA and Los Angeles, CA: California University Press, 2002.

Topdar, Sudipa. 'Duties of a "Good Citizen": Colonial Secondary School Textbook Policies in Late Nineteenth-Century India'. *South Asian History and Culture*, annual issue (2015): 417–439.

Tripathi, P. K. 'Free Speech in the Indian Constitution: Background and Prospect'. *Yale Law Journal* 67, no. 3 (1958): 384–400.

Upadhyaya, Prakash Chandra. 'The Politics of Indian Secularism'. *Modern Asian Studies* 26, no. 4 (1992): 815–853.

Vajpeyi, Ananya. *Righteous Republic: The Political Foundations of Modern India.* Cambridge: Harvard University Press, 2012.

Varshney, Ashutosh. 'Contested Meanings: India's National Identity, Hindu Nationalism and the Politics of Anxiety'. *Daedalus* 122, no. 3 (1993): 227–261.

———. *Ethnic Conflict and Civic Life: Hindus and Muslims in India.* New Haven, CT: Yale University Press, 2002.

Veer, van der Peter. 'God Must Be Liberated! A Hindu Liberation Movement in Ayodhya'. *Modern Asian Studies* 21, no. 2 (1987): 283–301.

———. *Religious Nationalism: Hindus and Muslims in India.* Berkeley, CA University of California Press, 1994.

Venkatesan, V. *Constitutional Conundrums: Challenges to India's Democratic Process.* Gurgaon: LexisNexis, 2014.

Verma, Vidhu. *Non-discrimination and Equality in India: Contesting Boundaries of Social Justice.* Oxford and New York, NY: Routledge, 2012.

Weiner, Myron. 'The Political Consequences of Preferential Policies: A Comparative Perspective'. *Comparative Politics* 16, no. 1 (1983): 35–52.

———. 'The Struggle for Equality: Caste in Indian Politics'. In *The Success of India's Democracy*, edited by Atul Kohli, 193–225. Cambridge: Cambridge University Press, 2001.

Williams, Melissa. *Votes, Trust and Memory: Marginalised Groups and the Failings of Liberal Representation.* Princeton, NJ: Princeton University Press, 1998.

Willinson, Steven. *Votes and Violence: Electoral Competition and Ethnic Riots in India.* Cambridge: Cambridge University Press, 2004.

Zachariah, Benjamin. *Developing India: An Intellectual and Social History, c. 1930–50.* New Delhi: Oxford University Press, 2005.

Zavos, John. *The Emergence of Hindu Nationalism in India*. New Delhi: Oxford University Press, 2000.

Zeillot, Eleanor. *From Untouchable to Dalit: Essays on the Ambedkar Movement*. New Delhi: Manohar, 1996.

Unpublished PhD Dissertation

Elangovan, Arvind. 'A Constitutional Imagination of India: Sir Benegal Narsing Rau amidst the Retreat of Liberal Idealism (1919–1950)'. Unpublished PhD diss., University of Chicago, 2012.

Dasgupta, Sandipto. 'Localizing the Revolution'. Unpublished PhD diss., Columbia University, 2014.

About the Authors

Bidyut Chakrabarty is Vice Chancellor of Visva Bharati, West Bengal. He was a professor in the Department of Political Science in the University of Delhi until November 2018. He completed his PhD from London School of Economics and has been associated with teaching and research for more than three decades. He has taught in several prestigious educational institutions, such as the London School of Economics; Indian Institute of Management Calcutta; Monash University, Australia; National University of Singapore and Universität Hamburg, Germany. He has authored several textbooks and academic books. Among his publications are *Public Administration: From Government to Governance* (2017), *Winning the Mandate: The Indian Experience* (2016, SAGE Publications), *Communism in India: Events, Processes and Ideologies* (2014), *Indian Politics and Society since Independence: Events, Processes and Ideology* (2008) and *The Governance Discourse: A Reader* (2008).

Rajendra Kumar Pandey is Associate Professor in the Department of Political Science, Chaudhary Charan Singh University, Meerut. He earned his doctorate degree from the University of Delhi. He has taught graduate students at two prestigious colleges of the University of Delhi—Delhi College of Arts and Commerce (1998–2003) and Hindu College (2003–2009). Subsequently, he shifted to the UGC-Centre for Federal Studies, Jamia Hamdard (Deemed to be University), New Delhi, where he played a pivotal role in establishing the Human Rights programme in the Centre, apart from making substantial contributions to teaching and research in federal studies. Besides publishing research papers in reputed journals, he has co-authored three books—*Local Governance in India* (2018,

SAGE Publications), *Modern Indian Political Thought: Text and Context* (2009, SAGE Publications) and *Indian Government and Politics* (2008, SAGE Publications). The current focus areas of his academic pursuits are public policy and governance with special reference to the issues of disaster management and human rights.

Index